D0062122

If Mama
Ain't Happy,
Ain't
Nobody
Happy!

Lindsey O'Connor

HARVEST HOUSE PUBLISHERS

EUGENE, OREGON

Cover by Terry Dugan Design, Minneapolis, Minnesota

IF MAMA AIN'T HAPPY, AIN'T NOBODY HAPPY!
Copyright © 1996 by Lindsey O'Connor
Published by Harvest House Publishers
Eugene, Oregon 97402
www.harvesthousepublishers.com

Library of Congress Cataloging-in-Publication Data
O'Connor, Lindsey, 1961–
  If mama ain't happy, ain't nobody happy / Lindsey O'Connor.
    p. cm.
  ISBN-13: 978-0-7369-1845-9
  ISBN-10: 0-7369-1845-0
  1. Mothers—Psychology. 2. Mothers—Religious life. 3. Contentment.
  4. Optimism. 5. Family I. Title.
  HQ759.03234 1996   96-10715
  248.8'431—dc20   CIP

Printed in the United States of America

06 07 08 09 10 11 12 / DP-MS / 10 9 8 7 6 5 4 3 2 1

For my mom,
Judy Earlene Britton,
who now truly lives in the fullness of joy

❧ Acknowledgments ❧
My heartfelt thanks to…

My wonderful children: Jacquelyn, Claire, Collin, and Allison. Thank you for loving me even when Mama ain't happy and for making it easy for me to make the choice to rejoice. And my soul-mate Tim: You are my sparkle.

Susan Gragg, my creative consultant, manuscript reader, and research assistant—not to mention my cohort in joyful living! Thanks for always knowing which hat I needed you to wear, for cheering me on at all the right places, and for making your feet like wings, Sahib. I'm looking forward to "winging it" for you over your manuscript!

Lois Ash, the personification of a soul who serves with joy. Thank you for serving me and my loving children. I am blessed to have you as a friend.

Susan Weisiger (child nurturer), Marguarite Mutchler (meals on wheels), Robin Murray, and Lisa Rutledge. Thank you for your help and, most of all, your prayers.

Dad and Barbara, who bonded with the grandkids when I needed to bond with my manuscript. Thanks for the gifts of time and love.

Brenda Koinis and Posy Lough: You two have added to this manuscript and to my life.

Lael Arrington and the Tomball Christian Writers' Group: "As iron sharpens iron," you have sharpened me.

Lisa Guest, for your enthusiasm for this project, prayers, and skillful editing. The Process has been . . . a joy.

And a special thanks to all of you who filled out my survey. Your input was invaluable.

～ Contents ～

Part Three
Practicing Joy and Contentment in Our Homes
What We Do

A Bit About
Being Joyful

Y ou've probably seen the T-shirt that proclaims, "I am woman. I am invincible. I am tired!" Is it too much to ask to also be joyful? To maybe find a sparkle here and there in life?

That's what I wondered years ago when, on top of trying to be a good wife and mother, I was juggling my work, church activities, home, and to-do list—and looking for a little bit of joy at the same time. I thought, "What's the point of going through the motions of life—what's the point of the accomplishments or the struggles—if there's no joy along the way? And what does God's Word say about joy anyway?" Besides, if I wanted to teach my children how to be joyful and content, I'd better figure it out myself. And so began my joy journey—a journey I'm still on and the journey I share with you in these pages. But a funny thing happened on the way to the word processor . . . I discovered a bit about "being."

Now, any one of us can learn how to do something, but learning how to be something—ah, that's harder. I had "doing" down pretty well, but "being"? Well, that transformation (and I'm still in process!) has been one aspect of the journey that led to this book. A book about being. About being joyful. About being content. It's about using our heads, hearts, and homes to know and share joy where we are. And, although it's primarily about being, I do offer you a few how-to's to make it practical. (If I just said, "Be joyful" but didn't help show you how, you could just listen to Bobby McFerrin's song "Don't Worry, Be Happy" and be done in three minutes!)

So why the title? Well, apparently lots of women can relate to the idea that "if Mama ain't happy, ain't nobody happy." When people heard the title while I was writing the book, most smiled or laughed or thoughtfully murmured, "Oh, yes"—perhaps picturing themselves as that mama. I asked 50 of these people to fill out a survey about their own journey toward joy, and I will share with you what they told me.

But before I begin telling my story and theirs, let me be quick to say that this book is not about making Mama happy. I am simply using a tongue-in-cheek colloquialism to point to the influence of the woman in the home and the important role she plays in the well-being of her family. I am not suggesting that our happiness is paramount or more important than our family's needs. In her book *Choices*, Mary Farrar has some strong words about that false premise, and I couldn't agree more:

> I am deluded if I think that what my child and husband need most is for me to be "happy." What a can of worms this opens up! What about a man who decides to leave his wife and children for the sake of personal happiness? Men have tried to argue the same point—that everyone will be much better off in the long run. Not so, life tells us. My personal happiness simply cannot be the plumb line for family decisions. Personal responsibility always precedes personal happiness if a family is to survive and thrive.[1]

Mary Farrar is so right. I've seen families torn apart as husband and children drown in the wake of Mama's pursuit of happiness. Besides, being happy isn't necessary for us to experience joy. And every Mama can use a little more joy than what's in her dishwater!

You may be up to your neck in more than dishwater. We women are busy, sometimes stressed, sometimes hurting, often tired. Can we possibly get through today's list and find a little sparkle along the way? Can we learn to be content where we are even when we don't like where we are?

Yes, we can! My Father told me so. In fact, He told me that savoring the sparkle was quite all right—and I always trust my Father. He says, "These things I have spoken to you, that My joy may be in you, and that your joy may be made full" (John 15:11). Our heavenly Father wants us to be joyful!

So if you're overwhelmed, tired, hurting, or maybe just missing the sparkle in your life, get cozy as I take you on a joy journey. And by the way—loosen up a bit and find your smile, maybe even a chuckle or two. This trip should be fun!

Sparkles in the Rocks
Life Is Hard;
We Need a Little Sparkle!

Stress can make you stupid. I know. My trip to Canada proved it.

It started even before I left. The stupidity, that is—the stress had been present for a while. The night before I left, I stayed up until 2:30 A.M. trying to find the bottom of my desk. (I was sure all those papers were busy multiplying in the dark while I slept.) There had been so much to do before leaving. Find this...call so and so...pack tickets...get cash. Finally I was ready. I said goodbye to my family and drove to the airport for the brief trip.

Juggling my luggage, I glanced at my watch. *Oh, no! Only 27 minutes! I hope I'm at the right terminal,* I thought. I knew I didn't have time to catch a shuttle to the other terminal, so I bypassed the line and quickly asked the nearest agent if I was at the right place. She curtly asked me if I'd checked the departure monitors. *Whoops! Didn't even think of those! I've practically grown up in an airport. What am I thinking?*

I quickly scanned the screen and was surprised to find that I was indeed at the right terminal and even at the right gate—to no credit of my own. I waited in line and guess which ticket agent I got? Of course the one who'd reminded me about the invention of departure monitors. *Great.* She processed my ticket and said, "May I have your passport, please?" *My WHAT?*

"Umm, I don't have it," I told her.

"You don't have your passport with you?" she asked.

"No," I replied. *And I'm not about to tell her I don't have one at all.*

"How about your birth certificate?" she continued.

"No, I don't have that either," I said, starting to feel quite foolish. *I think my parents still have it.*

"OK. Just give me your voter registration card," she persisted. *I wonder if mine is current.*

Not finding it, I said, "You're not going to believe this, but I don't have that either."

"Well," she said, a bit irritated, "you can enter Canada, but you may have trouble leaving."

"Fine!" I responded. "I just have to get to Canada and I can't miss this flight!" Desperate women are capable of desperate moves.

However, I came to my senses long enough to hear her say something about calling the customs office downstairs. I suddenly considered being stranded, alone, in Canada, in self-imposed exile. "Yes, please call," I said.

She did and then told me to go ahead to my gate. I smiled and said, "Thank you. I'm really not this stupid—really!" She sort of smiled back, probably thinking, *Sure you're not! Would you like some crayons for the flight?*

I walked up to the flight attendant at the gate and asked where the nearest restroom was. "On the plane," she said, "but you only have six minutes and you still need to check in at the desk." *Oh, yeah. How could I have forgotten?*

I checked in with the gate agent. "May I have your documents, please?" she asked. *Same song, second verse.* I explained my dilemma and told her the other agent had approved it. She skeptically pulled my ticket and gave me a boarding pass. Then I went to the jetway to board the plane. The flight attendant there asked, "May I have your boarding pass and travel documents, please?" *Again? Maybe I should wear a sign saying, "YES, I'M TRYING TO GO TO CANADA WITHOUT ANY TRAVEL DOCUMENTS."*

"I don't have any," I replied.

"And they let you through?" he asked in disbelief. "Let's see if they wrote that little love note anywhere on here." At this point, I think even a note from my mother would have helped.

While he looked, I asked him if I could just have my documents faxed to me there.

"Let's see. Do they have faxes in Canada?" he quipped. *OK. I deserved that.* I told him I would have my documents sent to me, and he stamped the magic words, "Documents OK" on my ticket. Then he added, "Be a good girl and be sure to do that, honey."

"Be a good girl"? I was a grown woman. I had a family. I had a business. But I also had to admit that my daughter could have done a better job getting to Canada than I was doing so far. How could I have considered leaving for a foreign country without any travel documents? What was worse, the thought of getting documents hadn't even crossed my mind. I had navigated flights many times before, but this time I had acted like a freshman flier.

I boarded the plane and slumped in my seat with a sigh of relief. *I made it. Now, if I can just regain my brain before we land....*A little later, during the meal service, I managed to get salad dressing in my lap and up my sleeve. How I did that I'll never know. The man next to me was somewhat amused and, no doubt marveling at my grace, offered me napkins. Then, to top it off, I didn't even have a pen in my purse to fill out the customs form before landing. *Maybe I should have asked that first agent for a crayon after all!* I borrowed a pen from the napkin man.

After we landed, Canadian airport personnel said, "May I see your passport, please?" *Oh, no. Here we go again!* I reiterated my situation (quite succinctly by now), and they let me through, muttering, "Where'd you think you were going, lady? Idaho?"

As I walked through the airport toward a taxi with everything intact but my dignity, I noticed that most people had coats with them. *Terrific. I just flew north and didn't even think to bring a coat. That confirms it. I'm an idiot!* Disgusted with being fuzzy-headed, I thought of all the people who had witnessed my "untogetherness." I imagined them all—the ticket agent, the flight attendant at the gate, the second ticket agent, the boarding pass collector, the man next to me on the plane, and the Canadian official—standing together shaking their fingers at me and saying in unison, "Get your act together, woman!"

I was in Canada to be interviewed on TV about my book *Working at Home.* I was supposed to have my act together. At least when the interviewer asked about the pitfalls of combining family life and a home business, I could share from personal experience that sometimes the combination is stressful—and I could warn with first-hand knowledge that stress can cause stupidity. Then I prayed, *Thank You, Lord, that I'm here in spite of myself—and please don't let any of those people see me on TV!*

Walking outside, I realized that for the first time in a long time I was walking slower than everyone else. *This feels pretty good!* As the stress began to loosen its vise-grip on me, I began to relax. Then I saw something that I hadn't noticed since I was a little girl. The sidewalk sparkled!

Immediately I was taken back to when I was about seven years old and I paid attention to things like sidewalks and sparkling pavement and shiny rocks. I remember walking down the sidewalk on a hot summer day (stepping over the cracks of course) and marveling at all the sparkles in that concrete. With the sun shining on it, the sidewalk shimmered. It had little diamonds stuck in it! I was amazed. "How wonderful! Has everyone noticed this incredible thing?" I wondered. The sidewalk was actually a pretty boring shade of gray, but at the right angle and in the right light, it sparkled!

Most of us adults never pay much attention to sidewalks. We just keep our eyes straight ahead and rely on our peripheral vision to help us stay on track. But stepping across that sidewalk and back in time that day made me think about that sparkle. Those glimmering diamonds in the sidewalks of my childhood—and in the sidewalks of my city today—really are diamonds. Actually,

I try to look on the bright side of life and ignore the dull.

~Beulah G.

they're diamond dust. It's added to the concrete of some side-walks to increase their hardness and durability in high traffic. So as a kid I was right all along. Those really are diamonds glisten-ing in the gray!

That got me thinking during my trip. *That's what's been missing from my life lately—the sparkle! I've been working so hard to balance all my responsibilities and be the kind of woman, wife, and mother that I should that I've slipped into the rut of a life without sparkle. Or maybe, just like the side-walk, the sparkle is there and I just haven't noticed.*

Then it hit me. *The sparkle in life is the glimmer of joy! That's what I need.* A life of disciplines and duties and dailyness without joy is a life without sparkle. I'd been so busy *doing* for so long that I'd forgotten the value of *being*. And what I des-perately wanted was to be...joyful. I wanted a life with a little sparkle.

Sparkles in the Rocks

Perhaps you've seen the bumper sticker/T-shirt slogan: "Life is hard—and then you die." For many people, that has the same effect of fingernails scraping on a chalkboard. While cer-tainly factual, it's a grating statement because it leaves out all the hope and joy and points only to life's hardship and death. It misses all the beauty in the journey. It skips all the flowers and refers only to the rocks. The dull, gray rocks—not even the kind with sparkles.

Sometimes life is as hard as the hardest rock and as colorless as the dull, gray ones. Sometimes there just aren't any flowers growing in the crevices. We find only rocks—the rocks of pain, disappointment, or difficult circumstances; the rocks of busyness, tedium, or stress—littering or even blocking our path. Perhaps right now you find some of these rocks looming between where you are and a point of joy and contentment. Sometimes the rocks of life can form a huge mountain, blocking our path to joy. Or maybe the rocks are just pebbles of irritation that get in the way. We will always find rocks of some type along our journey. But in-stead of letting them hit us on the head or push us six feet under, we can learn to navigate our way around them and—just as im-portant—to notice the ones with sparkles.

Sometimes rocks sparkle only because they are polished. When I was about eight, my parents gave me a rock tumbler for Christmas. It came with some dull, ugly rocks. I put them in the tumbler and plugged it in, and the slow polishing process began. When the tumbler finally stopped, those ugly rocks had been beautifully transformed into shiny stones. Their streaks of color made them suitable for hanging on chains and wearing around my neck, which I did. In fact, not long ago, my daughter found such a piece of jewelry in my things. "Mom, *what* is this?" she asked as she pulled out my creation.

"Oh, that's a work of art!" I replied. When she looked dumbfounded, I explained, "I used an ugly rock and a rock tumbler to make that necklace."

When I explained how it worked, Jacquelyn was truly amazed. She asked, "Oh, may I have this necklace? I won't lose it! I'll take good care of it so I can pass it down to my children!" (Oh, those lucky future grandchildren of mine!)

What intrigued me about that rock tumbler when I was a child—and what intrigued my child—is the fact that something pretty, colorful, and sparkling can come from something as ugly as a gray or brown rock. None of us would ever hang a plain, dull rock around our neck, but a polished gem—now that's another story. With a little friction and a little time, something hard and lackluster comes to reveal the sparkle that was there all along. And so it is with us.

There are several ways to think of the rocks in the tumbler. Sometimes the rocks are the hurts and trying circumstances that litter our life. When we look at these rocks of pain or unpleasantness, we don't see anything beautiful in them; we don't see any sparkle. But God can smooth things out so that at some point we will be able to see the beauty. He can also polish the rough edges off someone who's causing us pain. Sometimes He simply changes a situation and brings beauty out of ugliness.

Another way to think of the rocks and the tumbler is that sometimes we ourselves need to undergo the polishing process. We must get in the tumbler and allow God to polish us. Time and friction have to do their job on us before the sparkle in us is revealed. This refining work has to be done before the dull rock can shine. And, just as rocks are polished by time and friction, God can use both the passage of time and the friction of difficult circumstances or challenging people in our life to smooth our rough edges. When we submit ourselves to His polishing process, He can produce a beautiful shine in us, a reflection of the joy of the Lord. We can be joyful knowing that, even though the process may not necessarily change the circumstances in our life, God is changing us. As He refines us, we gain His perspective. As we are polished, others see the sparkle of His joy as it is reflected in our life.

What are the rocks in your life? And how's the tumbling process going? Perhaps the tumbling seems to be taking much too long or you're a little tired of the friction. Maybe you feel like nothing beautiful can be made of the ugly rocks in your life. But, friend, with just the right amount of friction and His perfect timing, God can make something beautiful out of even the ugliest rocks. He can polish them so that you can see the sparkle, and He can also polish you and produce His shine in your life.

There's still another way to see sparkles in the rocks. While some rocks sparkle on the outside because they are polished, others sparkle because of what's inside. Have you ever seen a geode? The outside can be very rough, with no shimmer at all no matter what angle or in what light we look at it. We can throw the geode in the tumbler for a spin, and we'll get a pretty, polished rock. If we stop there, we may be pleased with the shine, but we'll miss something much greater—the real beauty within. The inside of a geode is far more beautiful than a polished crust can ever be. Geodes contain gorgeous crystals in beautiful and varied shapes, sizes, and colors. Even in the shadows, these crystals are lovely. When they're held up to the light at just the right angle, they are exquisite. Before this beauty can be revealed, however, the rock must be cracked open. Only with enough pressure to fracture the rock do the sparkles become visible. Without that breaking, we have only a rock—rough or polished—and we miss the real beauty within. The treasure remains hidden.

We are like the geode. Sometimes the sparkle is within us. Just as the treasure of a geode's crystals lies hidden inside the rock, such a treasure can be inside us, too. Even if life is dull or hard and completely without sparkle you can know that the sparkle lies within you if you are a child of the King, having named Jesus as your Savior and Lord. Scripture teaches that the

Holy Spirit lives in those of us who put our faith in Jesus: "the Spirit of Him who raised Jesus from the dead dwells in you" (Romans 8:11). And one of the ministries of the Holy Spirit in the life of the believer is giving joy: "The kingdom of God is not eating and drinking, but righteousness and peace and *joy in the Holy Spirit*" (Romans 14:17, emphasis added). The Holy Spirit also produces fruit in believers who are the likeness of Christ—and one characteristic is joy (Galatians 5:22). The sparkle of joy can be found within believers because the Holy Spirit dwells there.

Sidewalks, rock tumblers, and breaking open geodes aren't the only way to see sparkles in the rocks. Just imagine the sparkle in the eyes of the early gold prospectors who said, "There's gold in them thar hills!" Gold rushes began and entire towns were established practically overnight because men hoped to find the glimmer of gold and claim it for themselves. Even today, in a privately-owned gold mine in Colorado, tourists can see shiny gold veins embedded in the rock. As you walk down the tunnel, you see how a narrow vein gradually widens until it reaches the mother lode where the vein of visible gold is about as wide as a car. The parking lot even sparkles with flecks of gold dust. But gaining the glitter isn't easy. About three million pounds of ore must be processed to produce a single approximately-30-pound brick of gold. That's a lot of sifting!

Although I'm no geologist or rock hound, I've seen quite a bit of gleam in rocks. I've seen sparkles in sidewalks, admired the shine after a rock has been tumbled, collected a few geodes, and panned for gold dust. Why? Because seeing the sparkle in the rocks is fun and often valuable. So is seeing the sparkle in the rocks of life. And joy is that sparkle in the rocks of life.

Seeing the joy in life is fun because it makes the dull places shine. Joy adds a touch of beauty to life. Seeing the joy is also valuable. It gets us through some rocky places on our journey when happiness can't be found. But the value of joy doesn't lie in the fact that it makes us feel good. It lies in the fact that it enables us to live a life that gives. Joy is the fuel for a life of service. To live life fully and richly—to live in service to God and others—is a wonderful thing. Joy helps us do just that.

Besides being a fruit of the Spirit, joy is also a gift from God. Jesus Himself said, "These things I have spoken to you, that My joy may be in you, and that your joy may be made full" (John 15:11). What a precious gift Jesus wants to give us! At times we simply stumble across joy. Sometimes joy is an attitude we deliberately choose. Often, joy is a gift freely given. That's why this book isn't about searching for joy. (If we do that, we may never find it.) This book is about living a life that yields joy and seeing joy in everyday miracles. It's about external joys like a beautiful sunset and internal joys like a sweet spiritual discovery at just the right time. Throughout this book, I will refer to all of these things, different ways of looking at the joy we have in Jesus and different ways of receiving His touch of joy.

After all, it seems to me that experiencing joy and contentment is a lot like seeing sparkles in pavement and rocks. The sparkles we see in sidewalks are like the external joys scattered across our path. The road may still be hard and gray, but when we look from the right angle (God's perspective) and in the right light (the light of God's love), we can see the sparkle. Sometimes we miss it simply because we're not paying attention. Stopping to take in a beautiful example of God's handiwork in nature, holding hands with someone you love as you walk along together, or looking into the eyes of a child saying, "I love you"—these are sparkles in life. So are good books, intellectual stimulation, heart-to-heart conversations, and ice cream. Joy can be found all around us when we pay attention. In fact, often it's the small things in life that add joy. Look for them and be thankful, for thankfulness is the heart of joy.

But maybe everything around you right now seems colorless and drab. Like the gray sidewalks, dull rocks, and rough geodes, your life may not have a lot of sparkle either. After all, sometimes we're like sidewalks on a cloudy day. People have walked all over us all day long and, since the sun is hidden, no sparkle is visible. On other days, we're like rocks—cold, hard, rough, and dull to the bone. (Sounds like a PMS day!) But every day we really are geodes: the outside can be polished, but the real sparkle is within. So, when all we see and feel is the hardness of life's rocks, we must remember that joy can be found sparkling, precious, and beautiful like gold. But getting to that golden joy isn't always easy.

The Struggle to Know Joy

Have you ever wondered why it's sometimes so hard to be joyful? We all want to be happy. None of us deliberately sets out to be miserable, discontent, or bored. Even when we desperately want to know joy, it can prove frustratingly elusive. Since life is hard and we need a little sparkle, why is finding it sometimes such a struggle? Because . . .

- Life can be so . . . **overwhelming**—as in *"Joy is probably here somewhere if I can just find her under this pile before she smothers. But where do I start?"*

To overwhelm means "to submerge" or "to cover over completely." Do you ever feel submerged in a pile of things to do that require far more time than you have available? No matter how progressive our society seems, most women still meet the majority of the family's needs whether we work for pay or not. We usually do the majority of the housework, meal planning, shopping, cooking, gift buying, card giving, and boo-boo kissing.

Then there are the holidays, another responsibility that falls mostly on our shoulders. And, frankly, those special times probably wouldn't have quite the pizzazz if we left the planning to the men. What man would sit down with the kids to watch a Martha Stewart TV special, and then actually try making wreaths and gingerbread houses? (I do draw the line at gilding and drilling nuts with a Dremel drill [whatever that is] for stringing on garlands. My house looks just fine with the nuts we already have.)

Often the many balls women struggle to keep up in the air simultaneously require us to be both juggler and magician. The act is stressful and exhausting, and all that effort can really get to

> *When* I find it difficult to remember my last experience of pure joy, it sets me back.
>
> ~Carla F.

us. As Barbara M. says, "I feel overwhelmed at times, trying to balance household chores, bills, our children's activities, and my drama and church work, all the while trying to be a supportive wife to my husband."[1]

Single moms and moms working outside the home or at an in-home business know a lot about juggling many balls and a very full plate. Lisa V. describes this struggle quite well:

I Am Overwhelmed!

I have three young children—
> And I'm working full-time.
I have two bathrooms to clean and no time for one—
> And I'm working full-time.
I have eight loads of laundry (not including the pile on my husband's side of the bedroom)—
> And I'm working full-time.
I'm late for work, the kids won't cooperate, the lunches aren't made, and I just put a run in my last pair of pantyhose—
> And I'm working full-time.
All I want to do is go to the movies with my friends for the first time in a year—but the groceries aren't bought, dinner's not planned, laundry isn't done, the house isn't clean, the kids have Girl Scout cookies to sell, and my husband "just wants to be able to watch football."

Even when fatigue—whether physical, emotional, or spiritual—and the pressure of balancing our many roles make life overwhelming, we can choose to find joy in the Lord.

- Life can be so . . . **daily**—as in *"What's so joyful about the 367th load of laundry?"*

We plan, buy, prepare, and serve a meal—only to find that the people we fed have the nerve to get hungry again within four hours or so! We finally get the last of the laundry gathered, sorted, washed, dried, folded, and put away—and then discover three days' worth of our son's dirty laundry stuffed in the toy box and moldy socks next to the wet towel under the bed. And, of course, more dirty clothes will be in the hamper again tonight. We get the whole house decluttered, organized, dusted, mopped, and swept—and in one short weekend the whole thing looks completely undone.

Iva H. expresses the feelings that go along with this cycle: "I believe the thing that keeps me from being joyful is getting bogged down with everyday things. I know if I could be a little more organized, I'd be happier." Robin M. struggles with "the fact that I would like to spend most of my time creating (writing, decorating, teaching my children arts and crafts), but I feel obligated to spend it maintaining my homelife (cleaning, cooking, disciplining the kids)." Betty M. adds, "The dailyness gets to me when I am physically exhausted and overwhelmed with household chores." Haven't we all been there?

Life happens daily. Monotony and tedium can be huge rocks in our path—but I maintain that we can see the sparkle even in those rocks if we look from the right angle.

- Life can be so . . . **busy**—as in *"A joyful life? I can't think about that today. I'm too busy. I'll think about finding joy tomorrow. Gotta run."*

America does busy quite well. Perhaps you've asked friends over to dinner only to hear, "Oh, we'd love to get together, but we're so busy right now." Or maybe someone has invited you somewhere and that's been your reply. And why is it that our immediate response to "How've you been?" seems to be "Really busy"? We have our Day-Timers, our schedules, our commitments. We coordinate car pools, sports, church events. We rarely sit down to take a deep breath. Is this how God intended us to live?

Microwaves, minivans, modems, and miscellaneous machines are supposed to make life easier. They do—and I'm not ready to give them up—but these timesavers also make our lives busier. We don't use these tools to do our work more quickly and gain more leisure time. Instead, too often, we fill the time saved with yet another item on our to-do list.

Do you find yourself busy but barren? Are you filling your days with countless activities but finding yourself not really fulfilled by those things? Barren busyness can stifle joy and contentment, but having the Lord's perspective on what we do can bring real joy. Keep reading!

- Life can be so . . . **disappointing**—as in *"I never thought life would be like this."*

Are you looking back at unfulfilled dreams or unmet expectations, wishing things had turned out differently? Are your current circumstances discouraging? Have people let you down? One woman writes, "I thought my life would turn out like I pictured when I was young. I had such high hopes. I just never counted on my husband having an affair and my son turning out like he did. I still love them, but the disappointment is huge."

What disappointments are keeping you from joy?

One of my favorite lines from the movie *Steel Magnolias* comes when Julia Roberts tells her mother (Sally Field) that she doesn't want to go through life always playing it safe and missing out on really great moments, like having children. She says, "I'd rather have 30 minutes of wonderful, than a lifetime of nothin' special." She doesn't want to get to the end of the road and, looking back, see only the gray disappointment of "nothin' special." I don't want a lifetime of nothin' special either, and neither do you. The good news is that we are not destined to "nothin' special." Despite the inevitable disappointments, we can live life joyously!

- Life can be so . . . **painful**—as in, *"How can I be joyful when all I feel is pain?"*

Different people can tolerate different levels of pain. Some of us can handle a great amount of pain and still function, but others of us are more sensitive and react at a much lower pain threshold. Whenever we reach our threshold, however, our main focus is usually the relief of that pain. When it's unrelenting or unmanageable, when we can't make it stop or get it under control, joy can become a mere memory.

Former flight attendant Janetlee H. knows about pain, both physical and otherwise. Since 1985, when she was hurt in an accident, she has been in chronic pain. I asked her if her pain makes finding joy and contentment a struggle. Her reply was:

It totally does. My pain brings migraines, and sometimes my thought processes aren't as clear as I'd like. I feel like my pain robs me. Pain is the enemy trying to take over and keep me from a joyful life, and it's just as subtle as Satan, creeping up on me without me realizing it until suddenly I'm not in control anymore. Sometimes I get weak, shaky, and extremely stressed because of pain that gets out of control. Sometimes the little things snowball and I just explode. Then I have to go back to the people in my life and apologize for reacting like that instead of simply responding.

Maybe you, too, know the rocky path of physical pain, or maybe you know the rough road of emotional pain.

Pam R. knew about emotional pain. It seemed to dominate her life. You see, she lost a child. Her precious two-year-old daughter was killed in an accident. Ever since then, Pam has struggled with the pain caused by a gaping hole in her heart, a hole created when her child was taken from her. Whenever she saw a child of the same age happily playing or holding a parent's hand, she felt as if her heart would break. Pam still thinks of her child every day, and every day her heart aches. For a long time, Pam thought she would never know happiness again, but over time it's returning. More importantly, she has learned that even in the most painful moments of her heartbreak—when the joy of life is missing—the joy of the Lord is still present.

Whether your pain is a hurt in your body or an ache in your heart, you know how it can mask much that is good and happy and joyful in life. But let me hold out to you the hope that God's joy can penetrate that pain.

The Storms of Life

Life is indeed hard, and sometimes seeing the sparkle in the rocks is difficult because we're engulfed in a storm, and when that happens joy can seem to be in the clutches of the undertow or dashed on the rocks. And, like you, perhaps I know such storms. I don't write to you from the mountaintop shouting down, "Be joyful, O ye women!" I'm not sitting above the hubbub of life, having never been touched by high waters or rough winds. No. I write to you as a fellow sojourner whose lived in the valley and on the mountaintop and along the somewhat rocky path between the two. Like you, I know from experience the over-whelming, busy, disappointing, and painful days of life—espe-cially the painful ones . . .

Six years ago, when the seeds for this book were first sown, I began to study what God's Word said about joy. I started think-ing about, praying over, and writing down what God was teach-ing me about being a joyful woman, about being a mama who was happy. Not too long after that, the storms began, and I des-perately wanted to keep from losing all my joy in the gale. That turbulence tested everything I had learned about joy, and it tested my faith as well.

The first storm broke when my husband's company down-sized and Tim was laid off. Needless to say, finances got tight. When he found another job, he began traveling Monday through Friday. We were only together as a family on the week-ends. Then one Wednesday afternoon I got a call from my dad and the second storm was unleashed. I knew my mother had been feeling bad for some time and had gone in for some test-ing, but I wasn't at all aware there was anything seriously wrong. Dad called from her hospital room, and I'll never forget his words: "Honey . . . well . . . we've got a little problem with your mother."

My insides began to quiver. "What kind of problem?" I was afraid to hear his answer.

"We've got a little cancer."

A little cancer! Is that like a little pregnant or a little dead? A little cancer? Oh, Lord, please! Not my mom!

As my father described the recent events and explained the diagnosis, I struggled to keep my composure. The word "lym-phoma" hung in the air, a dark cloud that had just descended over our lives. Little did I know how familiar I would become with that word. Dad, Mom, and I were quite strong until he asked, "Do you want to talk to your mom?"

"Yes, please."

As soon as I heard her familiar, "Hi, honey," the shock of the news gave way to grief. Neither of us could say anything for some time. I had been all right until I heard her voice, and she had been strong until she heard mine. Mom and I were very close. She was my cheerleader, my advisor, and my best friend in a different way than Tim is. Mom met needs in my life that only a mother can. The news that she had cancer was devastating.

While I was on the phone, my good friend Jill dropped by. Seeing that something was dreadfully wrong, she took care of my children while I talked. After I hung up, I had in Jill the shoulder, the hug, the helping hand, and the prayer warrior I desperately needed. How sweet of the Lord to send my unexpected visitor. With Tim gone, I needed Jill's support. I had just had my first taste of grief.

Within days, we made the decision to put our things in storage and move to Houston where Tim was working and my parents were living. (We were homeschooling at the time, so the quick move was possible.) Tim was still employed out of his Dallas office, so we weren't moving to Houston permanently. We were just going to live with him in his corporate apartment for about six weeks until we knew where his job would take him—or so we thought.

The next few years brought pain into my life like I'd never before experienced. I came to understand the meaning of what some people call the tear in life's membrane—the point where the protective envelope around you breaks and life's hardness comes crashing into your world. It had come into mine. I was dealing with two separate struggles simultaneously: my mom's health and my immediate family's uprootedness. I felt so misplaced.

The corporate apartment was just down the street from my parents' home. Although the apartment was very convenient, it was very small—and some of the walls were painted red. I would come home from consultations, scans, tests, and hospital visits with my mom to a very tiny and dark apartment with red walls. They weren't a beautiful, bold cranberry color. They were fire-engine red walls that represented to me the harsh, jarring intrusions in my life.

After one month there, we moved to another small but brighter corporate apartment nearby. We kept thinking that we would be permanently moved to Houston or relocated back to Dallas at any time. Then we'd get our things out of storage in Dallas; I had only packed for six weeks, but we stayed away for well over six months.

That period of time was a roller coaster of emotions for me. Not only was I struggling to cope with the harsh reality of my mother's cancer, but I was also struggling with our less-than-ideal and very uncertain living situation. And, to top it off, I was pregnant with our fourth child—a blessed event, but it was wreaking havoc with my hormones. I call those days our Nomadic Period. Boy, could I relate to those Israelites!

Every Friday, Tim came home with some tidbit of news, but the situation changed almost weekly. For seven months we lived from day to day, not knowing where home would be. I'd like to say I trusted in the Lord and never worried, but I can't. Oh, there were days when I rested in Him, but there were also days when, taking Scripture literally, I entered my "prayer closet." (The only way I could get away from everyone was to go into my bedroom closet. I'd shut the door, turn off the light, pray . . . and cry.)

My maternal nesting instinct had also kicked in by now. There I was, in an apartment with none of our things and nothing we needed for the baby. So we made an overnight trip to Dallas to get the crib and the rocking chair out of storage. As we started getting ready to check out of the motel and head back to Houston, I realized that our daughter Claire, five years old at the time, was having a hard time figuring out where home was, too. When we began packing our suitcases, baby things in tow, Claire said in a forlorn little voice, "We're moving again? I thought we were going to live here!"

I started to laugh, but suddenly I felt like crying! My child thought we were changing our address to the Motel 6! She had no idea where home was. Of course, the children didn't understand. *I* was struggling to understand. Much that was stable in our lives—our home, our church, our friends, and the health of loved ones—had been stripped away. I didn't know if my mother was going to live or die or where home was going to be. For most of my fourth pregnancy I didn't even know in which city the baby would be born. Our insurance company kept me guessing about whether I'd go into labor and have to make the four-hour drive to Dallas, hoping Baby Number Four didn't debut in the parking lot of the Corsicana Dairy Queen along the way! (She didn't—much to the relief of the Dairy Queen manager and me!)

But our tiny apartment got even smaller when we brought our fourth child home. "Cozy" took on new meaning as the six of us shared two tiny bedrooms. Knowing others have much worse living conditions did nothing for my post-partum days of "displacement." With Tim working a lot of overtime, I had many hours alone (as alone as one can be with four children) during which I pondered all the uncertainties of my life while the noise of the neighbors' quarrels and bathroom habits wafted through our thin walls. (I got to know those people quite well, although they never knew it.)

That period of my life would have been hard even without the pain of my mother's battle against cancer. My lifeline during that time was the quiet moments I had with the Lord before the children awoke. I would read my Bible and pour out my heart to God: "Lord, how can you possibly have me writing about joy? I'm not joyful! In fact, I'm miserable. I hate my circumstances, and I'm certainly not content. I want my mom whole, I want my husband to be here with us, I want to know where home is. I want my old life back!"

I kept waiting for God to say, "OK, Lindsey. Here's your old life—or at least part of it—back" or, "This is hard, but here's My joy on a silver platter." He didn't. Instead, everything I ever knew, or thought, or thought I knew about joy was put to the test. Before this, I knew about joy on the mountaintop, joy in the mundane, and joy in unpleasant circumstances. This experience, however, taught me about joy in the valley—and this valley was littered with more rocks than I'd ever had to face at one time. Although I didn't know it then, bigger and heavier rocks lay ahead. But during my struggle in that valley, God began to show me the sparkles.

Finding Joy in the Journey

Perhaps you're facing struggles that make my story seem like a walk in the park. I know many of you are. However, as a friend of mine who has lived through more tragedies than any woman should have to endure, once told me, "It's not always the traumas in life that are difficult to get through. God's grace is very encompassing. Sometimes the everyday stuff is a challenge." Even the everyday struggles and less-than-traumatic events can rob us of our joy when we try to operate in our own strength and when we forget to look for the sparkles in the midst of trouble. Instead of trying to climb over the rocks or haul them off ourselves, let's learn to navigate among them, guided by the One who can move the whole mountain. It's only in Him that we find joy that lasts—joy that weathers life's storms and shines like the sparkle in the rocks.

As you've probably sensed, this isn't a five-steps-to-joy book. Instead, it presents a lifestyle and perspective in which joy is the result, not the goal. It's a look at life where joy—the attitude, gift, and fruit—is possible, both internally and externally. We can make choices that cultivate joy in our heads, hearts, and homes.

It is my prayer that as you read these pages you will discover new truths about the joyful, abundant life God offers us and, in turn, learn to cultivate contentment and find joy in your journey, whether the path takes you up to the mountaintop, down through the valley, or somewhere between the two. In the triumphs, tragedies, and dailyness of our lives, each of us can find a sparkle in the rocks. It might be shining right in front of us in simple external joys like the glitter in the sidewalk. The sparkle might be the reflection of the joy of the Lord in our lives when we allow Him to polish us like a rock in a tumbler to produce that shine. And, as Christians, the sparkle—the Holy Spirit's capacity for the fruit of joy in our lives whether we feel it or not—is always within.

So where are you in your journey? Are you enjoying the sparkles along your path? Or are you staring at immovable rocks in a valley? Are you longing for a deeper joy and greater understanding and experience of the God-given sparkle that lies within? Are you struggling with

> *The fruit of the Spirit is love, joy, peace, patience, goodness, faithfulness, gentleness, self-control.*
>
> ~Galatians 5:22,23

some of the things that keep us from seeing the sparkle in life? Are you overwhelmed? Stuck in the dailyness of life? Or are you so busy that you're missing the joy in the moment? Are past disappointments keeping you from experiencing joy today? Or are you simply looking for relief from your pain?

Life is hard. There's no denying that, but there's a way, my friend, to find joy in the journey. You can experience joy in the moment, regardless of the circumstances of your life. You can know a deep and abiding sense of fulfillment and purpose, whatever the unsettledness, struggle, or discouragement you are dealing with. Making the choice to rejoice, connecting with the Giver of joy, and being attentive to the sparkles in the moment are worth every ounce of effort involved. When we cultivate a lifestyle conducive to joy, this attitude and fruit *is* ours! And sometimes our heavenly Father surprises us with a sparkle in the rocks when we least expect it—a glimmering, shimmering gift— simply because we are His children.

~❧ 2 ❧~

If Mama Ain't Happy,
Ain't Nobody Happy
So Maybe I'd Better Smile

It had not been a good day. I woke up late, spilled coffee grounds on the clean floor, and burned the toast all within minutes of my reluctant entry into the morning. I had a headache and felt like everything needed to be done at once. My toddler had an accident just as we were walking out the door (naturally), and Pearl, our new kitty, had an accident on my white comforter. To make my already partly cloudy day worse, I began to detect a storm of PMS hovering on the horizon. If only I could find that number and call in sick as a mom!

That afternoon I raced home from the grocery store (shopping is such fun with four children) and pulled into the driveway to find that the overnight company I was expecting later that evening had just arrived! And there I was with dinner in grocery bags! So I did what any savvy, together woman does. I pretended I'd planned it this way and, through clenched teeth, feverishly directed the children when the guests weren't looking. "Pssst! Jacquelyn, quick! Could you make the salad? . . . Claire, run upstairs to see if anybody pottied on the bed in the guest room . . . Collin, quit thumping Allison . . . Allison, quit eating the butter!"

31

No, it had not been a good day. Later that evening my third-grade daughter, Claire, slumped down on her chair to write about her day in her journal. "Mom," she said, "how do you spell 'horrible'?"

If Mama ain't happy, ain't nobody happy! Male or female, most people agree with that statement. Women usually smile a knowing grin, saying, "Oh, have I been there!" Men usually chuckle and add a bit too loudly, "Boy, isn't that the truth!" When people hear this statement, they think of themselves, their mate, their mother, or someone they know. It's widely recognized that Mama's happiness is important to the happiness of the rest of the family.

Have you ever heard the expression, "If Daddy ain't happy, ain't nobody happy"? I used to say, "Never!" until I read Colleen A.'s comment: "The phrase that would more accurately describe our family experience would be, 'If Daddy ain't happy with his job, ain't nobody happy.' I've been surprised to discover how much I am a reflector of my husband's happiness. I've found that I can be happy anywhere and in most situations if my husband is content and happy, especially in his career." Hear! Hear! Daddy happy on the job and Mama happy in general—we may be on to something!

$\mathcal{I}$f Mama ain't happy, ain't nobody happy.

It is better to live in a corner of the roof, than in a house shared with a contentious woman.

~Proverbs 25:24

Although the father profoundly influences the family, Mama gets the credit (or, in this case, the rap). Besides, when Daddy loses his...uh...happiness, Mama is often there to smooth things over. Made by God to be relationally oriented, we women tend to be the peacemakers and nurturers in the family. Here's a case in point.

One morning, after I'd worked on this manuscript long into the night, our entire family woke up late. I hadn't gotten enough sleep—and apparently neither had anyone else. It was a look-at-me-wrong-and-I-might-box-your-ears kind of morning. I commented (politely, I thought) that Tim needed to hang his bath towel (the size of Rhode Island) on the towel bar or shower door to dry. (After all, I knew *he* wasn't going to be the one scrubbing mildew off the bathroom door!) Well, his three hours of sleep sharply responded to my five hours of sleep, and my claws came out. Then, hearing myself, I thought, *Oh my! Who is this person—and why is she screaming at my husband like this?*

Tim went back to shaving and commented to his shaving buddy, three-year-old Allison, "Boy, if Mama ain't happy, ain't nobody happy, Alli. Somebody ought to write a book about that!"

I put on my shoes while the darts of conviction fully lodged in my heart. I thought, *I am pond scum. And he has the wherewithal to humor this old amoeba, swimming in sometimes murky waters!*

Our Circle of Influence

You and I influence—for better or worse—the people we are close to whether or not we intend to. When we recognize the incredible influence we have and direct it in a healthy, nonmanipulative, encouraging way, we can change a person's life. And that person may be someone we love.

• *We influence our husbands.*

Encouraging words and loving support can enable a man to go farther than he could go alone. Likewise, a critical, judgmental spirit can tear a man down. The truism "behind every great man is a great woman" is often just that—true! We can help our mate become the person God intends him to be by being a wife who builds up, comforts, loves unconditionally, and cherishes her husband. We are in a unique position to encourage our mate in ways that no one else can or would. Our respect and support can have a profound and positive impact on his self-image and, in turn, on who he is, what he does, and what he accomplishes. The book *Building Your Mate's Self-Esteem* points out how vital we are in this process: "Your mate's self-esteem will either hinder or enhance his ability to learn, make decisions, take risks and resolve conflicts with you and others. It will either restrain him or refuel him."[1] Our mate needs us.

• *We influence our children.*

Nineteenth-century English writer John Ruskin was well aware of this. He said, "My mother's influence in molding my character was conspicuous. She forced me to learn daily long chapters of the Bible by heart. To that discipline and patient, accurate resolve, I owe not only much of my general power of taking pains, but the best part of my taste for literature." Some have called Ruskin the most influential English writer of the 1800s. His art, literature, and writing on social issues helped form the tastes of Victorian England and influenced many people. That mother influenced a son who then influenced a nation.

The children you and I have a chance to influence come into this world moldable, malleable, and ready to be gently shaped into the kind of person God created them to be—and we are the dominant force in that molding. What an amazing privilege! And, as moms know, the wonderful bond between mother and child begins at (and even before) the moment of birth. Some psychologists call this early interaction "the dance." Dr. Brenda Hunter describes it: "Through her voice pitch, tempo, [and] facial expressions, a mother communicates her emotional state to her baby, and he dances synchronously in response to the messages he receives."[2] Other child development experts have called the mother/baby attachment the foundation stone of personality with the mother being the touchstone in a child's life.

Children need their mother's love as much as they need food. They learn they are loved and develop their self-concept from attachments to their parents, significantly their mother. "Simply put," says Dr. Hunter, "if a child's parents are consistently loving and sensitive to his needs, the child incorporates the message: 'I am loved, I am worthy, others will love me just as my parents love me.' If, on the other hand, the child's parents are rejecting, emotionally inaccessible, or absent, then a child may come to feel: 'I am unloved. Therefore, I am unworthy. How can I expect others to love me if my parents don't?'"[3]

Tell a child that he is special and watch him blossom. Treat a child as if she is special and watch her flourish. We influence children by the things we tell them, by the lessons we teach them, and, most powerfully, by how we live. Children learn what is modeled before them (more on that later). We profoundly influence the children God has entrusted to us. What an awesome responsibility and tremendous privilege.

• *We influence people in our circle.*

Whether we are married or single, mothers or not, we influence our extended family, our friends, our neighbors, and our coworkers. We can be the light that draws a family member back into the fold or a friend back to faith in God. We can be the person who makes a difference in the life of a neighbor. We can be salt and light to coworkers. We can show "random acts of kindness" in a world where kindness is much too rare.

In *Disciplines of the Home,* Anne Ortlund describes the influence we women can have on others as she gives three cheers for Mother:

> Over the centuries she's worked as hard as father, and for very different reasons.
> He has built the houses; she's added the colors, the smells, the music.
> He has shaped constitutions to make citizens protected; she has sewn flags to make them weep and cheer.
> He has mustered armies and police forces to put down oppression; she has prayed for them and patted them on the back and sent them off with their heads up.
> He has shaped decisions; she has added morale.[4]

The fact is that we women greatly influence our mate, our children, and the people whose paths we cross each day, and we do so through our personality, worldview, degree of optimism (or pessimism), character, and faith. Created by God distinct and very different from men, we women view life and people through a very different filter than men do. We often approach life focused more on relationships. We tend to be more intuitive and emotional. We exercise our influence on others differently than men do. It's no surprise that Mama's happiness (or lack thereof) affects the people in her circle of influence; it does so because we women function as thermostat, chief operating officer, and heart of the home.

Living Thermostats

Think about what a thermostat does. It regulates the temperature, controls the atmosphere, and can be adjusted to meet the need of the moment. If things need warming up, we raise the setting of the thermostat. If they need cooling off, we adjust the thermostat and lower the temperature.

Now the *World Book Encyclopedia* has a great description of a thermostat, which I will share with you (embellishments, no extra charge).

> A thermostat [us] is a device that helps control the temperature of an indoor area or an appliance [like a home or a husband]. A thermostat is set to keep an area or an appliance [the home/or husband] at a certain temperature [cool on the outside and hot on the inside—the husband that is]. It measures temperature changes [like when your husband wrecks his car] and automatically controls the heating or cooling [we instinctively and immediately soften our voices and cook his favorite dinner].[5]

Then *World Book* gets into some boring stuff about coils, uncoils, and bimetallic strips. The really interesting part (although that last bit would certainly interest *my* husband) is this: "Most thermostats turn heating or cooling equipment completely on [with the kids at Grandma's, we greet hubby at the door wearing !!!] or completely off [we suggest he might be more comfortable under Rover's roof tonight]."[6]

Some thermostats, however, use a method called proportional control. These "measure the difference between the actual temperature and the desired temperature and then adjust the amount of heating or cooling according to this temperature difference. Proportional control thermostats [our goal] can provide an extremely even temperature [and more consistent comfort]."[7]

Clearly, you and I are the thermostats in the home. By our very presence, we regulate the temperature of our family and therefore control the atmosphere in our homes. Properly set, we can—by our attitude and actions—meet the specific need of a given moment. (Have you ever noticed, for instance, that if you raise your voice, your children raise theirs? If we talk softly, our children talk softly. Whisper to a toddler and that little person will often whisper back.) Furthermore, we are able to read family members to determine the proper setting. When things get too heated, we can lower our setting and cool things off. If things are a bit too cool, we can take action to warm the place up. Our very presence can be the thermostat that keeps the family from sweltering in the jungle of life or freezing in the coldness of an uncaring world.

Chief Operating Officers

While fathers may be the chief executive officers in the home, mothers are the chief operating officers. (I wonder if COOs are paid the same as CEOs? Of course, any pay at all for COOs would be a step up!) We are the managers who usually run this enterprise known as "family." Often single-handedly, we oversee the day-to-day operations of the family unit—although I don't know a woman alive who wouldn't like an extra hand or two (either to grab an extra dishtowel or applaud her amazing juggling act—probably the former the most!). We are chef, chauffeur, chief bottle

We need to take [family management] as seriously as career success, because home is where success really matters. . . . Whether we're changing a diaper or closing a deal, our work has dignity, honor, and value.

~Kathy Peel,
The Family Manager

washer, social director, and, often, maid. We plan, prepare, and perform everything from cleaning clothes to remembering to buy food and toilet paper so that daily life is doable.

As chief operating officers of the family, we also know who is supposed to go where, at what time, with what, and with whom. We often schedule the family activities, and, as the members grow (in number and age), managing that schedule can feel like we're directing fast-moving freeway traffic with mere hand signals. We try not to schedule Aunt Rose's visit when the house has just been fumigated or little brother's birthday party when older sister has the debate team over. Simple stuff like that. Someday when we're old ladies, I just know our kids will come back and thank us for that. Until then, we can take pride in knowing that being the family's chief operating officer is a just, noble, and very important endeavor, if not a little arduous and sometimes downright exhausting.

Heart of the Home

Often nobody's happy if Mama ain't happy because we are the heart of the home. Dad may be the backbone, but we are the heart, the feeling center. Mother tends to be the one person in the family who is in touch with every other member of the family. We usually know where each family member is emotionally, physically, and, hopefully, geographically—although that's not always the case. Once when I was quite busy with my many COO duties, I took a minute to visit with a friend who stopped by. When she left, I went back to what I had been doing, thankful that the children were all playing so quietly. About ten minutes later the phone rang.

"Lindsey? This is Susan. Are you missing anybody?" she asked.

I thought for a second. Then, thankfully, before I could answer, she added, "Are you missing Collin?"

"Do you know where he is?" I asked, too embarrassed to admit that I didn't. (Oh, I would have missed him...eventually.)

"Yes. I got all the way home and when I pulled into the driveway, Collin jumped up from behind the backseat with his hands high in the air and yelled, 'Ta-da! I'm here, Mrs. Weisiger!' He nearly scared me to death! Since he was so proud of himself, I just told him it was very nice of him to pay me a visit and next time we might even let Mom know. I'll have Dirk bring him home."

Yes, it does pay to know where everyone is—geographically and otherwise. I feel somewhat comforted knowing that I am not the only parent to ever temporarily misplace a child. Another mother once called me after a birthday party to make sure her daughter had been picked up by her husband. She said, "I'm just checking. I told him her schedule, but he gets confused. Once when I had to be gone, I told him where and when to pick her up, but he forgot and had no idea where she was. If I hadn't come home, she could have stayed there for days!"

Besides keeping track of where everyone is geographically (usually), we also keep up with the condition of their lives. We intuitively know when our child is upset or when our husband has had a bad day. We can read a face, a voice, even a walk because we are students of those we love. God gave us mothers a heart for our family members that is very different from the loving and caring heart He gave fathers.

Now, like most generalities, this statement doesn't hold true across the board. In some families, the husband is the nurturer, and in other families both the man and woman are equally nurturing. And, sadly, we've also heard tragic stories of child abuse or even murder by the hand of a mother, but most mothers cannot even fathom such acts. Most mothers intuitively put the needs of their children first and love their children so completely they would give their lives to save them. That's one reason why we're the heart of the home.

And, in this role, we women meet most of the emotional needs of the family. We don't just see that Janie has her homework and her lunch in her backpack, clean clothes for tomorrow, and cookies for the class party. We are also there to scrape her up off the floor after school because of another child's cruel and hurtful words. We provide that important hug and listening ear.

God has designed us to be able to keep up with where each of our family members is emotionally, academically, physically, and spiritually. The knowledge is intuitive. I can tell, for instance, when my husband needs my full attention at the end of the day and when he needs to unwind by himself. I know when Jacquelyn needs a little extra love after a hard day, when Claire needs extra snuggles more than extra sleep, when Collin needs time to talk and pray just with Mom, and when Allison is ready to learn a new Bible story and song.

Instinctively we women put our arms around a crying child, whether it be our daughter whose friends ignored her at school or the little lost boy at the department store who needs us to help him find his mom. We know which child needs an extra hug and who needs a little space. We can tell the difference between a baby's cry of boredom and his cry of pain. We usually know where our children are spiritually, delighting in their every move closer to our heavenly Father. We can also spot when a child is really praying in church and when she's sleeping! We can keep up with all these people at the same time and on many different levels because God gave women hearts and minds that reflect our amazing ability to do, think about, and keep track of many things all at once. Another reason we women can keep track of the condition of everyone's heart as well as their spiritual walk and geographical location is that our hearts are linked to theirs just as strongly as their body was linked to ours in the womb. We are the heart of the home because God designed us that way. He gave us a soft spot in our souls that yearns for the closeness and well-being of our family.

As the thermostat, the chief operating officer, and the heart of the home, we women influence the people in our family by adding warmth, managing the home and schedules, and nurturing each individual. Since we function in these vital roles, it's no surprise that our joy and contentment—or their absence— directly impact our family and, often, our friends, neighbors, co-workers, and acquaintances. Within our circle of influence, each of us has a tremendous opportunity to touch people with the love and joy of the Lord. What a privilege to impact another person's life through our friendship! How precious to be able to teach a child about Jesus and make a difference for eternity! And what joy to be the soulmate our spouse needs!

But Who's Happy—and Why?

Since Mama's happiness affects the people around her, let's consider for a moment who is happy and what makes them so. Are members of the opposite sex, younger or older folks, or people of a different nationality happier than you are? Psychology has long studied the darker side of humanity, but researchers in what's sometimes called "the science of well-being" are providing new information about the subjective mindset of happy people. In an attempt to determine who is happy and why, these "happyologists" have randomly surveyed people and asked them to report their level of happiness or unhappiness and how satisfied they are with life.

What did these researchers discover? In his book *The Pursuit of Happiness,* David Meyers reports that no particular age, race, gender, or nationality inherently enjoys more happiness in life. This finding dispels many common assumptions. So who is happy—and why? According to some studies, happy people tend to have several characteristics in common. Meyers says the most important traits of happy people are: optimism, extroversion, self-esteem, and personal control.

They also tend to have good health and a supportive network of family and friends; and enjoy productive work and an active faith.

This secular look at faith and its connection to happiness intrigued me. The study defined "active faith" as one which meets people's deep needs—our needs for a greater joy, for strength during a crisis, for a support system, for an eternal perspective of life and death, and as something for which to live and die. Science is verifying what many of us have known for a long time!

As you look at the study's findings, however, you may be saying, "I want to be happy and I want my family to be happy, but that list of characteristics doesn't exactly describe me." Many of us are naturally introverted, some of us struggle with self-esteem, and others tend to be rather pessimistic. If we're not outgoing, confident, or optimistic, are we destined to less happiness? Statistically speaking, it seems so. The science of well-being suggests we're not in the running for high levels of happiness without those traits, but studies also indicate that those traits are hardly genetically encoded. The researchers used random surveys and merely noted these common threads in people's answers. These traits are quite logical contributors to happiness, and they serve as a wonderful springboard for identifying areas we might work on if we aren't as happy as we wish.

The real question for us, however, is, "Can I have joy without these traits?" Yes, yes, yes! And you can because the joy God gives is far different than the happiness the world offers. You and I may have less happiness in life than someone with all these "happiness qualities," but the only way we are sentenced to less joy is if we are missing the last characteristic listed above—an active faith in God.

Happiness vs Joy

Many people use the words "happiness" and "joy" interchangeably, but I don't. The two words mean far different things. Oh, if Mama isn't happy, everyone can feel the effects, but this book talks about joy which is something far deeper than happiness. Although happiness is wonderful and greatly enhances family life, being a woman of joy is far more important. And each of us can be a woman who chooses to be joyful, who radiates the joy of the Lord, who experiences joy in this journey, and who lives out and gives out joy to our families.

Perhaps contrary to popular opinion, happiness is not a prerequisite for joy. The two are quite different in nature: happiness is external, joy is internal. Happiness is based on circumstances; joy isn't. Happiness is defined as a "state of well-being and contentment or pleasurable satisfaction." Joy is defined as "a feeling of great pleasure or happiness that comes from success, good fortune, or a sense of well-being; something that gives great pleasure or happiness." Clearly, joy looks like the better pursuit, but the meanings are still

I doubt whether anyone who has tasted [joy] would ever, if both were in his power, exchange it for all the pleasures in the world. But then joy is never in our power and pleasure often is.

~C. S. Lewis,
Surprised By Joy

quite similar. Webster is saying, essentially, that happiness is well-being and joy is just a little bit more well-being.

But that's not exactly what the epistle-writer James had in mind when he wrote, "Consider it all joy, my brethren, when you encounter various trials" (James 1:2). Consider trials "great well-being"? I don't think so. James is referring to the kind of joy Jesus spoke of when He told us that His joy would be in us and it would be full (John 15:11). In these words of promise, Jesus is surely not describing something as ordinary as mere or even great pleasure (flowers give me great pleasure) or telling us that His well-being would be in us (eating my vegetables gives me a sense of well-being). I want something better than pleasure and well-being, something better than flowers and vegetables. I want the joy Jesus offers!

Joy is a special gift from the Creator—a fruit of the Spirit, an attitude of the heart, an element of the very nature of God—and that joy is available to us. Happiness is the result of things; joy can be in spite of things. Happiness responds to circumstances; joy is possible even when the circumstances are difficult. Barbara B. put it simply for her children when they were young: "Happiness is based on happenings and joy is based on Jesus." This difference between happiness and joy is the reason James can write, "Consider it all joy, my brethren, when you encounter various trials, knowing that the testing of your faith produces endurance. And let endurance have its perfect result, that you may be perfect and complete, lacking in nothing" (James 1:2-4). Encountering trials in my life certainly doesn't give me pleasure or a sense of well-being, but knowing what God can do as a result of that work in me—the work that James is talking about—enables me to "consider it all joy." So don't think you need to wait for happiness before you can know joy. It's not a prerequisite!

Our Female Makeup

When I glance in the mirror in the morning, I am so glad to know that my makeup is in my drawer waiting to help me put my best face forward. But that's not the kind of makeup I'm talking about here. Instead, I'm referring to that inner makeup we have that is unique to us as women and which affects how we feel and respond. Several aspects of who we are as women warrant special attention because they can rob us of joy. Oh, sometimes Mama isn't happy because she really isn't happy or the joy robbers have attacked (we'll talk about them in a later chapter), but sometimes what's affecting Mama is simply fatigue, hormones, or emotions. Recognizing the role this threesome plays in our lives and, yes, explaining it to our families can mean the difference between "ain't nobody happy" and "let's ride this one out together."

Fatigue

We women work at our jobs or in our home businesses or homeschooling our children or volunteering at church and in the community—and then we pick up our COO responsibilities. Most women, including those working outside the home, do at least twice as much housework and childcare as men. With what's left of us, we try to be the loving wife and mother that everyone—including us—is expecting. (No pressure there, ladies!) In light of that job description, it's no wonder that we fight fatigue—and I won't even mention the fatigue that comes from...shhhhhhhh...aging.

Remember when you had a little more energy, like, say, when you were three years old? I've often dreamed of the rich and energetic woman I'd be if only I could figure out a way to siphon off some of the energy from my preschooler, infuse it into my tired body, and sell the surplus. (I'd be happy if anybody could figure out how to do that. Forget the rich part. I'd pay for more energy—and I'd pay a lot!) Many of us women fight fatigue—particularly mothers of preschoolers, working moms, and single moms. So often when we blow it—when we lose our temper and our tongue with our families—what was really talking was our fatigue.

Sleep experts say that nearly every American adult is sleep deprived. The rate of illnesses, accidents, and ulcers is up because our sleeping time is down. The Better Sleep Council says we are the "walking weary as a society," getting an average of 7½ hours of sleep a night, but really needing an extra hour. And to some bleary-eyed souls, 7½ hours would be a dream! Could you use an extra hour—or two or three? (Personally, I could go for an extra week right about now!)

So many times I try to be the wonderful, fun, energetic mom with lots of patience and tenderness for my children—only to get to the end of the day with an empty tank. Even if it's been a good day and I've been that kind of mom, I'm running on fumes by the children's bedtime. I'm sure you know the feeling: *If we do the 30-second teeth routine, leave baths for the morning, and read the abridged version of the story (one or two lines per page), I may be able to keep from collapsing until I'm near the sofa.*

Then there are those days when I totally lose the battle against fatigue, and, once again, my children pay the price. Although I start out trying to be Wondermom, I decide that simply being very patient and a little bit of fun is a more realistic goal and shoot for that. But before I get to "Goldilocks walked into the three bears' house, broke some stuff, got scared, and never went back again," my energy is gone. It's then that things like toothpaste on the toilet seat and wet clothes on the bathroom floor after bath time really take their toll on me. When I recently got to that place, I noticed that my voice started rising. Every word was clipped and terse, building to a full-fledged, *"HOW MANY TIMES HAVE I TOLD YOU?"* routine, followed by the "NOW, GO TO SLEEP AND I DON'T WANT TO HEAR A PEEP!" line. Nobody peeped. Yes, I know the saying well. Mama wasn't happy—nobody was.

I went downstairs and flopped on the couch, in tears for reducing my children to tears (again) all because I was tired. *I don't want to be this way. I want to be that patient-loving-kind-fun-wonderful mother. Where does she go at the end of the day?* I'm learning that on nights like I just described, I am not really an ogre. I'm just completely exhausted, and in my tiredness that ogre-like behavior emerges. So I'm trying to take precautions during the day to prevent that total drop-dead feeling. I'm even learning to nap. Since I get up early with my children and frequently stay up late with my husband, I often take a catnap during the day. When I do, it's amazing how much happier I am during the arsenic hour.

I have also stopped feeling guilty about those naps. One day, when I told Tim I was really tired, he said, "You should take a nap tomorrow. I'd take one every day if I worked from home."

"You would?" I said, in shock that my hard-working husband had spoken those words.

"Yeah. They ought to build that into the corporate structure like some cultures do. The break makes you much more productive." (Viva, Mexico! Everything there shuts down for a nap after lunch. I wonder if we can lobby for internationalizing the siesta? It would no doubt make the world a kinder, gentler place!)

"They" also ought to write that bit of wisdom in an instruction manual for all: Naps make Mama happier! In fact, I'm about ready to lobby for an addition to all birth certificates in bold type: **Naps required for all babies, toddlers, and mothers of such.**

It really is OK to sit down. I don't know why I (and you, too?) keep forgetting that! If you work outside the home, a short rest after work and before entering the "wild zone" can help. Don't feel guilty about plopping down on the sofa for a few minutes after you get home. "Taking ten" like that will help you get through the end of the day. Or you could do what a friend of mine does. Most days, during her lunch hour, she takes a 15-minute nap. She says it makes a huge difference in her energy level later that evening when she's with her family.

Yes, fatigue is an enemy we all know, but it's an enemy we shouldn't try to fight standing up. Let me say it again: It really is OK to sit down! Rest is rejuvenating.

Hormones

Another aspect of our makeup that influences whether or not Mama is happy is our fluctuating hormone level. Just consider this entry from one of my journals:

> What an emotional week for me! Hormones. YEEEEK! I began to sense my patience waning and my tension rising, and for three days I turned into this barely recognizable crazy person. I screamed and cried and asked myself, "Who is this woman? I don't know her and I wish she'd leave." Then, three days later, the hormone rage died down, and she left as suddenly as she had come. Was I ever glad to see her go!

The medical profession continues to document that hormone-driven premenstrual syndrome affects our personality and feelings. Those hormonal shifts in our bodies make a Dr. Jekyll/Mr. Hyde transformation seem tame. Our Mrs. Hyde routine can really make us wonder who is living in this body of ours! Being aware of our hormonal patterns and learning how to navigate the rough seas they stir up is crucial to our well-being and our family's! A friend of mine is ready to rent a garage apartment from her mother-in-law just for "those days"—and she's thinking of opening it up to women everywhere. She'd call it "The PMS Hospice: An Escape for Hormonally-Harried Women." Imagine the marketing possibilities! It would be a nice break for us and a great relief for the family as well. After all, as far as I'm concerned, Kathy Peel's description of PMS in her book *Do Plastic Surgeons Take Visa?* is right on target. Surely those letters stand for "Psychotic Mood Swings"!

But hormonal shifts in a woman's body are not a laughing matter, as Janetlee H. knows. Battling with major hormonal fluctuations was a way of life for her, but it wasn't until her hormonal imbalance got to dangerous levels and nearly immobilized her that she saw the problem for what it was. She says, "I didn't realize the effect my hormones were having on me. At first I thought I was going crazy. Then I thought it must be a spiritual attack or there was something wrong with me as a person, wife, mother, or friend. I tried to make changes on my own, but nothing worked."

Janetlee didn't realize there was anything wrong for a long time because she was so busy taking care of her family, her job, and other people. She had stopped looking out for herself. She says, "I had gotten caught up in the world telling me I could do it all—but I couldn't. I looked at others who appeared to be doing it all and wondered why I couldn't. Women 20 years older than me and single mothers with kids and without household help were functioning. I couldn't make myself do it all any longer, and I wondered, 'What's wrong with me?'"

What was drastically wrong, Janetlee discovered, was a major hormone imbalance which led to a hysterectomy. As Janetlee's case illustrates, sometimes hormones cause problems much more severe than your average PMS. Listen to your body. Physical problems need to be found and treated. With the right help, we can manage hormonal fluctuations. We can even learn to manage garden-variety PMS.

A friend of mine, for instance, has learned to read the warning signs in her body and anticipate her moods. "I note on my calendar when I am most likely to suffer from hormonal shifts, and I plan my schedule accordingly," she explains. "I try to never make major decisions during that time because my perspective isn't quite right and my thinking isn't quite as clear as normal. I also make sure that I get lots of extra rest on those days."

That kind of planning ahead is a great idea. However, I'm usually not that together, nor can I always predict those days. Too often I find myself short-tempered, emotional, or being a screamin' meanie, and wonder, *What is wrong with me?* Then the light will go on. *Oh, yeah.* Maybe you can relate? Some women don't know they are dealing with PMS because of an irregular monthly cycle. As one woman said, "It was hard to ever blame PMS for how I felt or acted because I never knew when it was my hormones and when it was just me."

Once some health concerns prompted my doctor to, in her words, "play around" with my hormonal balance. "Great! I'll be sure to warn my family to batten down the hatches," I said—and I did. I find it helps to explain to family members that there is a physical reason why Mom is being less than her wonderful self. Women can use a little extra support and nurturing during that time, but we won't get it if we don't ask for it. We also need to quit beating ourselves up when we blow it and remember that sometimes Mama is simply experiencing the physical effects of hormonal shifts—a victim of her own physiology.

Emotions

Sometimes women are emotional because of fatigue or hormones, but other times we're emotional because we are uniquely female. Perhaps this fact about us is what gave rise to the "If Mama ain't happy" saying in the first place. We've gotten a bad rap by bewildered men and perplexed children. "Women are too emotional" is a common response to us. Some women, perhaps. At times, perhaps. But just as disturbing is the woman who has too little emotion. What is called for, but difficult to achieve, is a beautiful balance of emotion and control so that emotions are shared in just the right amount at just the right time. And—may I put your mind to rest?—the only person who was ever capable of that perfect balance was Jesus. His emotions were always appropriate to the given situation, and He is a model for you and me. But sometimes we need more than His example alone.

Dee D. is a woman who knows all too well the power that our emotions can have over us. She struggled with hormonal problems, extremely fluctuating emotions, and a difficult marriage. One day while she and her husband Brynn were arguing, her emotions and hormones were raging out of control. Naturally quiet, Dee found herself standing at the top of the stairs yelling down at Brynn. Without thinking, she picked up a huge plant and hurled it down the stairs as easily as if it had been a baseball, narrowly missing her shocked husband. Realizing that she was out of control, he simply began to clean up. Soon after that event, Dee found medical help for her hormone problems.

She and Brynn became Christians soon after that, but her fragile emotions and difficult marriage were still realities. One day she completely shut down emotionally. She explains:

> Brynn and I were in the car, and I began thinking how I was so tired of feeling this way and fighting. I thought, "I'm not going to take this anymore." So I just started staring out the window. It was like I had turned off my emotional switch and took myself out of myself. For three days I was in a daze, not uttering a word or leaving the house. Some men from the church prayed with me, and I just watched them, thinking, "It's nice that they're doing this," but there was no feeling whatsoever. My body was there, but my emotions were someplace else. My husband then admitted me to a psychiatric hospital.
>
> I struggled because I knew that, as a Christian, I wasn't "supposed" to be this way. I got on my knees and cried out to God, "Lord, what am I doing in here? You've got to give me something to hang on to." Then I read Psalm 31—"Because Thou has seen my affliction, Thou hast known the troubles of my

soul....I am forgotten as a dead man, out of mind, I am like a broken vessel....But as for me, I trust in Thee, O Lord, I say, 'Thou art my God.'" I read that psalm for the six weeks I was there and kept getting different things from it. That was the beginning of my healing. For the first time I began to know God and know that I could trust Him.

When Dee was released from the hospital, the Lord led her through a slow, gentle time of recovery, marital counseling, spiritual growth, and healing. Today she is active in her church, a testimony to the healing that God can do with even the most fragile and damaged of emotions.

Emotions—Can You Trust Them? asks the title of one of Dr. James Dobson's bestselling books. I think the resounding answer would be "Not usually!" We aren't to live in the emotions, letting them wildly rule us. We're to live in the will, allowing our emotions to reveal what's inside. That's a big difference. Oh, I praise God that we are emotional creatures, for this God-given attribute helps us be nurturers. Our emotions allow us to feel happiness and joy, to cry with someone who's hurting, to be compassionate, to laugh, to mourn, to smile, to love. Even as we strive for balance, we can still cherish this aspect of our femininity. It truly is a gift. After all, without our emotions, we'd be nothing more than Mr. Spock in heels—efficient but as cold as ice.

Now, the next time you slip into your "Mama ain't happy" scenario, remember that fatigue, hormones, and emotions may be at work in you. Recognize when fatigue is reaching a toxic level and rest before you lose your cool. Understand how hormonal shifts affect your body and figure out what you can do to stay on an even keel. Strive for that healthy

> $\mathcal{W}$e have no more right to consume happiness without producing it than to consume wealth without producing it.
>
> ~George Bernard Shaw, *Candida*

balance between emotions and control. Accepting these aspects of our female makeup can help us take precautions before we, in our "unhappiness," make "nobody happy."

Trickle-Down Joy

Finding joy and contentment in life is the driving force behind most of what many people do. That inner satisfaction affects our thoughts, our attitudes, and our actions which, in turn, affect other people. This is trickle-down joy, and that's what the rest of this book is about. We'll examine this trickle-down effect and see how we can choose joy and contentment with our head, cultivate joy and contentment in our heart, and practice joy and contentment in our home. We can indeed be women who choose to be joyful, who radiate the joy of the Lord, who experience joy in this journey, and who live out and give out joy to those in our circle of influence. We don't have to wait for happiness based on happenings. We can make the choice to rejoice!

❧ Part One ❧

Choosing Joy and
Contentment in Our Heads
What We Think

❧ 3 ❧

It's All in Our Heads
Making the Choice to Rejoice

I f your mother ever told you "that's all in your head," she may have been right! Oh, I'm not suggesting that you make things up. I am suggesting, however, that feeling good about who we are and where we are in life often starts in our heads. It starts with what we think—in a word: *attitude.*

Attitude is a state of mind and heart. It colors how we respond to all that happens in our lives. Our attitude is the filter through which we view the world and the perspective from which we interact with it. Some people perceive and approach life through a beautiful rosy filter (most of the time). Others have a filter that could use a little cleaning. And some folks (and we all know at least one person like this!) have a filter that's so damaged they ought to pitch it and get a brand-new one. (If only changing attitudes were that simple!) Through what kind of filter do you see life? With what kind of attitude do you approach each day?

It's in Our Heads

Old Webster was a funny guy. He first defines "attitude" as "the arrangement of the body or figure (posture)." That sort of gives new meaning to having a bad attitude, doesn't it? Then he snaps out of it and explains that attitude is "a mental position or feeling regarding a fact or state." I would add that it's an outward expression of our inward feelings. Again, it's in our heads. And Scripture supports that fact: "As a man thinks within himself, so he is" (Proverbs 23:7). What we think determines who we are and how we act.

Now we may be able to hide how we feel for a time, but sooner or later our behavior and demeanor will be affected by how we feel. When we least expect it, our attitude sneaks out and gives us away. Sometimes our attitude makes its appearance rather subtly at first. We may think we're doing and saying things ever so pleasantly, but then our attitude slips out, revealed by our words or actions, and we're discovered. Attitude reflects what's really going on in our hearts. Let me give you an example.

I have served on a number of committees in the past and have found that, while often effective and occasionally fun, they accomplish things in a rather...umm...interesting way. (Just ask the folks who think that camels are really horses put together by committee!) At one such meeting, I had some definite and rather strong ideas about one of the issues we were going to discuss, but I went to the meeting fully intending to just listen. Well, my brain forgot to remind my mouth of that great plan, and before I knew it I was expressing myself.

At first I thought, "This is good. These things need to be said." Perhaps, but the problem was that my words, body language, and facial expressions were dripping with attitude—and it soon became quite apparent that it wasn't good. I proceeded to offend some, make others defensive, and I ushered in a big chill—all in one liberated moment of self-expression. *Boy, it's getting a little tense in here,* I thought. Then I realized that I was a chief contributor to the mood. When all was said and done, God used that meeting—as is His custom—to draw us together and teach me that my attitude sometimes peeks out of my actions just as easily as my slip peeks out from under my dress. Neither one makes us look very good.

At other times our attitude is about as subtle as a 400-pound monster wearing gold lamé. There's no missing it for the world! You can see it coming a mile away! One unnamed daughter of mine occasionally battles that kind of attitude, although without most of those pounds or the gold lamé. (What kind of mother do you think I am?)

"So, honey, how was your day?" I asked cheerfully one day when she got home.

"Fine," she said with the same tone of voice I'd use to exclaim, "The neighbors' dog pooped in our yard again!"

"Oh, that good," I replied, while stirring the night's dinner.

She slammed her books on the table as she walked by. One of them fell on the floor. She ignored it and bumped into her brother on her way to the fridge.

"'Scuse me. You're in my way," she barked at him. "What's for dinner?" she asked me.

"The world's best vegetable soup. How 'bout that?"

"Again? I'd rather eat cat food!" she complained, rifling through the refrigerator.

"No problem—that can be arranged."

"What's for snack?" she asked, first searching a cabinet unsuccessfully and then slamming the door.

"Popcorn."

"Again? How come we *never* have anything good to eat?" She checked the fridge one more time to be sure something good hadn't appeared in the 20 seconds since she last looked.

"Honey, would you take this laundry upstairs, please?"

"OK. But why is *she* getting to watch *Reading Rainbow?* She *never* has to do any work," this daughter said of her sister.

She grabbed the basket and headed upstairs, each footstep proclaiming her attitude.

"Did anything happen at school today?" I probed when she returned to the kitchen.

"No!" she said sharply—and then she screamed, "Mom, look! Allison just spit on my math homework. Scat, you!"

As I removed Allison from the scene of the crime, Collin entered and helped himself to the hot popcorn sitting on the table next to the unnamed and clearly unhappy daughter's backpack. It spilled—into the backpack, of course. When my daughter with an attitude returned from cleaning her homework, she shrieked, "Mom, get them outta here!"

Whether our attitude is camouflaged and subtle or screaming out at the world in no uncertain terms, three things are certain: our attitude helps shape who we are, it affects other people, and its appearance—what it looks like when it does appear—is completely our choice.

The Power of Our Attitude

The attitude with which we approach life determines the kind of woman we are, the kind of wife we are, and the kind of mother we are. It shapes the kind of friend we are and the kind of servant we are. It affects how we view our circumstances, our world, and our future. To a great extent, our attitude also influences our goals and the enjoyment we find in reaching them.

In the words of Christian writer and pastor John Maxwell, our attitude rather than our aptitude determines our altitude. Our attitude, not our ability or knowledge, determines how high we can soar. In his book *The Winning Attitude,* Maxwell gives several reasons why our attitude is so very important:

1. Our attitude determines our approach to life.
2. It determines our relationships with people.
3. Often our attitude is the only difference between success and failure.
4. Our attitude at the beginning of a task will affect its outcome more than anything else.
5. It can turn our problems into blessings.
6. It can give us an uncommonly positive perspective.
7. It is not automatically good just because we are Christians.[1]

> *How* ow good is man's life, the mere living! how fit to employ All the heart and the soul and the senses forever in joy!
>
> ~Robert Browning, "Saul"

Let me say it again: Our attitude shapes who we are and what we are able to accomplish.

Abraham Lincoln is a great historical example of a man with a wonderful attitude in spite of tremendous adversity and a teacher's disparaging remarks: "When you consider that Abe has had only four months of school, he is very good with his studies, but he is a daydreamer and asks foolish questions." Woodrow Wilson and Albert Einstein encountered similar teachers during their school years. One of Wilson's teachers said, "Woodrow is a unique member of the class. He is ten years old and is only just beginning to read and write. He shows signs of improving, but you must not set your sights too high for him." And one of Einstein's teachers said, "Albert is a very poor student. He is mentally slow, unsociable, and always daydreaming. He is spoiling it for the rest of the class. It would be in the best interest of all if he were removed from school at once."[2] Without a positive attitude, these men might have believed their teachers! Thankfully, they didn't listen. They kept on going.

And that ability to keep on going when the going gets tough is part of the good attitude that employers look for in employees. Hiring managers have reported that, when choosing between two equally qualified job applicants, they would pick the one with the better attitude—the one who values and enjoys working—over any other quality. Over half of the managers surveyed care more about a potential employee's *attitude* than their *aptitude*.[3]

Read what Charles Swindoll says about the importance of attitude:

> The longer I live, the more I realize the impact of attitude on life. Attitude, to me, is more important than facts. It is more important than the past, than education, than money, than circumstances, than failures, than successes, than what other people think or say or do. It is more important than appearance, gifting, or skill. It will make or break a person, a school, a church, a company. The remarkable thing is we have a choice every day regarding the attitude we will embrace for that day. We cannot change our past.... We cannot change the fact that people will act in a certain way. We cannot change the inevitable. The only thing we can do is play on the one thing we have, and this is our attitude....I am convinced that

life is 10 percent what happens to me and 90 percent how I react to it. And so it is with you.... We are
in charge of our attitudes.[4]

What kind of shape is the attitude that you're in charge of?

A Positive Look at Life

Would you say that your attitude is basically positive or basically negative? Are you a natural optimist or a die-hard pessimist?
Is your water glass half-full or half-empty? Or maybe you're like
Ziggy, who said, "My glass may be half-empty, but there will be
less to clean up when I spill it!" He gives his pessimistic outlook
a positive twist—which is better than being positively negative!
Or—yet another possibility—maybe you're like my husband.
When I asked Tim if he considered himself an optimist or pessimist, he replied, "Neither. I'm a pragmatist." And he is, always
choosing the practical approach to life's problems and situations.
But I contend that even a pragmatist can choose to be optimistic.

An optimist is someone who naturally sees the brighter side
of things and hopes you do, too. I think of a waiter I had recently.
After I finished a mediocre Mexican food lunch, he came to my
table and said with a Texas-size smile and south-of-the-border accent, "Everything was just about perfect?" I didn't know if that
was a question or a statement, but he seemed so cheerful and
confident that it had been good, that I just agreed with him. "Yes,
it was," I replied. I could have mentioned that the enchiladas
were lukewarm and a little dry, but I didn't want to spoil his impressive optimism.

Another impressive thing about optimists is their ability to
see problems as challenges. Optimism turns roadblocks into
bridges. Whether we choose to be stopped or to travel to the
other side depends on our attitude. And hundreds of studies and
thousands of anecdotes support the fact that people with a positive attitude excel in college, on the job, in sports, in politics,
and in most other fields, often despite some really tough circumstances.

While working on this book, I met two folks who know the
importance of this kind of positive attitude in their employees
and who view problems as opportunities for blessings. Jim and

Joycelyn McLachlan Clairmonte are the hosts of the beautiful McLachlan Farm Bed and Breakfast in Spring, Texas, where I spent several days alone to write this book. (Most of these pages, however, were written with a child nearby or occasionally on my lap.) The Clairmontes greeted me warmly and immediately made me feel like family. (I knew when I first heard her name— *Joycelyn*—that I'd like the hostess!)

One night I took a break from my self-induced sequestering when they invited me to join them for dinner. As we visited (and they didn't even know I was working on this chapter!), Joycelyn and Jim told me stories about some of the many weddings they have hosted—like the one where the groom showed up for an abbreviated service so he could get back to the hospital from which he'd been given a three-hour leave. Then there was the rainy-day wedding when the entire set-up—from the chairs to the arches—had to be moved three times and the bride (choosing to keep the wedding outside) had to wade through ankle-deep water in her wedding gown in a pouring rainstorm to get to the outdoor pavilion. But then there was an indoor evening wedding when a storm blew out the electricity, but a multitude of candles set in beautiful porcelain teacups around the room turned what could have been a disaster into one of the most beautiful weddings they'd hosted.

Clearly, Joycelyn and Jim's quick thinking and great attitude have made special memories out of potential chaos, but as I heard these stories, I wondered how the brides handled these emergencies as the most special event of their lives was about to take place. Joycelyn said, "There's one thing I tell all of my brides when they consider having their wedding here: 'Honey, don't get your heart set on things. Lots of things can happen at an outdoor wedding, and you have to approach this with the right attitude. With the right attitude, we can handle anything that comes up.'"

"You talk about attitude with all the brides that come here for their weddings?" I asked.

"Absolutely," she said. "I can handle about any situation— except a hysterical bride. I also make sure that the employees I hire have a good attitude. I won't hire them if they don't. Hard work is just hard work, so it helps to tackle it with a good attitude. A bad one affects everyone, and we try to have fun while we work." By George, I think she's got it! And this woman, with her great attitude toward life, is influencing countless brides and employees! Way to go, Joycelyn!

Optimism Is Good for Your Health

A positive attitude does more than help success come your way and make life more fun. At the same time that medical science continues to point to chronic stress, anger, and depression as leading causes of a host of diseases and even death, doctors are finding that a positive attitude is good for our health and our life expectancy. One article reported: "Scientists suspect that sensations like optimism, curiosity, rapture—the giddy, goofy desire to throw wide your arms and serenade the sweetness of spring—not only make life worth living, but also make life last longer. They think that euphoria…is good for the body, that laughter is protective against the corrosive impact of stress, and that joyful people outlive their bilious counterparts."[5]

A *Good Housekeeping* article entitled "The Secrets of People Who Never Get Sick" also reported that optimism is key to good health. Optimists have fewer sick days and doctor visits. They are also more inclined to take care of themselves by exercising and taking medications as prescribed. The author wrote, "Optimism strengthens the immune system…and optimists are also healthier because they encounter fewer bad life events [such as divorce or job loss]; they anticipate problems and do something before disaster strikes, and they have more social support."[6] Bring on that optimism and joy!

Our Attitude Affects Others

Our attitude affects not only us, but everyone with whom we come in contact. Unless we live in Siberia, we will rub elbows with other people, so a good attitude is helpful. (Of course, Siberia is so cold, I don't think anyone's expected to have a good attitude there!) It's a simple fact of life that people who have pleasant attitudes are pleasant to be around. Those who don't, aren't.

Whatever our attitude, we carry it with us everywhere we go, and people form opinions about us based on that attitude.

When we happen to share our bad attitude with the butcher, baker, or candlestick maker, you can bet that's who we'll run into the next time we go shopping. When we're irritated with the cashier at the checkout line and let her know it, we can rest assured she'll be the visitor sitting in the next pew on Sunday morning. More important than saving face after our bad attitude slips out is realizing what that bad attitude communicates to those who don't know us or the Savior we represent. If our attitude stinks, so does our influence for Christ.

Our Children

Artist Mary Engelbreit has a wonderful print depicting a young child looking up at her mother from the threshold of their door, facing the world beyond. A book and world globe sit on the floor, and a picture on the wall reads "Dare to Dream." The mother is looking at the outstretched world before them, gesturing toward it with one arm and holding her child with her other arm, as if to say, "This, my child, awaits you. Go! Do! I am behind you!" At the top, the artist has written, "All that I am or hope to be, I owe to my mother"—the words of Abraham Lincoln.

We mothers do indeed have an amazing opportunity and responsibility when it comes to shaping the attitude of our children. After all, each of us picks up much of our outlook toward life when we are young and carries it with us into adulthood. (At that point, change is difficult but not impossible—which we'll get to in a minute.) When we are young, we take on the traits we see modeled, and they become very much a part of us. Child development experts say that future success has its roots in a positive environment in the early years. Our children, therefore, deserve to have a mom who lives out before them a positive perspective and attitude. What we teach them with our words and, more importantly, with our lifestyle can affect who they become and what they try to accomplish.

If you and I constantly complain, so will our children. If we see the negative in life before we see the positive, our children will learn to do so, too. If you feel you're a pessimist by nature ("That's just how I'm wired") and are content to remain a pessimist forever, your children will probably be destined to the same gloomy perspective. If we are optimistic, our children have a better chance of learning to be that way, too—as Colleen A. knows. Saying that her attitude affects her ability to be joyful and content, she explains that she had a great teacher: "In situations where I've decided to be content, I have been. I credit a wonderful mother with a very positive attitude about most things as a significant role model for me." Of course many a positive mom has negative children. After all, each child comes into this world with his or her own unique temperament, but a child has a much greater chance of becoming optimistic about life if mom is.

Now having a bad attitude from time to time is human nature. It's the habitual bad attitude that becomes a problem. In fact, I doubt that I could find a mother alive who hasn't had an occasional bad attitude. (I think it goes with the territory.) But moms are usually very aware of the fact that, when it surfaces, that bad attitude affects our children. Just ask Pam H. She had just come home from running errands with her young sons, Caleb and Clay. She was tense and tired and furious with Caleb for disobeying her. As they walked through the living room, she began to read him the riot act. When she got to the bedroom, three-year-old Clay was talking on his toy phone, but she was in no mood to pretend with him now.

He looked at her and said, "Mama, you have a phone call. It's God."

That took her aback. Curious, she looked at him and asked, "Oh really? What does He want?"

"He said He's not very happy with the way you're treating Caleb," Clay said. "He wants to talk to you."

Pam stopped short and took a deep breath, surprised by her

> *The greater part of our happiness or misery depends on our dispositions, and not on our circumstances. We carry the seeds of the one or the other about with us...wherever we go.*
>
> ~Martha Washington

young child's words. She took the phone and said, "Hello...!
Yes, God...You're right.... I am angry and I am out of control....
You're right...I have been a little bit rough on my children today.
I know it's partly my fault because they're tired and hungry and
I should have fed them and put them to bed sooner.... Yes, God,
I'm sorry. I'll try to do better, and I will apologize to my kids."

Pam handed the toy phone back to Clay, knelt down so she
could look her boys in the eyes, and said she was sorry. Then
she prayed with them and asked God to forgive her for her bad
attitude. She told me, "I have learned to take time out to learn
from my kids and to let them learn from me by asking for forgiveness and an improved attitude." Pam could have snapped at
Clay to put the phone down and be quiet but, instead, she made
the choice to change her attitude.

Our Attitude Is Our Choice

Choice is key to attitude. We alone are responsible for our
attitude. We can choose it, and we can change it. "We are either the masters or the victims of our attitudes," says John
Maxwell in *The Winning Attitude*. "It is a matter of personal
choice. Who we are today is the result of choices made yesterday. Tomorrow we will become what we choose today. To
change means to choose to change."[7] Put simply, we can make
a choice to rejoice.

And whether we are wealthy or poor, filled or hungry,
healthy or ill, intelligent or simple, we all have an equal opportunity to choose the kind of attitude we will have. We all possess
that freedom. Mary H. has learned to choose wisely and well:
"I've learned that I have control over my attitude. I choose to be
joyful the same way that I choose to be in a funk. I refuse to be
a victim, and I choose joyfulness as often as possible."

I'm trying to consistently make the same choice that
Mary has learned to make. Some years back, when I was
struggling to complete a Bible study on prayer, I realized how
important that choice is. The study part wasn't the problem;
the rising-early-and-praying part was. One day I didn't wake
up until almost 8:00, my alone time gone and my morning
routine shot. I was frustrated with myself for my lack of commitment and inconsistency, and that frustration soured my

whole attitude. All morning I felt apathetic and couldn't seem to shake it. About midday, I wondered what was robbing me of my joy, and it suddenly struck me: My enemy was my attitude! Simply pinpointing that I wasn't very joyful because of what was going on in my head helped a little. I tried to change my course for the rest of the day. I changed scenery, too. I took the kids out for lunch, we went home for their nap, and then I enjoyed a visit with a friend. The change in my head and in my location helped me change my attitude, and my joy began to reappear.

It helped to realize that only I could change the way I was outwardly expressing my inward feelings and that it was my responsibility to do so, and I did change my attitude that day. If only I could say that it's been in perfect shape ever since! But, alas, sometimes it slips back into the mucketymuck, and I have to drag it out, wipe it off, and try again. Sometimes others in my family (and occasionally people outside that circle) gently remind me to do just that.

Tim and I try to teach our children that an upbeat, positive attitude is right up there with cleanliness and godliness. After all, nothing can ruin a family outing, a family dinner, or any other kind of family time more completely or more quickly than for one person (or more!) to have a bad attitude. When trying to explain the importance of a good attitude, I have found myself telling my children things like "That kind of an attitude, young lady, will not be tolerated!" Tim would often add, "You change your attitude right now!" You know how it goes.

Well, one day I hadn't yet made my choice to rejoice. I didn't have a good attitude at all, and I knew it. It was one of those days when I felt like running into the street in my pajamas yelling, "Yeah, I'm in a bad mood. Wanna make something of it?" The thought of doing that sort of tickled me. I pictured my oldest daughter shaking her finger at me for going outside in my pj's and screaming in the street and then telling *me* that my attitude just would not be tolerated so I'd better change it right now. (After all, I tell her to do that.)

And that's when the light bulb went on. At that instant, I could no more change—or be forced to change—my attitude than I could fly to the moon. Why did I think my children could do so? First of all, I didn't feel like changing my attitude. Second, if I were told to perform such an instantaneous attitude transformation, my ol' human nature just might kick in with, "Oh, yeah?

Let me see ya make me!" (Now I would never actually say that, but those hidden little thoughts sometimes creep up.) Issuing a "change now" demand to my children was unfair, and that realization has helped me try to replace the demand with gentle reminders that only they can improve their attitude. I can't change their attitude for them, nor can I make them do it. They are in control, and, for children, that's a very big deal since there's not a whole lot that young ones are in total control of.

Back to that bad-attitude day. I want you to know that I resisted the urge to run outside in my pj's and scream in the street. Far more importantly, I was reminded that I cannot make my children change their attitudes just as no one can make me change mine. Choosing our attitude—making the choice to rejoice—is an individual freedom and responsibility.

Changing an Attitude

Knowing that we can choose to develop and maintain a positive and joyful attitude leads to the question, "How?" And the answer is "by remembering that your desire, decision, direction, and deep roots in Christ enable you to make and live out the choice to rejoice." One very important note: I am not offering these four ideas as the "be-ye-joyful-plan." Being joyful is much too complex to be reduced to four (or even 14) easy steps. But these four points may help you begin—or begin again—to choose a joyful attitude and maintain it.

Desire

Before we can ever change anything about ourselves, we must have the desire to change, and that desire often comes once we realize that we need to change. Some of us, however, walk around with an attitude that could use some adjusting, but we don't see that there's a problem. So take a moment to evaluate your attitude. Is your attitude in good shape? When is it—and when isn't it? Does your attitude need to be adjusted very often? Are you as positive as you'd like to be? Write down your answers and then ask someone who knows you well and loves you to assess your attitude. After evaluating your attitude and considering the reasons for developing a positive one, you may find the desire to improve yours. You may realize you want to change. That's the first step.

Decision

Once you realize that you want to change, your next step is deciding to do something about making that change. Confirm that decision by saying to yourself or writing in your journal, "I hereby make the choice to rejoice!" Such a decision is required, a deliberate act of the will to make the choice to rejoice. Paul made the decision when he said, "I will rejoice" (Philippians 1:18), and we can, too!

But sometimes making that decision isn't as simple as it sounds. Sometimes our mind is willing ("Yes, that sounds like a great idea"), but our will is not ("but I can't possibly do that!"). That is when we have to be willing to be made willing. We have to be willing to let God change our heart or mindset so that we can be willing to choose a joyful attitude over a negative one. If you aren't yet at the place where you have decided to make the choice to rejoice or you don't know how to actually make that decision, you can start with a simple prayer: "Lord, please make me want to choose to incorporate Your joy into my attitude. I am willing for You to make me willing to do Your will. I'm willing for You to make me willing to rejoice." Imagine the possibilities of God at work in a willing heart and mind "for His good pleasure" (Philippians 2:13)!

Direction

When we desire to change our attitude and we've decided to make that change, we must then have a sense of direction before we can change our location on the attitude spectrum. We must know where we're going and have a plan to get there. As you make a plan to alter your attitude, consider the following:

1. *Know that attitudes follow actions.*

We don't have to wait until we feel good to start living out a good attitude. If we did, we could be waiting a long time! Besides, attitudes have a funny way of following actions and feelings often follow behavior. When we begin to act in a certain way, our feelings often catch up. So, if you and I want to have a good attitude, we must start acting as if we have a good attitude. If you want to be more joyful, start acting more joyful. If you want to be more patient, start acting that way. The feelings often follow the actions—as I tried to help my two older daughters learn this concept recently.

One thing I can't stand is their bickering, and one day they were really going at it. Since there was no end to it in sight, I took each one of them aside, separately, and said, "I know you don't feel like being kind to your sister right now, but you may not continue to act this way. Even if you don't feel like being kind to her on the inside, please show her kindness on the outside—and then watch what happens." And I stopped there. I didn't offer any further explanations, and each daughter thought the talk was for her ears only.

Well, their curiosity piqued, my girls weren't about to miss seeing what would happen, and I quietly observed them the rest of the day. I could tell they were still mad at each other, but each took on the newly-assigned role with great gusto. "*You* go first," one said. "No, after you," the other responded, both of them speaking with saccharine sweetness. They practically knocked themselves out being kind to each other as they waited to see what would happen.

And you know what happened? Although initially they may have been expecting candy to fall from heaven because they were being pleasant, the phoniness gave way to the real thing, and they didn't even notice. Their attitudes began to follow their actions. And so can ours. When we make the choice to rejoice, the feelings can follow. But I must mention here that lasting change comes only with a changed heart, not merely with changed actions (that's the topic of chapter five). Right now changing your actions is a good first step toward a better attitude.

2. Replace bad thought habits with good ones.

The only way to replace bad thoughts is to work at developing good thought habits. (Replace "I always do things wrong" with "I'm just having a bad day," for instance.) Our thoughts influence our actions which affect our attitude which, in turn, affects our thoughts, and so the cycle goes. We start with a thought, we dwell on that thought, and then we make a decision and act based on that thought. This action reinforces the thought, leading to a habit. That habit influences our future thoughts, and the cycle starts again.

For example, we start with the thought, "I'm down today ... again." Then we dwell on that negative thought: "I feel so crummy. I think I'll help myself to some comfort food." Then comes the decision: "Yes, that's just what I need! There's a whole bag of Oreos in the pantry"—and off we go for the cookies. Next comes the negative action and negative attitude: We eat half the bag and think, "I'll never feel good or be thin." And the cycle continues.

Replacing those bad thought habits with good ones might look something like this: "I feel down today, but I don't want to stay like this." Then we dwell on this positive thought: "Hmmm, what I need is some fresh air and exercise." Then the decision and action: "I think I'll change into walking shoes right now"— and out the door we go. Good habits yield good attitudes: "I feel better already." Our habits affect our attitudes and our attitudes affect our habits. Although our thought habits are often deeply ingrained, we can train them to be positive.

3. *Change what you can.*

If you can change something that is causing your bad attitude, do so. If, for instance, you are frequently late (a bad habit) and the frustration makes you cranky (a bad attitude), you can change your habit and thereby positively affect your attitude. You can learn to become punctual (by setting the alarm a little earlier, minimizing what you try to get done before you leave the house, and so on), which will limit and maybe even eliminate your reason to be cranky—and your attitude will be better. So look for what is causing your bad attitude and do what you can to change those contributing factors when you can.

4. *Commit to work on improving your attitude daily.*

Change isn't easy; change takes work. To successfully change your attitude, commit to work on it daily. The fruit of your efforts will definitely be worth the energy you spend cultivating a good attitude.

5. *Find someone to hold you accountable for your attitude.*

Ask that person to remind you (gently and lovingly, of course!) when your attitude needs adjusting. Too often it's hard to recognize when our own attitude is in need of adjustment, and that's where a friend or loved one's constructive comment can open our eyes. If I'm exuding negativity, sometimes a lighthearted, "What are you so cheerful about?" delivered with a wink can be just what I need to realize that my attitude could use a tune-up.

6. *Look for mentors and models.*

If you want to be more positive, try to surround yourself with positive people. Nothing can drag you down more quickly than negative folks.

7. *Press on when you slip up.*

You will slip. We all do. I haven't heard of anyone in the last 2000 years or so who had the right attitude all the time. When you mess up, forget what lies behind and reach forward to what lies ahead. Press on just as Paul did: One thing I do: forgetting what lies behind and reaching forward to what lies ahead, I press on toward the goal for the prize of the upward call of God in Christ Jesus (Philippians 3:13,14).

You now have a sense of direction and some ideas about how to get going that way. There's one more point to consider as you undertake permanent attitude adjustment.

Deep Roots

If we stop with the above suggestions for improving our attitude, we are limited to a self-help fix. While that superficial effort may do the job for some, we don't want to be the only help we have in this major reconstruction job. And, as a Christian, we are not in this alone. God's Word tells us that we have a helper in the Holy Spirit who enables us to accomplish God's will when our strength isn't enough. To develop the kind of attitude that is pleasing to God, pleasant for others, and a worthy model for our children, we need to turn to our heavenly Father, His written Word, and His Holy Spirit. Making the choice to rejoice a decision that will last requires us to dig our roots deep into God and His Word, relying on His Spirit to transform our heart as we do so. (There's more on this in chapter five.)

Choosing Joy

If joy is an attitude of the heart (as we saw earlier) and we can choose our attitudes, then I can choose joy—and you can choose joy! Each of us can choose to live a joyful life. Being joyful begins in the head, with our choice to have a good attitude, be positive, learn optimism, and model these things for our children. Taking that first step—choosing to think this way—is a deliberate act of the will. Other factors are involved—as we'll see—but an attitude of joy begins with our thinking. We can indeed make a choice to rejoice!

That fact is the basis of *Happiness Is a Choice,* by Doctors Frank Minirth and Paul Meier, in which they write, "Both of us can say with a deep inner conviction that a majority of human beings do *not* have the inner peace and joy about which I am thinking. We are also convinced that all human beings are capable of having this inner joy and peace if only they will choose it and follow the right path to obtain it."[8]

Making the choice and following the path won't always be easy, though. Sometimes we can simply say, "I choose joy!" as Christian singer Larnelle Harris does in his song by that title, and that's all there is to it. More often than not, however, making the choice to rejoice is only the beginning of our journey.

Even when we're in pain, we have that choice to rejoice. Perhaps you've heard of Lucy Mabery, the wife of Trevor Mabery who was one of the Focus on the Family board members killed in a plane crash. Lucy knew tremendous pain and grief at her husband's tragic death, but she learned from that experience that we have to work through our pain and that we can find joy again. She told me, "When Trevor was killed, I could have chosen to crawl into a hole, but instead I chose to allow others to watch me walk through the process. You can choose happiness. You can change your mindset. You can say, 'These are bad circumstances, but I'm not going to let them overwhelm me, so I won't drown.' I also decided not to be stoic. I allowed people to see me being real. The more I did that, the stronger I got."

Like Lucy, the apostle Paul knew about choosing the right attitude. Despite all his sufferings for the Lord (2 Corinthians 11:23-27), he stands out as one of the most joyful people in the Bible. In the first chapter of Philippians, for instance, Paul describes some of his afflictions and then says, "... and in this I rejoice, yes, and I will rejoice" (verse 18). He decided to rejoice today ("in this I rejoice") and he decided to rejoice in the future ("I will rejoice"). You and I can do the same.

Choosing Is Not Creating

Let me add that choosing joy does not mean trying to conjure up joy by your own power. You and I can never create joy, but we can make the choice to develop joy as an attitude of the heart. Joy is much more than just an attitude. It is also a gift from the heavenly Father and a fruit of His Spirit, and those things can never be created. We can choose joy in the sense that we can choose our attitude. We can choose how we look at life, express ourselves, relate to people, and relate to God. We can choose to look at life through a rosy filter of a joyful attitude or one that is gray or cracked. Choosing to have a joyous attitude can help make a ho-hum, lackluster life one that sparkles. Which do you choose?

Different Temperaments, Same Joy

The various ways people approach life and express their joy is fascinating. We are all so different. My husband and I have completely different personalities, as this simple story illustrates.

One day I went to a new salon. I was ready for a transformation from my "college hair," a style I had worn for too many years, to a totally new "do." My friend Robin went along to offer moral support—and to make sure

We can live as though Christ died yesterday, rose today, and is coming tomorrow, or we can live as though Christ died, period. We can count blessings, or we can count calamities.... It's our choice.

~Barbara Johnson, *Splashes of Joy in the Cesspools of Life*

that I didn't chicken out. When Sal got done, I was (to my surprise) quite pleased and decided I just had to stop by Tim's office and show him the new me immediately. (Temperament clue here.) Tim casually walked out (another temperament clue), surveyed the big change, and calmly said, "That's nice."

"But do you like it?" I asked.

"Yes, it's nice," he replied. I could tell he liked it, but I continued.

"'Nice' is boring. I want you to be gaga!" I said.

"OK, consider me gaga," he said flatly, but with a smile.

I have learned that, for Tim, he was being gaga! I would have been thrilled if he'd exclaimed, "*WOW*! Honey, you look incredible! How about a night on the town?" I knew that's what he meant, but he would never think of saying it quite like that. After all, his temperament is different than mine.

We all express ourselves differently, and our display of joy is no exception. All of us can make the choice to rejoice, but our approach to that decision can vary widely. Here's a fun look at how four different personality types might handle that choice:

• *Fun-loving Sally Sanguine,* looking for an exuberant approach, might make the choice to rejoice by bouncing across the room in her bright red outfit, laughing just for the fun of it, and loudly exclaiming, with her arms open wide, "Hello, world! It's gonna be a great day!"

• *Controlling Carol Choleric,* looking for her own approach, might make her choice to rejoice very decisively. Deliberately and confidently, she might stride across the room, get everyone's attention, and say, "I have decided to rejoice for the rest of my life. I'll begin with this big grin. [Smile.] Now here's the rest of the plan, so all of you get out something to take notes on. You can be joyful, too."

• *Perfectionist Milly Melancholy,* looking for the proper approach to joyfulness, might straighten her skirt, carefully gather her data on the subject, and say, "I will make the choice to rejoice after I've analyzed this book and completed my attitude graphs. I certainly can't jump into this joyfulness thing without first giving it careful and thorough consideration. Can I get back to you next week?"

• *Laid-back Felicia Phlegmatic*, looking for the simple approach, might say, "This is no big deal. It's certainly nothing to get excited about. I made the choice to rejoice years ago. I'm just smiling on the inside!"

Each person—depending on his or her temperament—is going to approach joy and express it a little differently. (In some cases, a lot differently!) You may laugh uproariously, you may flash a big toothy grin, you may smile only when you deem it appropriate, or you may laugh on the inside. You may be exuberant in your expression of joy or you may have a quiet sense of contentment, a calm sense that life is good. Whatever your expression of joy, whichever your approach, you can make the choice to rejoice. It's up to you—and don't worry if your joy looks different than someone else's joy.

❧ 4 ❧

Taming the Monster
of Discontent
Wanting What We Have

Have you ever thought, "I'll be happier when..."? Perhaps you're thinking, "I'll be happier when I have more money" or "I'll be happier when I have a better job." Maybe it's, "I'll be happier when I feel good again," or even "I'll be happier when I get all my children potty trained!" Have you ever muttered, "I'd rather be anywhere but here?" I have. I know all too well that menacing monster of discontent and how difficult a monster it is to battle. The problem is that just when we think we're the conqueror, it's breathing down our necks again. Since it keeps rearing its ugly head, I've decided to try to tame it.

Why a chapter on contentment in a book about joy? Because the monster of discontent has a way of pushing aside joy. It's very difficult to be joyful and discontent at the same time. But the opposite is true as well. The more joy I have, the less room I have for discontentment. And part of being joyful is learning to be content.

What does it mean to be content? Contentment is not so much having what we want as it is wanting what we have. (Go ahead and read that sentence again!) "Content" is defined as "happy enough with what one has or is; not desiring something more or different; satisfied." Now there's a concept that's foreign to lots of people! Some of us have fought off the ugly monster and can say that we're genuinely happy with what we have. (But maybe you struggle with this.) Many of us can say we are happy with who we are. (But too many people don't like themselves.) The part of the definition that sounds so foreign is the phrase "not desiring anything more or different." That almost sounds downright un-American. I can just hear that monster asking, "How can you be happy with what you have when so much more is available? How can you be happy with who you are? Don't you desire personal growth? And how could you possibly not desire anything more or different? Don't you ever go to the mall?"

Contentment—not desiring anything more or different—is a rare trait today. Mention it and you could get lambasted for discouraging others from bettering themselves and improving their lives. After all, isn't wanting more and better the American way? And there are times when there's nothing wrong with that. Bettering ourselves with an education, improving our life with tools we need, or buying a better house *is* the pursuit of the American dream. These are good things in themselves. But there's a fine line between obtaining from need and obtaining from greed. Contentment falls somewhere on the line between want and excess—a line that's in a different place for different individuals and that shifts during one's own life. The question that occurs to me, then, is: "Where is my heart? When do my wants take me over the line of contentment and into the monster's territory?"

Being Happy Where We Are

Learning to be happy where we are is one of the more difficult lessons in life. One reason is that "where we are" is always changing. Just about the time we get used to one place—be it an address, an age, a job, a season of life—we have to move to a whole new place and get used to it. After all, first apartments make way for starter homes, and fall precedes winter. Babies stop being newborns and learn to sit up and crawl away. The twenties always lead to the thirties and then to the forties (which hopefully doesn't lead to midlife crisis!). Even "aging gracefully" can't go on forever, for physical life must eventually end, allowing our spirit to go home to a new address. Nothing stays the same forever, so throughout our lives we always have an opportunity to learn to be content in whatever place or season we find ourselves.

Greg P., a man who filled out one of my surveys, has learned the value of contentment. He said, "Meeting, dating, and marrying my wife, Donna, taught me that God's will is perfect and sovereign. I learned to be content in His will as a single, even though I sometimes doubted God would ever send me the soulmate I desired. That was important because being content where I was helped me establish who I was as a man in Christ prior to meeting my wife."

But sometimes we are too busy looking ahead to the perfect moment when contentment will be easy. Aware of this fact, a mother wrote these words to her college-age daughter:

> Don't you get the feeling that nearly everyone you meet has the same ideal—to be about 30 years old, at the peak of their powers, healthy, and in control of their life? It's as if there is one ideal moment in life and all would be well if we could just freeze the action right at that point.[1]

We delude ourselves—whatever our age—if we think there is one ideal moment in life when all will be well and contentment will become as natural as breathing. That's not how life works, and an ideal world is not the best breeding ground for real contentment.

True contentment is being able to say, "I am happy right here where I am"—and mean it *regardless of the circumstances.* Getting to that place isn't easy, but that's the point to which God calls us: "Godliness with contentment is great gain" (1 Timothy 6:6 NKJV). Thankfully, I know what it feels like to live in that place—but I have struggled to

Joy is peace dancing.

~Tim Hansel,
Holy Sweat

get there. I also know what it feels like to be scared away from that place by the monster of discontent—but I know it can be tamed. Contentment is a virtue worth pursuing for it brings great joy and incredible freedom. Continuing her letter, that mother writing to her daughter wisely added that we must "learn to cultivate the virtue of contentment—which frees us from forever wanting to exist in just one stage of life."[2] Contentment also frees us to savor the gift of the present and to know the joy God wants us to experience today.

The Seeds of Discontentment

We can better pursue contentment when we understand the strategy of the monster of discontent. We can strengthen our stand against that monster when we realize that it rears its ugly head through comparisons, commercialism, and circumstances.

Comparisons

One of the quickest ways to breed discontentment in your life is to make comparisons. Comparing yourself, your possessions, and anything else connected to you with someone else can lead to only two things: pride or discontentment. Let's first consider pride.

If we compare ourselves to people who have less than we do, pride can take root. We can become smug about the things we have and begin to lose sight of the fact that everything we have and everything we are is a blessing from God. The self-made man or woman is a myth. He or she has simply been blessed by God. Wise and wealthy King Solomon knew that "it is the blessing of the LORD that makes [one] rich" (Proverbs 10:22).

The kind of comparing which leads to pride might begin with, "Look, Bill! The Smiths' car is broken down in front of their house. I think it's the third time this month." There's no problem with this simple observation, especially if it leads you to see if the Smiths need your help. But the path can get treacherous. *Hmmm. It sure looks bad sitting there jacked up. I wonder how long they're going to leave it there. I hope it's gone before our company comes. I am so glad we got our new car before they got here.* Ah, the seeds of pride have been sown before we realized what was happening.

Pride is like that. It can start small, taking root as a tiny seed in our hearts but growing into one of those seven deadly sins. Comparing what we have can lead to pride in our possessions. Comparing who we are or where we are can lead to self-pride. Both are sins and contrary to the self*less* attitude of Christ, which should be our goal.

Again, if we compare ourselves with those who have less than we have, we risk becoming proud. But if we compare ourselves with those who have more than we do, we risk becoming dissatisfied with what we have, where we are, and even who we are. We find ourselves becoming discontent.

Comparing ourselves with others can begin so subtly: "Look, Bill! The Smiths got a brand new car. It sure is pretty." This simple observation seems safe enough. "I'm so happy for them. They really needed one. She was telling me just the other day how she was stranded three times last month." This time the observation includes some rejoicing in the blessing another has received. But at this point, if we don't watch it, we can find ourselves walking the dangerous path of making comparisons. *Hmmm. I hadn't noticed our car looking quite this ratty.... The paint sure is faded. The upholstery is even torn. The car runs, but it sure looks bad. In fact, I don't think I want to be seen driving it.* Before we know it, the monster of discontent is behind the wheel and has taken control, driving away the awareness of our blessings. We find ourselves wanting more than what we have, and we lose sight of the fact that we are very blessed to have a vehicle that runs well and is dependable.

"Well, that's rather simplistic," you may be thinking. "Besides, I would never do that." Maybe not—maybe not with a car, or at least not in one sitting and not intentionally. To better understand the destructive power of making comparisons, maybe you need to consider something other than a car. What if the object of comparison was a house or new furniture or your children's accomplishments or...? You plug in the thing that lights your fire. Satan knows our vulnerabilities, and he will find ways to tempt us. Comparing what we have with others seems so harmless—and it is when we stay within the confines of noticing their blessings and sharing in their joy. But when we take the next step (and this move can be subtle) and start making comparisons between us and them, Satan can use it as a tool to scatter seeds of discontent. The rate of their growth can be quick if they were sown in fertile ground (if we're focusing on something we value) and if we water them with continued comparison. The seeds germinate with that kind of nourishment and grow into a field of weeds that chokes out our ability to enjoy the blessings we've received.

I learned early on that my parents wouldn't tolerate the complaining that comes with being discontent, and my father shared a lesson he learned in junior high to explain why. He had a teacher who hung a sign at the front of the classroom. It said, "I complained because I had no shoes—until I met a man who had no feet." No matter what our situation, there's usually someone worse off than we are. My dad never forgot this message and, subsequently, neither have I.

Again, maybe you're not real picky about what kind of car you drive. I'm not. Satan has never brought me pride or discontentment because of someone else's car. (If you could see my car, you'd know pride in that area is no problem!) However, plug in something that touches me a little more personally—like, say, a house or decorating or achievements—and that's where I need to guard my heart. After all, the effects of pride and discontent can be devastating and far-reaching. Ministries have toppled because of pride, and marriages have been ruined by discontentment. It's no simple thing, and Satan knows it. He will sow seeds using things that tempt us, so protect your soil.

One way we can protect our soil and stop making comparisons is by realizing that comparisons aren't always what they seem. What we see in other people doesn't always tell the whole story. The grass isn't always greener in someone else's life—as a friend of mine learned at the beauty shop.

When Posy was getting her hair done one day, she saw this beautiful girl with gorgeous hair. "Wow," she thought. "Why can't I have hair like that?" At first she wasn't going to say anything since she figured the girl was probably tired of hearing everyone tell her how beautiful her hair was, but she changed her mind.

"You have beautiful hair!" Posy exclaimed.

"Thank you. I kind of like it, too," she said. "It's what came in after the chemotherapy."

No, the grass isn't always greener, as my friend saw. But it often looks greener when we don't see the big picture—and that's a lesson Maria can teach us. You undoubtedly have a Maria in your life. She has a clean and well-organized home; she feeds her family wonderful, nutritious meals; her children seem well-mannered; and you just can't imagine her ever running out of groceries or clean clothes. She even finds time to serve at church, take part in a Bible study, and entertain. She makes us feel rather inadequate.

To counter such feelings, read what Carol Mader wrote in an article entitled "Dare to Not Compare" from the newsletter "The Proverbs 31 Homemaker."

> Many women compare themselves to others, whether consciously or otherwise. We use yardsticks such as the neatness of a house or how many extra activities a woman appears to be handling. We contrast and compare only to feel that we never measure up. Judging by externals, we fail to look beyond the facade. So it occurred to me, if I were going to compare my household with Maria's, I needed to compare *every* aspect.
>
> Maria's son, Shawn, and my son, Ivan, were close in age. While Shawn nursed three times a day, my son nursed every two hours even with solids. Shawn would play happily with his toys for hours, but my son screamed if I got more than two feet away. Shawn took two long naps each day and slept twelve hours at night. My baby napped once a day for 45 minutes and never more than nine hours at night. While Maria changed eight diapers a day, I was changing a whopping 22 diapers a day! Maria's husband happily assumed child care duties every evening, yet my husband was busy fourteen hours a day, seven days a week, with graduate school. No wonder I was exhausted.[3]

Carol found that Maria had 35 hours free of child care that she didn't have—and that didn't count the help from her husband and the fact that she had a happier baby. With 35 extra hours a week, Carol could get her act together like Maria. Carol adds:

Maria's life and my own, I realized, were simply very different although on the surface they appeared similar. I found that comparisons were really an exercise in futility. Each family and their priorities are unique.[4]

Think again about the Maria you know. If you're discouraged by the comparison, stop comparing. Dare to not compare! After all, you can't have a clear picture of that other person's life. You're only dealing with what you see on the outside from a distance, and that's hardly an accurate picture.

Like Carol's Maria, your Maria is a real threat to your level of contentment. But maybe the Maria in your life is a little different from Carol's Maria. She always looks great, does the appropriate thing at the appropriate time, and meets her family's every need, in a gorgeous and orderly home, with gentle, lovingkindness. This woman is impeccable, unflappable, punctual, and—more importantly—impossible! This Maria lives only in your imagination, and Satan can use her to destroy your self-esteem and rob you of the contentment God wants you to have.

We must not allow that old monster to put this fictitious woman on a pedestal before us. Take in a big breath of reality and blow her off. Stop looking around and comparing yourself to other people (real and fictitious). Instead, look up to God and realize that He calls you to be a Proverbs 31 woman, "an excellent wife...[whose] worth is far above jewels...a woman who fears the LORD...[whose] children rise up and bless her; her husband also, and he praises her saying: 'Many daughters have done nobly, but you excel them all'" (Proverbs 31:10, 30, 28). Don't be seduced by the charms you see, whether in a real-life Maria or the Maria of your imagination. Comparisons lead to pride or discontentment. Comparisons cripple contentment.

Commercialism

We are a people who want more, and our society breeds that desire. Everywhere we turn, we are offered something newer, bigger, or better. Advertisers threaten our contentment with what we have by trying to sell us what they have. Our clock radios wake us up with a call to buy. During breakfast, interruptions to the morning television show invite us to purchase. Then, as we drive around running errands, billboards remind us of what we could acquire. Our culture is saturated with advertising—and the pace picks up during December!

Advertisers put a lot of money into this call to consume. Some reports say that every year the industry spends almost $500 per American. Advertisers are banking on the fact that they can make us discontent with what we have, help us discover needs that we weren't aware of, and compel us to spend our money. In the bestselling book *Your Money or Your Life* , authors Joe Dominguez and Vicki Robin say, "Advertising technology, armed with market research and sophisticated psychology, aims to throw us off balance emotionally—and then promises to resolve our discomfort with a product. Fifty to 100 times before 9 A.M. every day."[5] (I don't know about you, but I don't like being thrown off balance emotionally by 9 A.M. With that much of the day left, I need every emotion I've got! Who knows which one will come in handy later? Besides, sometimes I can lose my balance all by myself.)

Advertising exacerbates our perceived needs and can, in turn, steal our contentment. You know how it works. You go to the mall to get that gift you have to buy, and on your way out you spot this cute outfit in the window. You stop. *Now that's a great outfit.* You leave. You turn around and glance one more time. *I bet that would look great on me.* You go back and try it on. *I was right! But I really can't afford this now.* You leave—for real this time—but you take a bit of the mall with you mentally. During the week, you think about how much you'd love that outfit, even though it wasn't on your list when you entered the mall. Later, when you're trying to decide what to wear, nothing quite holds a candle to that outfit at the mall. Your wardrobe is fine, but you left your satisfaction with what's in your closet at the store window. As you think about the outfit some more, you begin to see your want as a need, even though it isn't. And that's the goal of advertising.

The situation is different if we need the clothing and have the money. Then we can make the purchase and enjoy the new outfit. But when we allow our "needs" to be determined by what we see in the mall and hear in the ads, we are letting our commercial culture influence what we buy as well as how we feel about what we already own. We are letting the demon of commercialism define our needs and rob us of our contentment.

Now I'm not knocking the advertising industry. First, I've worked in the business and, second, I'm always grateful when advertising alerts me to products, prices, and services that are useful. However, we all need to be aware that repeated exposure to ads can make us think that we need things we really only want. There's nothing inherently wrong with wanting things—as long as that wanting doesn't interfere with our contentment. Most people want things occasionally (some of us want more frequently than others!). The danger comes—and it often comes subtly—when our wanting blurs our thinking about what we really need and makes us unable to see the blessings of what we already have. Maybe that's why we're told in a famous top-ten list not to covet—and that's a word you don't hear much today. You never hear someone say, "I'm sure coveting that outfit which I don't need and can't afford." After all, can it really be coveting when there were three others on the rack? You don't want what someone else has. You simply want one just like it! Fine line, isn't it?

How can you protect yourself from the appeal of commercialism? Here are some basic ideas. If you're struggling to be content with your wardrobe, for instance, don't go window shopping. If you're becoming discontent with your home decor, slack off on those magazines that feature decorating ideas. If frequenting the mall makes you want stuff, try frequenting some place else. Often window shopping, women's magazines, the mall, and other exposure to material goods and services are wonderful, but if you begin to find commercialism turning your contentment to discontentment, do your best to disconnect.

Circumstances

A young man runs into his professor one day. The professor asks, "How are you doing?" The young man replies, "Okay, I guess, under the circumstances." The wise professor quickly responds, "Under the circumstances? How did you ever get under those?"

It's all too easy to get under the circumstances of our life, isn't it? Well, when I feel that circumstances have piled up and piled up, I sometimes imagine God holding that pile in the palm of His hand and watching me squirm and sweat under there. He's lifting the edges so I can breathe, but I've been so busy screaming about the hugeness of the pile that I haven't heard Him say, "Hel-LO in there! Have you forgotten that you're still in My hands?" I need that reminder that "Thou hast enclosed me behind and before, and laid Thy hand upon me" (Psalm 139:5). Don't we all?

We humans certainly tend to let our circumstances affect whether we are content or discontent. When things are going well, we are content. Mama is happy. But when the tide turns and our circumstances change, discontentment creeps back into our lives and tries to edge out our joy. It is so easy to adopt straightjacket thinking about this pattern: *If things are as I wish, I am content. If things are not as I wish, I am discontent.* With this very human and very binding line of thinking, we let bad circumstances restrict our contentment, holding us hostage until more favorable circumstances come along and, Houdini-like, free us from the straightjacket. Rick, an attorney friend of ours, experienced this recently.

Rick had been working on an extremely difficult case. Preparing to bring it to trial had been exhausting, both physically and emotionally. So when he went home, he decided to unwind with some channel surfing. He, the remote, and the sofa became one! He sat there, blindly flipping through the channels, a victim of the bleary-eyed blahs. The next day, he won the case and was thrilled. That night when he went home, he noticed the drastic difference between how he felt then and how he had felt the

> *My* content-ment comes from knowing that I rest in God's will and that He has protec-tion and provision should I ever need it.
>
> ~Nancy N.

night before and started thinking about how the circumstances had affected him. If he'd lost the case, he knew he would have been more down than the night before even though losing the case wouldn't have meant losing his job or personally paying the settlement. The Lord turned on the light for him, and Rick realized how closely his contentment was tied to his circumstances.

Now there are some circumstances in life where we cannot be content, nor should we be (an abusive situation or a situation that is painful beyond description, for instance). I'm not saying we should accept such circumstances and endure them. Sometimes we must take bold actions and do what we can to change those circumstances that are damaging and clearly out of God's plan for us. But most of the time, when we're under the pile of life, we can learn to cultivate contentment despite our crummy circumstances. After all, those circumstances don't come to stay. They "come to pass," and our heavenly Father is holding us—and the pile—in the palm of His hand. And God has taught me that that fact is key to our contentment.

A Lesson in Contentment

When we moved into the house we are currently living in, I was very grateful to be out of those dinky corporate apartments and into a place that would allow us to get our things out of storage. After living in a motel-like setting for seven months, we had great fun watching our belongings come off the truck. "Oh, look, honey! There's the table....And here come the kids' toys....Yea! *our bed!*"

"Settle down," said my calm, cool, and usually collected husband, but even he was thrilled at the prospect of once again sleeping in the comfort of our own familiar bed.

Unpacking was actually fun, and I was content...for a while. The house was (and is) a real blessing, but as soon as the boxes began disappearing from the living room, we began to notice just how much work the place needed. I kept repairmen coming and going for the first three weeks. The house is not just older, it's brittle. Quite often when we would open a cabinet or drawer, part of it would come off in our hands. I've got pieces of woodwork all over the place begging to be glued together.

Does the scene in *It's a Wonderful Life*, where the banister knob keeps coming off in George's hand ring a bell? That's us.

In fact, one day as I looked out the back window, I noticed something lying in the yard and saw a big board hanging down from the top of the house. I went outside to find the siding coming off and some boards near the roof hanging on by a nail or two. Realizing that the house was literally falling apart, I yelled, "Kids! Whatever you do, don't play outside. You might get hit in the head by the house!"

There are days when the torn vinyl, rotting wood, and the carpet which is 15 years past its prime all get to me. And since the house is a rental property, we aren't able to personalize it at all. If we paint, the color must first be approved by the management company, and then, when we move out, we must re-paint it with their lovely beige. If I want to plant flowers, I must first ask ("Excuse me. Do you mind if I beautify your property with a pansy?"). Needless to say, I have been discouraged from doing much to this place.

Why am I telling you all this? Because God has taught me a lesson here. Let me back up. We all know that Satan attacks us where we live, and that's where he has attacked me—literally. Women tend to be more emotionally tied to our homes than men, and I am no exception. I don't like living in a place that's falling apart, and I don't like being unable to spruce it up without running my idea by Congress. But those haven't been the hard things. For me, the hard thing has to do with light. You see, I love sunshine and want as much of it flooding into my home—and my life—as possible. I like my home, as they say in real estate ads, "light and bright." That's good for me, as studies confirm. Researchers have discovered, for instance, that extended darkness can alter people's moods. Locales with long, gray rainy seasons and little sunshine tend to have higher depression and suicide rates than other places. People who work night shifts and see little sunshine over long periods of time can also succumb to a downward slump in attitude and depression. I can personally attest to the accuracy of these findings.

Yet right now I am living in what I call "my cave"—unless it's cold outside, and then I call it "our sieve." This house is so dark that we have to turn on the lights in the den at midday even in the summer. For three years, I've been "in the dark," struggling to keep a good attitude. "No big deal," you may say, and it's certainly not. I've faced *much* greater darkness in my life. However, often it's little irritants in life—like dark homes—that can steal our joy, rob us of contentment, and keep us from living the abundant life that God has promised us and wants to give us.

And this promise-making, promise-keeping God is using this house, as He uses everything in each of our lives, to teach me. For a long time, the struggle to be content in a dark, dingy abode was intense, especially since we're living near a very materially blessed area. I have to continually guard against falling into the comparison trap. At first I focused on how much I disliked the house, the repairs, and especially the dark. I began to ask God for a different house.

> Lord, You've called me to be in the home as a homemaker and full-time mom first and as a home-based worker second, and I thank You for that, but does it have to be in such an ugly place? Please, Lord, will You *GET ME OUTTA HERE?*"

I struggled with feeling unspiritual as I prayed that request. Then I decided it was OK to ask God for anything if the requests were made for the right reasons and with pure motives and a right heart. Then I found myself praying a bit more contritely. *Lord, please, if it be Your will, can we move?* Not yet. God wasn't finished teaching me. At that point my prayer became, *Yes, Lord, I'm beginning to see. Thank You for this house....* *Are we done yet?* Nope. Not yet. Try again—and I did after a little more time, a few more broken fixtures, and a little more darkness. *But, Lord, I want to be in the light. Please, will You take me to the light?* And then the light began to shine—not in my house (it's still as dark ever), but in my heart. The light began as a pen light, but then it grew to a night light, then to a flashlight, and pretty soon to a floodlight which illuminated my lack of contentment. I couldn't leave this dear old (emphasis on "old") house until God taught me true contentment. I began to feel and not just say prayers of thanks for where we lived. *Oh, Lord, thank You that this house is so big. Thank You for enough bedrooms, the big yard, a large kitchen, plenty of storage. And in Your will, I'll take that new address any time.* But I still had more to learn.

Sometimes we don't realize we're in a bubble until we get outside of it. That was my experience as I continued to learn the lesson God had for me. I began to realize that while I had been busy comparing what I didn't have with what my upwardly mobile friends did have, much of America didn't live the way they do or even the way we do. As I traveled, I saw how really blessed my family and I are. And, as I thought about other countries, I remembered that most of the world lives far below our standards. At that point, I began to appreciate a fact I'd known for ages: The blessings we enjoy as Americans are bounteous. As my genuine thankfulness increased, so did my contentment.

Now some of you might visit our house and say, "No wonder you prayed so hard!" (Some people have actually said this!) When I once told someone that I could stay in this house for another year or so, she replied, "I don't think it will last that long!" Yet another visitor even said, "It's nice things are sort of…like this, with your children and everything." (I loved that one!) Other people, however, might come and say, "Oh, how truly blessed you are! It would be so nice to live in a house like this." And people have said this, too. Your perception depends on your perspective; what you see depends on where you have come from.

Only now does my perspective agree with those who say, "Oh, how truly blessed you are!" God humbled me greatly by showing me how sinful my discontentment was. I have learned to be thankful for what I have right now. I now see that I have much. Oh, I don't *like* the house any better—it's as dark and drafty as ever—but I am quite thankful to be here. I am quite content. At first I was surprised I could actually say that. I am also very glad that God didn't remove His blessing of this invaluable lesson in contentment by giving me the blessing I had asked of Him.

At this point you need to know that I've lived in an apartment, a trailer, and an old school—where I slept on a cot—and I was content in each place. Then God blessed me with the biggest (albeit ugliest!) house of all to let me learn that we can be discontent anywhere no matter how much we have and that we can be content no matter how little we have. After all, contentment isn't based on the things around us. It's not based on our possessions or our position. Our contentment is based on the attitude we choose to have toward these things. Contentment comes when we hold loosely all that we are stewards of, for nothing is really our own. Everything is a gift from God. When we are grateful for these gifts—be they many or few—then we can know contentment.

And, as surprising as it may sound, knowing contentment can sometimes be a struggle even in a beautiful setting. Joycelyn Clairmonte knows this. The bed-and-breakfast inn she and her husband run is picture perfect. Standing in the middle of 40 acres, it has wood floors, rambling porches, rocking chairs, quilts, and a barn, and every impeccably decorated room looks as if it were taken straight out of a magazine. Even with all this, Joycelyn still sometimes wrestles with the monster of discontent:

> I love to decorate. When a place gets finished, I start feeling like it's time to move on so I can do another one....I'm certainly not unhappy, because we absolutely love to share our home with guests, but sometimes it's hard not having a place of our own to go home to at night....We share our home so much that we have to keep it as close to perfect as possible. I love things neat, but sometimes I just want to leave my shoes in the middle of the floor and be able to wear my pajamas around....We even have to move out sometimes when we rent all the rooms....This business is our gift, our calling, and our ministry, and we love it. But sometimes it's hard not living like real people, and I find myself getting discontent.
>
> Sometimes I want to put my head in a vise and yell, "Joycelyn, get your head together." I have to remember to take every thought captive and deliberately praise God for the blessings of this beautiful home, the property, my husband, the country, and so many other things. When I focus on my one lack and let that override all that's good, I feel discontent and ungrateful. I even feel self-pity.

As Joycelyn's words suggest, it doesn't matter how much we have. Satan can find a way to shift our focus from our blessings to our "one lack" and, in so doing, undermine our contentment. A grateful spirit and the expression of that gratefulness in thanksgiving to the Lord will help us tame that ornery and persistent monster of discontent.

We Have So Much—But Do We Want What We Have?

You and I, living in this country at this time, have more possessions, more conveniences, and more luxuries than any other place and time in history. We have some of the highest household incomes in the world. Two-thirds of us Americans own homes, six out of ten young people receive a college education, medical and health care advances are increasing our lifespans, and we have more luxury and leisure items than we have time for.

Technological advancements have turned backbreaking, daylong labor for necessities into simple and convenient acts. Instead of grinding the grain for home-baked bread, waiting months for a letter, and driving a day or more to the general store in a horse-drawn wagon, as the American pioneers did, you and I can heat a frozen entree in the microwave to eat in the minivan while we talk on our cellular phone on the way to the mall. I don't know about you, but I'll take a minivan over a buckboard any day! We are truly blessed.

You'd think that all this affluence and increased leisure have made us happier, right? They haven't. In fact, some experts say that only between 10 to 33 percent of Americans consider themselves very happy. Some psychologists say one-third of Americans are depressed, with more people suffering from this emotional problem than from all others put together. Furthermore, depression is the leading cause of suicide. Self-help books are hot sellers, psychologists' offices are full, and "personality-altering" drugs are at the center of a new controversy. A Christian counselor recently told me, "Every couple I counsel is unhappy. That's why they are coming. They want to be happy, to be transformed by their marriage partners, their jobs, their money. In short, their circumstances." It's no wonder America is singing the pop song, "All I Wanna Do Is Have Some Fun!"

Many people are even asking the very question researcher and author George Barna used to title his book: *If Things Are So Good, Why Do I Feel So Bad?* Despite our plethora of toys, tools, and trinkets, when we are asked if life gets any better than this, many of us are saying yes, explaining that we would like to know personal peace and fulfillment. Barna states, "Far from crowing about the supremacy of America and the joys of modern living, Americans are entangled in a battle for survival, striving to get through today, somehow, so they can take another crack at making things more fulfilling tomorrow. The sad truth, for most people, is that we are committed to minimizing our pain rather than maximizing our joy."[6]

We are a nation of people who have so much, yet we aren't very happy. We are richly blessed, but often we're not content. Is it because we forget to ask ourselves, "How much is enough?" When do we think we'll have *enough* money and *enough* things? When is our car, our house, or our job nice enough? Susan Gregory, author of *Out of the Rat Race*, recommends that we ask ourselves these questions and explains why answering them is important:

> We will not find satisfaction until we identify what is *enough*. Without *enough* we will continue to spend beyond our means. Without *enough* we will diminish our ability to realize our dreams and to fulfill our purpose in life....Just to remind you, the definition of *enough: adequate for the want or need; sufficient for the purpose or to satisfy desire.*[7]

Defining "enough"—with guidance from the Lord—is indeed key to contentment.

The acquisition of new, trendy, and better things without knowing how much is enough can obscure the joy that God provides when we live within His will and within our means. Sometimes we even forget to determine what enough is in our activities, filling a busy schedule with traveling or just go-go-going. Perhaps we need to teach our children to discover the line of enough as they juggle school responsibilities, clubs, sports, lessons, friends, church, and family. And we can all benefit from doing what Greg P. does: "I try to seek God's will for my contentment as I plan a budget and schedule." That poses a question we should all ask ourselves: "With what does God want me to be content?"

One woman learned a real lesson in contentment and enough when she flew from her home to another state to spend a few final days with her father. In her letter printed in *Focus on the Family* magazine, she described the last lesson he taught her:

> As I entered his room at the nursing home, he gestured with his arm to his half of the area and said with wonderment, "Just think... all this...is *mine!*"
>
> Startled, I looked around and saw a few pictures, his writing materials, a few clothes and toiletries. In that moment, I took an important mental snapshot of what genuine contentment and gratefulness is. He and Mom had made the climb from small living quarters to lovely parsonages and cozy homes—then back to an apartment, followed by an "assisted living" room, and finally, half of a room. Never had there been any complaint. Even at the end, there was still an amazement for God's goodness and provision.[8]

That reminds me of something someone else once wrote about enough and sufficiency. Two thousand years ago, the apostle Paul wrote, "My God shall supply all your needs according to His riches in glory in Christ Jesus" (Philippians 4:19).

I spent a summer in India and that taught me to be very thankful for our big, beautiful houses, clean water, hot showers, food without bugs and plenty of it.

~Colleen A.

In light of that truth, we need not continue our search for enough. It is being taken care of by our loving and generous heavenly Father. Our circumstances are in His hands.

When comparisons, commercialism, or circumstances threaten to move us from being content to discontent, stay in the first "tent." Don't even think about packing your bags. Instead, stay where you are by choosing a life of contentment and remember that "godliness with contentment is great gain" (1 Timothy 6:6 NKJV). When we stop comparing ourselves with others, when we reject commercialism's influence on our desires, and when we strive to live above our circumstances rather than under them—then we can begin to want what we have. When we view what we have as a blessing instead of comparing our possessions to what we don't have or considering what else we could obtain, we begin to be content. Getting to that point is not always easy, but then most worthwhile pursuits aren't. Being content with what we have and where we are calls for discipline of the mind. It demands changing how we think, which was not a lesson I learned easily, as you'll see next.

~∂5∂~

The Secret of
Contentment
What I've Learned Thus Far

Meanwhile, back at the ranch....Or I should say that I wished I were living on a ranch instead of where I was.

In the last chapter, I told you how I came to learn contentment. You may be thinking, *Yeah, but you didn't really tell us how.* Quite right. The "how" actually began long before I finally learned the lesson. And maybe the learning process has already begun for you. Perhaps, for instance, you agree with chapter three that your attitude is "all in your head," and you want to do more of chapter four and "tame the monster of discontent," but you're wondering, *How can I have the right attitude, choose joy, and be truly content?* I wondered the same thing.

Joy and Contentment in the Pits

Before I left the dinky corporate apartments that held none of my stuff to become discontent in a big house with all of my stuff, God started working in me. I told you how I would go into my closet to cry and pray. I'd try to distance myself from the children long enough to heave up a prayer and then listen for His voice, but I often just heard the neighbors in their bathroom.

When I couldn't hear His word, I went to see His Word. I took to reading my Bible in the morning right when the birds announced they were up, which was, thankfully, before my children did the same. I began to study Philippians because I'd always been taught that it was the joy book of the Bible and boy did I need some of that!

I loved the first few verses where Paul thanks God when he remembers his friends. I could relate to that. I missed my friends back home, so I joined Paul in thanking God for them. Paul prays joyfully for them and says he has them in his heart. *Yeah, Paul, me too. They brought me great joy, and missing them makes my heart kind of hurt.* He goes on about love abounding. *Good stuff, Paul. I miss my mother being healthy, my husband being home, and my friends being here. I need lots of love. Let's get on to the joy part.* He does, but first I had to learn more about his circumstances or—should I say, his afflictions.

This changed man—forgiven, cleansed, and living beyond the chains of his past when he persecuted Christians—was now preaching the gospel. Yet his ministry wasn't reaping him accolades, standing ovations, and appreciation dinners. Instead, he was beaten and jailed, thrown into a cold, dark, damp cell and bound with shackles and chains. There were probably bugs, rodents, and a minimal amount of food—not a pretty picture. Outside the prison people were trying to discredit him (Philippians 1:15-17). As he sat in prison, Paul was evidently waiting on the court's verdict—his very life was at stake!

If there were ever a situation where a complaint or two and a grumble here and there might be expected, this would be it. I doubt that Paul would have gotten much criticism if he'd expressed his discontentment and said something like, "The food here sure isn't homecooking" or "How come some of my converts are preaching from motives of envy and strife, but I'm the one in jail?" Instead, Paul says, "And in this I rejoice, yes, and I will rejoice" (Philippians 1:18). He was *in* prison urging those *outside of* prison to rejoice! He wrote the book of Philippians to tell the saints about having joy and contentment *during* adversity—and he practiced what he preached. *How could he do that? More importantly, how could I?*

I looked around my apartment and thought of Paul. Here I was with a clean place to sleep, freedom to come and go, plenty of food, and numerous other blessings—and I was complaining! I was discontent! I was struck by the sharp contrast between Paul's crummy circumstances yet incredible attitude and my don't-hold-a-candle circumstances and lousy attitude. What a dichotomy! I'd wallow in discontentment for a while and then follow it up with a dip into the guilt pool. *I'm so miserable.... I have no right to be.... I would make Paul sick! What does he say about that joy in adversity again?* and I went on to chapter two of his letter, trying to make what I knew of Paul real in my own life.

Have the Attitude of Christ

I call Philippians 2 the attitude chapter. The man who lived in the pits with joy did so, in part, because he had the proper attitude, and he tells us what that should be. In Philippians 2:5 Paul says, "Have this attitude in yourselves which was also in Christ Jesus." We are to be Christlike. We are to have the same attitude that Christ had—and His was one of selflessness and humility:

Although He existed in the form of God, [Jesus] did not regard equality with God a thing to be grasped, but emptied Himself, taking the form of a bond-servant, and being made in the likeness of men. And being found in appearance as a man, He humbled Himself by becoming obedient to the point of death, even death on a cross (Philippians 2:6-8).

There is no greater example of selfless living, no greater sacrifice. It is the sacrifice on which I base my faith, indeed the sacrifice on which I stake my very life. Christ was God, but He laid aside His privileges as God to become

I must not let earthly things distract me from my goal.

~Terri F.

a servant on this earth, humbly submitting to His Father's plan to the point of death—and He did this because He loves us. *And I feel like I'm sacrificing these days in my life—but nothing compares with that!* I thought long and hard about the issue of self-sacrifice.

In Philippians 2:3,4 (I love these verses), Paul tells us to have a selfless attitude:

> Do nothing from selfishness or empty conceit, but with humility of mind let each of you regard one another as more important than himself; do not merely look out for your own personal interests, but also for the interests of others.

This was Christ's attitude and it can be ours, too. In fact, after I studied them, Tim and I adopted them as the O'Connor Creed and Motto. I want to teach the children that we are to avoid selfishness, look out for others first, and do so for the right reasons and that, in so doing, we become more like Christ—and His is the attitude for which we strive. We added verse two to our creed because it describes the wonderful joy of unity: "Make my joy complete by being of the same mind, maintaining the same love, united in spirit, intent on one purpose" (Philippians 2:2). What a great goal for the family—the one under our roof as well as the one who shares our faith. Then I really got on a roll and, for obvious reasons, added verse 14: "Do all things without grumbling or disputing." As a mother, that one's my favorite!

Continuing my study of Philippians, I moved on to chapter three and began to learn more about attitude and perspective. Paul starts off boldly: "Finally, my brethren, rejoice in the Lord. To write the same things again is no trouble to me, and it is a safeguard for you" (Philippians 3:1). *Again, he's telling me to rejoice, but my joy's pretty thin. I could use a safeguard.*

I kept on reading and realized that I'm not just to take on Christ's attitude. I'm also to *know* Him. Paul tells us to "put no confidence in the flesh" (verse 3), to "know [Jesus], and the power of His resurrection" (verse 10). You and I are encouraged to fully seek to know Christ instead of having confidence in the flesh. When we have confidence in our own accomplishments, we have an attitude of arrogance, but when we "count them but rubbish in order [to] gain Christ" (verse 8), we begin to have an attitude of humility.

Paul tells us to forget what lies behind and reach forward to what lies ahead (verse 13) and to press on (verse 14)! *This is another aspect of the attitude he encourages me to have.* Don't put confidence in yourself, but strive to know Christ. Forget your past and press on to reach the prize of eternal life. Paul then says, "Let us therefore, as many as are perfect, *have this attitude*; and if in anything you have a different attitude, God will reveal that also to you" (Philippians 3:15, emphasis added). *Hmmm. Selfless, humble, knowing God, pressing on....Great attitude!*

But wait a minute, I thought. *There's no way I can have that kind of attitude. The verse even says "as many as are perfect," so that leaves me out.* Only one Person has ever been perfect—Jesus—but that doesn't mean you and I are off the hook. In the original Greek language, this word "perfect" means "mature." Paul is basically saying, "For those of you mature enough, this is the attitude to have, and when you mess up, God will let you know." So many times I am convicted about my lack of a selfless attitude. When my attitude stinks, it invariably has its roots in my selfishness: I'm thinking more of me and my situation than anything or anyone else. And when I have a bad attitude, I am never truly humble. Despite our humanness, you and I must not look at the attitude described in these verses as an impossibility. God did not give these words to Paul to pass on to us for our self-condemnation. (No guilt trips, please! Everyone has a bad attitude now and then.) Instead, we are to look on these verses as a goal to attain. And Jesus is our ultimate model!

From the Head to the Heart

I'd read Paul's letter to the Philippians many times before, but not until I got disgusted with my own bad attitude and my own lack of joy and contentment in my circumstances did my understanding of what he says change from head knowledge to heart knowledge. That change began with my study of Philippians 4. There I read a very familiar passage:

> Not that I speak from want; for I have *learned to be content* in whatever circumstances I am. I know how to get along with humble means, and I also know how to live in prosperity; in any and every circumstance I have learned the secret of being filled and going hungry, both of having abundance and suffering need (Philippians 4:11,12, emphasis added).

"For I have *learned* to be content." I latched onto that phrase. If Paul said he learned, then maybe I could, too. He didn't say he *was* content in his circumstances; he said he *learned* to be content in them. During the rest of our stay in the dinky corporate domiciles and during the first few years of living in my "cave," this teaching began to really cook for me. These thoughts were percolating in my head and stewing in my heart. I'd love to be able to tell you that I simply read all these verses and then, just like Jiffypop, I was done. I was content. I was "perfect attitude" personified. Sometimes God works that way, but not this time. He let me sit on the back burner awhile, His precious lesson simmering in my life until it was ready to be tasted. And how rich the flavor that comes with such simmering! If I may be so bold, let me share what I have learned thus far from the Master Chef.

The secret of having a great attitude and being content while we're in the pits involves three things:

- Renewing our thought life.

- Remembering the Source of our strength.

- Resting in that Source's sovereignty.

Let's look at each of these now.

There is no joy in the soul that has forgotten what God prizes.

~Oswald Chambers,
My Utmost For His Highest

1. Renew Your Thought Life: Know on What to Dwell

You and I need to choose joy and contentment in our heads by adjusting what we think. Attitude is purely a mental process—a head-thing—so to change it we must change how we think. We must *renew* our thinking. Adopting an "out with the bad, in with the good" approach, we must stop thinking one way and start thinking another way. Paul encourages us to renew our thinking when he says:

> Finally, brethren, whatever is true, whatever is honorable, whatever is right, whatever is pure, whatever is lovely, whatever is of good repute, if there is any excellence and if anything worthy of praise, let your mind dwell on these things (Philippians 4:8).

Sometimes instead of dwelling on what is true, however, we look at what we lack—which isn't a true picture. Instead of thinking on things that are honorable, our thoughts honor no one. Instead of pondering the lovely, we look at the unloveliness of our situation and surroundings. Sometimes we don't find anything excellent about things because we don't look for it, and when we can't think of anything worthy of praise, it's often because we aren't focusing on the One who is always worthy of praise.

But Paul knew on what to dwell! When we harness our thought life, choose (in our head) to think about things that are true, lovely, worthy of praise, and so on, and consciously choose to let our mind dwell on these things, we begin to train our attitude and tame the monster of discontent. When we think about the kind of things God calls us to think about in Philippians 4:8, our mind begins to be renewed. Our attitude begins to change. Contentment becomes attainable regardless of our circumstances! And there are two reasons why.

Our thought life determines our attitude. As we've seen, what we think determines how we feel which, in turn, affects our attitude. I love what John Maxwell says in *The Winning Attitude*. "Two things must be stated to emphasize the power of our thought life. Major premise: We can control our thoughts. Minor premise: Our feelings come from our thoughts. Conclusion? We can control our feelings by learning to change one thing: the way we think....Our thought life, not our circumstances, determines our happiness.[1] That's pretty straightforward.

Our thought life determines our contentment. Being content is not based on what happens to us (our circumstances) or how we feel about what happens to us (our emotional response to our circumstances). Being content is based on our thoughts. Contentment begins with what we think about ourselves and our situation. It's not based on what happens to us, but instead on how we think about and emotionally respond to what happens to us. If we can control what we think, we can better control how we feel, and our feelings determine our ability to be content ... or not be content. Renewing our thinking is renewing our mind, and Scripture says that doing so can transform us:

> Do not be conformed to this world, but be *transformed* by the *renewing of your mind*, that you may prove what the will of God is, that which is good and acceptable and perfect (Romans 12:2, emphasis added).

Instead of moaning about his circumstances, Paul knew on what he was to dwell. Instead of focusing on what was happening to him (which is so easy to do), he began to look at the bigger picture and was lifted above his circumstances. Then he found joy.

Renewing our mind involves "taking every thought captive" (2 Corinthians 10:5) and learning to think God's thoughts. It is a lifelong process, something that we must pursue daily. Renewing our minds sounds like work, but "along life's way...it brings a peace and delight that can only come from having embraced the mind of Christ."[2] It brings true joy.

2. Remember the Source of Our Strength: Know Who Is Empowering Us

Adopting the right attitude and changing our thinking will not make us content when we try to do it in our own power. That would be nothing more than simply practicing positive thinking, which can be good but which only goes so far. Our ability to harness what we think is limited, but there is a Source that knows no limits and is available to us as believers. The second part of the secret of contentment, then, is to remember that *God is the source of our strength.*

We need to ask ourselves, "In whose strength are we operating? Who is controlling my life? Is it me and my circumstances—or is it God?" Paul knew that he was not in control and that he was not operating on his own strength, but that it was Christ in him. He knew who was in control and providing the power when he wrote: "I can do all things through Him who strengthens me" (Philippians 4:13).

When we rely on our own strength, our ability to change is limited. Our strength is finite; God's strength is not. In our own might, our determination to be content is undermined by the limits of our willpower and our ability to accept our circumstances. To make the choice to rejoice and tame that monster of discontent, we must recognize the Source of our strength: God is at work in us. As Paul might say, I have "a confidence that I measure up to any situation I am facing because of the resources of strength that God has made available to me."[3]

Knowing the Source of our strength and His unending, omnipotent nature can give us the confidence we need to choose and live a life of contentment. To make sure you are accessing His strength and not just relying on your own, remember the source of your strength—dwell on it and keep it in the forefront of your mind. Do what Paul did and acknowledge that it is Christ in you who provides the power to change your thinking and, therefore, your attitude. Remind yourself of this and thank God that the things you do are really done through Him who strengthens you.

3. Rest in the Sovereignty of That Source: Know That God Is in Control and That God Is Good

God is sovereign. He is in control over each and every circumstance of our life. Here we just have to take God at His word—the Word.

God created everything and controls even the weather: "It is He who made the earth by His power, who established the world by His wisdom; and by His understanding He has stretched out the heavens. When He utters His voice, there is a tumult of waters in the heavens, and He causes the clouds to ascend from the end of the earth; he makes lightning for the rain, and brings out the wind from His storehouses" (Jeremiah 10:12,13).

God can do anything He wants to do: "Whatever the LORD pleases, He does, in heaven and in earth, in the seas and in all deeps" (Psalm 135:6).

God knows everything that happens to us and He cares: "Are not two sparrows sold for a cent? And yet not one of them will fall to the ground apart from your Father....Therefore do not fear; you are of more value than many sparrows" (Matthew 10:29,31).

Sometimes our circumstances appear completely out of control, and we feel tossed about by life. When that's the case, we must remember that God has the power to control anything and everything (even these circumstances in our lives) and that He can do so in an infinite number of ways (He can do as He pleases), and that—most importantly—He cares about what happens to us (remember the sparrow?). The God who sent His only Son to die for us and bothers to know the very number of hairs on our heads (see Matthew 10:30) also knows what is going on in our lives, and He cares greatly.

Many times we know that God cares about the big picture, but we need to be reminded that He is also always aware of what's in our little bitty viewfinder of life. I think of what God did for the Koinis family, my longtime friends. After much detailed planning and great anticipation, Steve and Brenda took their two children to Disneyland for a vacation. They had planned and prayed for this trip, and the kids were about to burst with excitement—when raindrops started hitting the windshield on the drive from their hotel to the

> *I* have to continually remind myself of who is in control. God knows all things and loves me more than anyone else.
>
> ~Vicki K.

theme park. Brenda said, "OK, we know that 'God causes all things to work together for good to those who love God, to those who are called according to His purpose,' and that's us, so let's pray." (See Romans 8:28.)

They did, and the children fully expected the raindrops to cease and the clouds to part. They didn't. When they got to the park, the drops had become full-fledged rain. By the time they got to the ticket gate wearing their yellow ponchos, rain was coming down in buckets. They got their tickets and went in even though it was raining so hard that Brenda thought her contacts were going to float away. She and Steve told the children that God could use this for their good—to help them learn to trust God as completely as Jesus did—even though He didn't answer their prayer for dry skies as they had asked.

Other good soon became apparent: They practically had Disneyland to themselves. Wearing their bright yellow slickers, they went from one attraction to another...without having to stand in long lines. They were having the time of their lives, and seeing everything in one day instead of the two they had planned. The next day they were able to visit a waterpark—a vacation bonus not on their itinerary, but on their Father's. It was a memorable trip for the fun as well as the spiritual truth the Lord had demonstrated. Now, years later, when the children wonder how good might come from bad circumstances, their parents remind them that God used a pouring rain at Disneyland for their good and that He can use this (whatever the situation at the moment) for their good, too.

I believe that God cares deeply about the little things in our lives as much as He cares about the big things when we allow Him to use them to reveal something about Himself. Sometimes we pray for the biggies because we desperately want an answer. But I think, somehow, God must be especially pleased when we pray even for small things because it shows that we care about His involvement in our daily lives. My friend, Betty, prays before she goes shopping and even before she chooses her clothes for the day, saying, "Father, You know what You have planned for me today. How can I best represent You?" Once she needed a safety pin to keep her dress intact, but she doesn't sew and knew she didn't have a pin. She prayed for a pin, and when she opened her eyes, there right at her feet was a safety pin. A coincidence or an answered prayer? Betty believes God answers even prayers about small things.

God recently showed me in a very personal way that He cares about the small things. I just got back from a wonderful women's ministry retreat which, for several years, has been held in a beautiful country setting. A shop in the nearby town sells prints of the big country house where we stayed, with an excerpt from the Psalms written on it in calligraphy. Last year I decided that I would get one the next time I was there. I told no one that I wanted this print, and this year, I was working on this manuscript during our free time and didn't have a chance to go shopping with everyone else. My little want would have to wait. However, when we were leaving the retreat, a friend handed me a simply wrapped gift. You guessed it. It was the print I had wanted for a year. I was touched by her thoughtfulness and awed once again that God even cares about the little insignificant desires that we have and loves to prove that to us! A coincidence? I think not. I agree with the little sign on my bulletin board that says, "A coincidence is when God does a miracle and chooses to remain anonymous." God cares about all the details—from life and death to pins and prints. Nothing escapes the notice or reach of our sovereign God.

In order to rest in God's sovereignty, however, we must know that He is completely good—good in character and good to us. His Word teaches that "the LORD is good, for His lovingkindness is everlasting" (Jeremiah 33:11), that He is "the good shepherd" (John 10:11), and that we are to "give thanks to the LORD, for He is good" (Psalm 106:1). We must simply

> $\mathcal{A}$s a single person, I want a husband and family like the picture in my mind I grew up with. However, only God knows what I need— my wants are not necessarily my needs.
>
> ~Tamhra L.

take God at His word. The Scriptures state definitively that goodness is part of God's character, and we must choose to believe that. The Bible also gives a clear picture of God's goodness from the beginning of creation, through His provision for and involvement with the people who have served Him through the ages, through His redemptive plan for us in Christ, and, ultimately, in His promise of what awaits us in the kingdom to come. Every page of Scripture points to a God who is indeed good despite what we see and experience in our fallen world.

Now, look for a moment at your own life. Recall the times that God has provided for you and consider all the things He has done for you. Reflect on His blessings—both material and spiritual. Remember the big things and the small. Don't forget His provision for the "pins and prints" in your life. Ponder what God has done for you and how He has demonstrated His goodness to you in both the big ways and the little ways. Reflecting on these things and becoming fully convinced that God is indeed good can mean the difference between choosing faith and choosing doubt when dark days come. We'll talk about this more in chapter eight, "Joy in the Dark." But right now determine in your heart to believe that God Himself is good no matter what your circumstances suggest. Goodness is part of God's character and He never changes.

When we choose to believe that God is in control and that He is good, we can rest in His sovereignty. We can relax knowing that because He loves us dearly, He is always at work to make us more like Christ in our faith and ability to trust Him.

Seeing God's Perspective

The apostle Paul knew joy and contentment because he saw all of life from God's perspective. Paul knew what to think about, he knew that God was his strength, and he rested in the fact that God was in control. His one objective was to know Christ as he continued the race for his prize in heaven, taking as many people with him as he could. His body was here on earth, but his heart was in heaven. His body was in prison, but his mind was not. This focus on what was unseen—this hope in the Lord—allowed Paul to continue to be used by God even when he was in jail. He just watched God alter the way in which he was used.

No longer able to minister in freedom, Paul began his letter-writing ministry behind bars, something for which Christians through the centuries can thank him. He surrendered his vision, his dreams, and his plans for ministry to God and allowed God to alter them. His imprisoned body but free mind truly knew God and saw God's perspective. Paul had been privileged to get a glimpse of heaven, and he knew what was waiting after this life. This understanding of God's plan for eternity dominated Paul's life and ministry and enabled him to have a heavenly perspective on his own sufferings. When we, like Paul, begin to live for the world to come instead of just living for this world, we begin to see everything from God's perspective. As we mature in our faith and choose to believe in His goodness and sovereignty regardless of what we're experiencing now, we grow in our ability to see those circumstances as God sees them.

Trusting to Joy

I would like to point you to something that I find very pivotal in the life of a joyful Christian. On the surface, it's a simple thing. It is also something quite rich, to be cultivated throughout one's life. It is this: "When we *trust* God and exercise our *faith*, then we can *yield* ourselves completely and experience the byproduct of joy." Let's look at those key words.

Trust

When we trust God. Many Christians are joyful because they are saved, but that is where joy begins and ends. Joy was meant to be much more than gratitude to God that He has made a way for us to escape hell. He also intends for us to live in joy in the present—no matter what that present is. But we can't do that unless we trust Him.

If we know that God has saved us (from eternal death, the penalty for our sins), is sovereign (in control over any and all circumstances that come into our life), and is completely good (in character and to us), then we can know that we are safe no matter what. Knowing that enables us to trust Him completely, which brings great joy. We trust God with what happens after death (because He has saved us from hell), and we trust Him with our life before death (because we have determined that He is sovereign and good).

Trusting God with all of our life like this is possible when we truly become intimate with Him. The better we know Him, the more we can trust Him. (We'll look closely at this in chapter seven.) When we trust God, we allow Him to work in us. We trust; God "does." So don't get caught up in trying to do joy. Just trust God first. The Lord will take care of what you entrust to Him. There is great joy in total trust.

Faith

When we trust God and *exercise our faith.* My intent here is not to dive into the deep theological waters of faith, but to look at it as it applies to joy. When we trust someone, we can have faith in him or her. When we trust God, we can exercise our faith in Him. Put simply, faith is absolute and complete belief regardless of proof. Being able to exercise such childlike faith is both the first step of our spiritual life and fundamental to our spiritual growth (see Matthew 18:3,4). Exercising faith as an act of our will is the beginning of our life as Christians. It is what takes us from death to eternal life. Continuing to live and exercise that faith is what growing and maturing is all about. As Hannah Whitall Smith wrote over 100 years ago in *The Christian's Secret of a Happy Life,* "The soul that has discovered this secret of simple faith has found the key that will unlock the whole treasure-house of God."[4] Without faith, there is no lasting joy.

We can learn about faith and trust when we look at our children. My four children have faith in their father and me because they trust us. They know we take care of them and that we are good to them. They also blindly trust us with their future because they know our character and they know we love them. They trust, and we take care of them. They are secure and carefree. My children play freely in my house, not fretting about their next meal or next week's schedule, and I want to be just as carefree and trusting in my heavenly Father's care. You and I can begin to know a life of joy when, like children, we put our total faith in Him because we trust Him with our present and our future.

Indiana Jones shows us how this works in one of his movie adventures. To reach the treasure he's seeking, he must get from one precipice to another but there appears to be no way to cross. Only a steep cliff and imminent death lie between him and the treasure. Yet, mustering up all the faith he has, Indiana attempts the crossing anyway and steps out into the open air. Wondrously, a bridge appears with each step he takes. He looks down, amazed that he's seeing something where there was nothing before his leap of faith. Step by step he makes his way safely across.

That scene is a vivid picture of what the Christian life is all about. And this scene is a call to trust. If you desperately long for a life of joy—the full and abundant life that Christ talked about—go ahead and make the leap of faith into total surrender even if you can't see the path beneath you. It is there.

Yield

When we trust God and exercise our faith, then we can yield ourselves completely. When we yield to oncoming traffic, we give up the right to go where we want to go. We either stay right where we are or we get out of the way to make way for what's coming. We can do the same thing with our life when we yield ourselves—body, soul, and spirit—to God. We can also think of yielding as consecration, complete obedience, and (my favorite) utter abandonment. These words and phrases all mean an entire surrender of our whole self to God. When we do this, we make it possible for God to bless us with His joy.

Why is this sometimes so scary? Many of us are afraid that the minute we say, "OK, God, I'm Yours. I completely surrender to You and Your will," God is going to look down on us and reply, "Aha! Now I've got you where I want you! With which misery shall I start? A mission trip to Africa?" But the truth is that God desires to give us good gifts just as we desire the best for our children. If our children were to tell us that they want to do exactly as we wish, we would not respond, "Great! Now, how hard can I make things for you?" What mother's heart doesn't soar when she sees her child trying exceptionally hard to be obedient? What mother isn't touched when her child shows sweet and complete obedience? I think the heart of God soars with compassion and love for us when we demonstrate that we want to be in total submission to Him. When we surrender ourselves with utter abandonment, we can trust Him. We can know that if He wants us in Africa, He will make Africa our heart's desire.

Furthermore, when we surrender ourselves to God, we are like clay in the hands of a skilled potter. A potter is able to make something beautiful of the clay when the clay is pliable, yielding to his hands, submitting to his touch. He shapes it, scrapes it, turns it, molds it, lets it dry, and puts it in the fire. The clay doesn't try to jump off the potter's wheel or run from the fire. The clay submits. It isn't expected to help the potter in any way; it is merely to remain workable in his hands. As a result, the potter is able to produce something beautiful.

But living in a culture that values doing, we find it a real challenge to merely *be* in God's presence—to *be* the clay in His hands. When we yield to the Master Potter's skillful and loving shaping of us as well as to the firing, the results are a beautiful vessel fit for use in His service. (By the way, whether we are an earthen crock, an everyday mug, or fine bone china depends on how long we are in the fire!)

When we offer our bodies and our minds to God (Romans 12:1,2) without thinking of the cost and we commit ourselves to do whatever God wants, we are yielding ourselves to Him. When we are consecrated (fully obeying Him) and abandoned (completely surrendering our whole being to Him), we are yielded. And when we are yielded to God, we can accept life with its rocks and mountains and shadows and, in the process, experience the beautiful by-product of joy.

But how do we do that? By whatever means we can—and I don't mean that flippantly. Scripture doesn't outline three easy steps for yielding yourself to God. But know that God can use anything in your life to bring you to this place and that He will take you however you come. In her books, Barbara Johnson describes this yielding point in her life as the time she told God, "Whatever, Lord!" Hannah Whitall Smith speaks of "utter abandon" as a means of yielding. Devotional writer Oswald Chambers puts it this way:

> It is a transaction of will, not of sentiment. Tell God you are ready to be offered; then let the consequences

> be what they may, there is no strand of complaint,
> now, no matter what God chooses....Go through the
> crisis in will, then when it comes externally there will
> be no thought of the cost....Tell God you are ready to
> be offered, and God will prove Himself to be all you
> ever dreamed He would be.[5]

Chambers also explains that to be truly abandoned to God also requires that we not consider the cost beforehand:

> Beware of talking about abandonment if you
> know nothing about it, and you will never know
> anything about it until you have realized that John
> 3:16 means that God gave Himself absolutely. In
> our abandonment we give ourselves over to God
> just as God gave Himself for us, without any calcu-
> lation. The consequence of abandonment never en-
> ters into our outlook because our life is taken up
> with Him.

The call to yield to God truly is an invitation to joy. Have you accepted?

For some people who have, yielding to God may happen with a simple prayer in the quiet of life. For others, it may come during a period of pain and darkness. It may happen on the oc-casion of a life-changing event that you will always remember, or it may result from a prayerful lifestyle. The odd thing about giving everything to God, though, is that we humans have the tendency to keep snatching it back even when we don't want it! We play "hot potato" with our problems and areas of self that we want God to control. But whenever we realize that we're car-rying all that around again, we can empty our arms as fast as we can. We must fling it all back to God as often as necessary.

However you want to describe your submission before God—surrender, yielding, consecration, abandonment, or "whatever, Lord"—consider this description from *The Chris-tian's Secret of a Happy Life*:

> ...an entire surrender of the whole being to God—spirit,
> soul, and body placed under His absolute control, for

Him to do with us just what He pleases. We mean that the language of our hearts, under all circumstances and in view of every act, is to be "Thy will be done." To a soul ignorant of God, this may look hard, but to those who know Him it is the happiest and most restful of lives.[6]

When we trust God and exercise our faith, then we can yield ourselves completely and experience the by-product of joy. The ability to surrender our whole selves to God with complete trust and childlike faith is the key to possessing the abundant life filled with the fruit and gift of the joy of the Lord.

As we learn to renew our thought life, remember who is the Source of our strength, and rest in God's sovereignty, we begin to see all of life from God's perspective and therefore truly learn the secret of contentment. Gaining this perspective and learning this lesson, however, isn't a one-time event; it's more of a process. It isn't a quick course to be gobbled up and never tasted again. New struggles and temptations will be put on our plates, allowing us to exercise what we've learned. I pray that my responses—and yours—will be savory to the Father as we continue to be nourished at the bounteous table of His Word and teaching, be life bitter or sweet.

The bottom line is, "Do I trust Him?" I think the longer we walk with the Lord, the truer, deeper our joy and contentment become because we are so acquainted with His faithfulness.

~Kellie M.

~&Part Two &~
Cultivating Joy and
Contentment in Our Hearts
What We Feel

~❧ 6 ❧~

How Can I Be Joyful When I Feel Like a Grump?

Where We Start When the Feelings Won't

Well, that's just great," you may be thinking. "I've made the choice to rejoice. I'm taming that monster of discontent, and I've chosen joy. But I still feel like an irritated junkyard dog—cranky and at the end of her rope." Maybe a birthday card a friend of mine received would be appropriate for you. It said, "I searched all day to find a birthday gift that matches your personality...but nobody carried a pit bull in high heels![1] Maybe you're a pit bull, or maybe you're a teddy bear that's happened to dehibernate. Some days, even the most gentle of us are cross. Sometimes we just don't feel joy in our heart.

Unfortunately, even if we choose joy and contentment in our heads, feeling it in our hearts isn't automatic. Although feelings often do follow actions (as we've talked about), they don't necessarily follow our thoughts. Just because we decide to choose joy—to change what we think, to see life from God's perspective, and to learn to think God's thoughts—doesn't mean we will immediately feel joyful, and that can be so frustrating. That is why many of us when we hear "happiness is a choice" advice and songs like "I Choose Joy" on the radio scoff, "Oh, yeah? I did, too, but it doesn't work!" Sometimes it doesn't work because we stop at the point of making a choice. We say, "OK, I choose." Period. Then we wait for some kind of magic to work in us—an instantaneous transformation from pit bull to pleasant puppy. But joy is not the result of magic. Besides, we must not expect that our choice to rejoice will make us laughing hyenas or playful otters if that is not our nature. Instead, we need to say, "I choose joy. Now what's next?" Don't stop with the choice; proceed from choosing joy in the mind to cultivating joy in the heart!

If you expect change to come simply because you've made the choice to rejoice, if you expect your behavior and your feelings to immediately follow suit, you will probably be disappointed. Often we can act our way into a feeling (and we can usually do that more easily than we can feel our way into an action), but we should not depend on this method for attaining real joy. We can't assume that once we begin to act as if we're joyful, joy will follow and will last over the long haul. Oh, we may know joy for a time with that "act first" method, but the charade will wear thin, then so will our disposition, and, if we're not careful, even our faith. To say that if we just change our behavior we will grow spiritually and emotionally is really a false assumption, as Doctors Henry Cloud and John Townsend say in their book *False Assumptions: Twelve "Christian" Beliefs That Can Drive You Crazy*. What, then, are we to do? They say this:

> The Bible presents an answer. Instead of attempting to fix our symptoms, we can actively take ourselves to good nutrients. Just as a tree planted in rich soil can flourish, so can we expose ourselves to God's healing resources.
>
> The only behavior we can practice that will move us to emotional and spiritual adulthood is picking ourselves up and taking ourselves to good nutrients— that is, to God and his people.[2]

In other words, we can't know lasting joy by finding an action that produces that feeling and trying to continue that action. We can only truly know joy by accessing the real Source of joy—which is God Himself.

"But didn't you just say, not too many pages back, that I'm supposed to *choose* joy?" you might ask. Yes, yes, yes—and then go straight to the heart. A person can't become joyful by an act of will alone any more than an alcoholic can simply stop drinking or a depressed person can cheer up just by deciding to do so. You and I must first choose joy in our head and then cultivate it in our heart. Although the will is quite powerful, real change must occur within the heart. Ultimately living a life of joy will be the result of inward change, not the other way around. Inward change does not come simply with new behaviors. Sustaining power to change is based on God above and not merely on our will within.

I've realized that from being in that certain spot between pit bull and otter, wanting desperately to splash in the joy instead of growling in the pit, yet realizing that the metamorphosis wasn't happening. I was trying to jump into the joy with my pit bull self and ended up all wet and a little bit mad. No, a pit bull can't swim like an otter (although I bet that would be quite interesting to watch, as perhaps I was). Nor can a pitbull change itself into an otter. But, unlike that pit bull, you and I are not destined to remain in the doghouse growling at the world and chewing on bones. We can live in peace and feast on the fruit of the joy of the Lord, but first we must let Him transform our heart.

I remember all too well what it feels like to be in that place of wanting to be the otter, of longing to feel "splashes of joy in the cesspools of life," as Barbara Johnson puts it in the title of her book. Sometimes we want more than anything else to know joy, but wanting it and finding it can seem worlds apart. But the goal is not light-years away; the distance between wanting and finding joy is

Fixing our eyes on Jesus, the author and perfecter of faith, who for the joy set before Him endured the cross,...

~Hebrews 12:2a

Imagine the joy that's awaiting us!

actually a little journey—a journey of the heart in our walk of faith. How can we be joyful when we feel grumpy, and where do we start when the feelings won't? Start with seeking the Source.

Seeking the Source

A young child stood close to his mother, clinging to her skirt as he watched a group of children tearing into beautifully wrapped presents. They were squealing with delight as they each opened their package. The little child, obviously not part of the celebration, looked longingly at the joyful children. Then he looked around to see where these lucky children had gotten their presents. He left his mother's side and wandered for quite some time around the room, hoping that the person who had blessed these children would think he was part of the party and bless him with a package. Finally he spotted the giver and ran to tell his mother. "Mother, look at all those presents! It looks like such fun! I'm going to go get one, too," he said expectantly. "No, child, you aren't," replied his mother. "Although you've found the giver, you may not get a gift from him. You don't know him."

And so it is with us sometimes. We desperately want the gift of joy, but we look in the wrong places. Like the child searching the room to find out where the children got their gifts, we search for joy by filling our schedules and lives and minds with things that we hope will lead us to that gift. We pursue this job and that hobby or sport and crowd our lives with various activities in an attempt to find joy. We think that marrying this guy, having this child, taking this job, pursuing this ministry, or buying this thing will finally bring us joy, and when we miss the sparkle we are dumbfounded. We are like that child searching for the source of the gift and, initially, coming up short.

Oh, many of our pursuits are wonderful, and they bring us great happiness and, yes, even some joy. But when we look to them as the source of our joy, we will eventually be disappointed. Our mate will let us down, our child will make a wrong choice, the job will not work out, the ministry will become difficult, the thing we bought will lose its luster. Then we will see only the rocks in life and none of the sparkle. The things that fill our lives certainly can and do add sparkle, but we must know that they are not the true source. The only real source of our joy is Jesus Christ. When we have trusted Him for our salvation and are in relationship with Him as our Lord, we have access to the wellspring of joy. We aren't limited to playing in the spring; we can drink from its very source! Jesus said, "If any man is thirsty, let him come to Me and drink. He who believes in Me, as the Scripture said, 'From his innermost being shall flow rivers of living water'" (John 7:37,38). He also said, "I am the bread of life; he who comes to Me shall not hunger, and he who believes in Me shall never thirst" (John 6:35). Not only will we not thirst, but the water that Jesus offers us "shall become in [us] a well of water springing up to eternal life" (John 4:14).

Just as the mother might ask the child who wants a present, "Do you know the giver?" I need to ask you if you know the Giver. Some of you may have never made the choice to get to know the Giver of eternal life and joy and to trust Him as your Savior and Lord. If you want assurance of eternal life and the incredible joy that comes from knowing Jesus Christ, put your faith in Him. Simply acknowledge that He is the Son of God, that He died on the cross as payment for your sins, and that He rose again, defeating death and the power of Satan. Then, having made that basic confession of faith— having chosen by an act of will to believe this wondrous truth—choose to pursue a relationship with Him. In other words, act on the promise we find in the gospel of John: "As many as received Him, to them He gave the right to become children of God, even to those who believe in His name" (John 1:12). And, as His child, you will spend eternity with God. Knowing that your eternal destiny is taken care of is a source of great joy, as the apostle Peter explains:

> Though you have not seen Him, you love Him, and though you do not see Him now, but believe in Him, you greatly rejoice with joy inexpressible and full of glory, obtaining as the outcome of your faith the salvation of your souls (1 Peter 1:8,9).

Or, perhaps you made the faith decision years ago, but you've never developed much of a relationship *with* God. Please know that it's never too late to start. God desires a relationship with you! Do you know Him, friend?

Now, you may have made these choices and have been a Christian for many years, but perhaps your joy stops with the knowledge that you are saved. Maybe you've thought, "Yes, I have joy knowing that God has saved me, but my problems far outweigh my joy." Oh, listen, dear reader. Joy is meant to be so much more than gratitude to God for making a way for us to escape hell. He also wants us—through His joy—to be free of the things of this earth that bind us up, whatever they are. We miss this joy and its accompanying freedom because we, like the little child, search for the Giver of the gifts and, not finding Him, look to external things to provide our joy. We miss that joy for another reason, too.

Sometimes we are like the child after he has found the giver. We ask for the gift, but we are asking someone we don't know. We know who the Source is, but we don't know Him well. And we don't receive gifts from strangers any more than the child receives a gift at the party where he doesn't know the host. Instead, gifts come from those people whom we know well. The gifts that mean the most to us are from those whom we know and love. How well do you know the Giver of Joy? How much do you love Him? *To receive the gift of joy, become intimate with the Giver.*

Enter His Presence

The only way to become intimate with someone is to spend time with that person, and this principle is true for God. Not only can we become more intimately acquainted with God when we spend time with Him, but we will also find joy when we are in His presence. "Splendor and majesty are before Him, strength and joy are in His place" (1 Chronicles 16:27).

Other versions of the Bible say instead that there is "joy in his dwelling place" (NIV). Would you like more than just your everyday joy? Would you like your joy cup full? Then enter into the presence of God, for, as David proclaimed in a song, "In [God's] presence is fulness of joy; in [His] right hand there are pleasures forever" (Psalm 16:11). There is indeed great joy in dwelling with God, as the psalmist knew when he wrote, "How lovely are Thy dwelling places, O LORD of hosts! My soul longed and even yearned for the courts of the LORD; my heart and my flesh sing for joy to the living God" (Psalm 84:1,2).

Are you there, dear reader? Does your heart sing for joy to God? Does your soul long for His courts? If so, then you know the joy of which I speak. You can join the psalmist in exulting, "How lovely are Thy dwelling places!" But what if you can't say that? What if all your heart and flesh long for right now is a little more sleep or freedom from pain or an end to the quarrels? In times like these, the dwelling place of God seems far off and very much out of reach. How can we possibly enter His presence when just getting through each day is a struggle?

And then, making the experience of joy seem even more unreachable, we are often victims of our culture: We are a people more interested in "seven steps to joy" than in learning how to live in the presence of God. Too often we want quick applications and simple how-to's rather than learning gradually how to truly experience all that God has for us. Titles like *Quick Tips for...*, *Secrets of Success in...*, and *Ten Ways to Instantly...*jump from the covers of magazines and books and fill the broadcast airwaves, offering ideas for how to solve our problems and satisfy our society that wants instant everything. We want a fulfilling marriage—tonight. We want to end our depression—today. We want and need answers to our troubles, but those answers won't always come with a ten-easy-steps approach. When we go for the quick fix, we often wind up with less depth. Finding true joy is no exception. Happiness is

By your own deliberate choice, by an act of your will, develop the holy habit of being consciously aware of Him and drawing on Him.

~Ray and Anne Ortlund,
In His Presence

a quick fix—nice, but temporary and undependable. Joy is different.

So I offer you no simple, quick steps to joy. Instead, I offer you my hand (in my heart, I can hold yours if you are hurting and longing for the joy of the Lord), and I say to you, "Yes, the joy is there and it is available to you! The Father longs for you to enter His presence and to bless you with His joy!" I also stretch out my hand to point you to the Way, to Jesus Christ Himself. I am pointing to His presence: "Jesus said to him, 'I am the way, and the truth, and the life; no one comes to the Father, but through Me'"(John 14:6).

Entering that presence, that dwelling place of the Lord, is not a specific, isolated experience. We don't, for instance, enter His presence only when we enter and worship in a church. Furthermore, we don't learn to enter His presence just during our quiet time. We need not be at a certain place, at a certain age, or in just the right circumstances to be in His presence. Through His blood shed on the cross, Jesus made a way for us to continually enter His presence (Hebrews 10:19), to learn to live in His presence—something Old Testament saints couldn't do (Leviticus 1:3; 1 Samuel 6:19,20). We *are* the dwelling place of God; we are the temple (1 Corinthians 6:19). Unfortunately, sick children, financial pressures, quibbling family members, scary medical test results, and a multitude of other problems and everyday circumstances can keep us from being in and sensing His presence.

"Yes, that's me," you may say. "How do I live in His presence when my life is so demanding. And just what in the world does 'living in His presence' mean anyway? How can I do that when I feel so unspiritual?"

I'm continually learning more and more about what "living in His presence" means in my life (and I don't mean theological learning). For me, living in God's presence is having a constant awareness of His love and presence in my daily life—in the sick kids, work pressures, dirty dishes, and everything else. He cares about it all, and He is in it all. I have learned, for instance, that I can enter into the presence of God while washing dishes or rocking a child in the night just as easily as I can when I'm worshiping in a cathedral. If I wait until I feel particularly "spiritual" to enter His presence, I may never even bother! But when I acknowledge His presence with me while I'm scrubbing the tub or buying broccoli or writing a book or doing whatever, I am practicing His presence in every part of my life, something Brother Lawrence describes in *The Practice of the Presence of God*:

> Attention to God was to be not just a slot of time every day, but all day long, every day. His presence was to permeate everything. We would commit our-selves to do everything for the love of God, in simple rest and without fear.
>
> We would seek to live as if absolutely nothing mattered except loving God, pleasing God, trusting God....
>
> The psalmists had sung to God, and so would we, "I am always with you; you hold me by my right hand" (Psalm 73:23).[3]

Read those words again and consider how close God is to you. These simple statements of Brother Lawrence changed Ray and Anne Ortlund, as they explain in their wonderful book *In His Presence*. When they were first learning this truth and making it a habit in their lives, they held each other accountable for prac-ticing the presence of God, and they worked on it in very practi-cal ways. Ray, for instance, set his wristwatch alarm to go off every 15 minutes as a reminder to think of God. He also put self-stick notes on his desk, mirror, and car with the letters "PTP" for "Practice the Presence." Anne put a paper with the word "JE-SUS" written on it on the floor beside her bed to remind her to begin her day by worshiping Him. The Ortlunds write that "the most important thing one person (or couple) can do for another is to bring him (or her) into the presence of God, and leave him there!...Living in His presence is the secret to living."[4]

Truly, I am just beginning to learn this secret and live this wonderful, life-changing truth. I am not writing to you as one who has reached that goal, but as one who struggles (as you may) but who is beginning to see how exciting it is to live in God's presence. I remember the day, before I had even thought about the phrase "practice His presence," that this principle first be-came real to me. I was at a time-management seminar led by a woman who explained that she had gotten very little sleep the night before due to a sick child. I was about to feel sorry for her *(That poor woman only got a few hours sleep and has to get up and speak all day),* but that thought went no further. She continued: "But I don't mind. In fact, I count it a privilege to have the pleasure of rocking a child in the wee hours of the morning, holding him, singing to him, wrapped in the presence of the Lord." I scarcely remember anything else she said that day because God spoke so clearly to my heart through those few, simple words and her attitude. I thought about what my attitude might have been: *Can you believe it? That child threw up all night and insisted on me rocking him. I only got a few hours of sleep and look at all I've got to do today!* Instead, this gracious woman pointed out that our difficulties can in fact be blessings because God is present in them. Even in the simple and not especially "spiritual" act of rocking a child we can be in His presence!

The seed the woman planted that day is continuing to grow deep roots. I am learning to choose to remember God in the routine and mundane moments of my day. I am learning that the phrase "abide in Christ" is much more than Christianese, that it is relevant to me in the car pool line and in traffic as well as in church. Abiding in Christ is a lifestyle that grows out of my growth in Him and my realization of His great love for me. It is a way of life that can be chosen and practiced. It is a way of life that brings great joy.

I have so much to learn about this way of thinking and living. It sounds simple, but its impact on us can be profound, as the Ortlunds describe in their book. They talk about how the great love the Father has for us can draw us into a life lived in the love of the One who loves us completely. They also caution:

> Please hear us carefully! "Practicing God's presence," unless it flows out of the nourishing, deep-rooted truths of our Christian faith, becomes purely experiential, shallow, and eventually silly.
>
> What you believe about God—your theology—is what shapes and defines the real you. More than what how-to seminars teach you (although they can be helpful), how you behave in marriage, raise children, and generally function as a person *will flow out of your knowledge of God and your life with Him.*[5]

We behave how we behave because we believe how we believe. It is that knowledge of God and our life with Him that I want to turn to next—our life as part of the vine.

The Vine Life

I remember the first time Tim and I ever experimented with gardening. We lived in a suburban neighborhood with a postage-sized backyard, but we wanted to do our share of tilling the earth. The first garden was actually his; I just got to help. And I'm glad he gets the credit because, in spite of his efforts, about the only thing that little plot produced was okra trees. We didn't just grow your average suburban tomato. We grew giant foliage, elephant ear-sized plants peering over our fence. My friend Donna commented, "I've seen a lot of gardens, but I've never seen okra trees." It was rather fun, if not a little humiliating. We got exactly half a bowl of okra from those enormous plants—enough for everyone in the family to have three fried okras. But that garden bore more than those okra. You see, I learned much from that little plot. Things I'd read and heard about vine-life living took root in my heart more deeply as I watched actual vine life unfold before me.

As I watched that garden grow, so did my fondness for John 15, that "vine life" chapter which describes so plainly our relationship to Christ. Those familiar words came to life as I watched our garden. I saw why Christ referred to growing things to teach so many lessons. Jesus says, for instance, "I am the true vine, and My Father is the vinedresser" (John 15:1). As I looked at our okra trees and the other more normal vegetation, I thought of God as my Master Gardener—and kept reading. Jesus continues, "Every branch in Me that does not bear fruit, He takes away; and every branch that bears fruit, He prunes it, that it may bear more fruit" (verse 2). I looked at the pile of recently pruned foliage that had been keeping the plant from producing more okra. "Abide in Me, and I in you. As the branch cannot bear fruit of itself, unless it abides in the vine, so neither can you, unless you abide in Me," Jesus teaches in verse 4. I got up close and personal with the vines in our garden. The branches were not merely attached or temporarily connected to that vine—they were part of the vine; they were grafted to it. I began to wonder,

Am I merely attached or am I grafted to Him? Abiding began to take on new meaning for me.

My favorite part of that passage of Scripture—and the basis of this book—is verse 11 when Jesus says, "These things I have spoken to you, that My joy may be in you, and that your joy may be made full." That's the reason Christ tells us about the vine life. He wants us to have His joy, and He wants that joy to be full! We are to live the vine life abiding in Christ so that we can yield the fruit of His joy! He doesn't tell us to abide in Christ so that we will be good Christians. He doesn't tell us to be part of the vine, willing to be pruned and abiding in His love, just because He says so. He lovingly tells us the reason for His call to abide in Him ("these things I have spoken to you") because He desires that we have incredible joy, His joy ("that My joy may be in you"). He doesn't stop at telling us we can have His joy (what a gift in itself!), but He tells us we can have gobs of it ("that your joy may be made full").

Vine life is about abiding in God's love, keeping His commandments, allowing Him to prune us, and bearing fruit for the kingdom. Joy is some of that fruit. Living the vine life is the foundation for joy. So often I had read that section of Scripture and focused only on the abiding, pruning, and bearing fruit. It hadn't sunk in that the reason Jesus tells us about the vine life in the first place is so that we can live with His abundant joy within us. Lots of joy! A fullness of joy! Knowing His joy is important to Jesus, as you can see from John 15. Never doubt that He wants you to have His joy. Never side with the philosophers and nay-sayers who suggest that joyful living is selfish. Read Christ's words for yourself. He wants you to live a life of joy, and you can do that by abiding in Him!

> *It is impossible for us really to live in Jesus, as a branch in a vine, and not have His joy flowing into us.*
>
> ~Colleen Townsend Evans,
> *The Vine Life*

~⊱ 7 ⊰~

Three Powerful P's
Becoming Intimate with the Gift-Giver

T he most formidable task of relocating is not unpacking a household of belongings; it's reconnecting. After we moved back to this part of Texas, my family and I faced that task again. Although I'm no stranger to moving (I've moved 24 times since birth), putting down new roots and developing friendships still takes time.

One month after we moved here, Tim and I were in a hotel lobby and I noticed a group of women with cute name tags who looked like they were really enjoying themselves. "I'll bet they're a church group," I told Tim. "In fact, they look like a group I could fit in with." But I never found out who they were. Later, we joined a church in our area, and a year-and-a-half after that I made plans to go on their women's retreat. One woman said to me, "This year we're going to the country."

"Where have you usually met?" I asked.

"At a hotel," she replied.

"At the same time of year?" I asked.

She nodded.

"Which hotel?" I continued.

She told me and, amazingly, my new church friends were the

same joyful women I'd observed in that hotel lobby a year-and-a-half before.

By now, my roots are deeper. God has blessed me with friendships and the joy of a couple of kindred spirits. Moving from observation...to acquaintance...to friendship...to kindred spirit—these are heartwarming moves. When we leave the casual, superficial realms of a relationship and begin to enter into intimate soul territory, the bond takes on a new value, for these relationships are rare. It is sweet when an acquaintance becomes a friend and a friend becomes a kindred spirit. When someone we love becomes our soulmate rather than just the object of our love, we have a precious treasure indeed, for soul-territory is where we are touched at our deepest level—the fiber of our being. Likewise, when we leave behind a casual, superficial, "religious" relationship with God and enter into soul-territory, we become intimate with the Giver of joy.

In the last two chapters, we've looked at the importance of knowing God's thoughts, renewing our mind, seeing His perspective, and abiding in and yielding to Him. *The extent to which we can do these things is a significant indicator of the extent of the joy we will know, for at this soul-spot the truest, deepest, most pervasive joy occurs.* The only way to know such profound joy is to get to know God in a deep and intimate way. As I point to three powerful P's for becoming intimate with the Gift-Giver, let me encourage you to read with your heart. Although these activities are probably familiar to you, ask God to show you the unfamiliar in them—the place where you may perhaps move from the casual to the intimate, from the surface to the soul.

The three P's for becoming intimate with God are:

1. Poring over His Word
2. Praising Him
3. Praying to Him

Doing these three P's will enable us to abide more deeply in Him, enhance the ease and frequency with which we enter His presence, and increase our ability to think His thoughts. The time we spend with God in these ways does indeed bear the fruit of His joy in our lives.

1. *Poring Over God's Word*

If you want to hear from someone who truly loves God's Word, read Psalm 119. The longest chapter in the Bible, this acrostic psalm (the writer devotes eight lines to each letter of the Hebrew alphabet) praises the Scriptures; and all but four of its 176 verses mention the Word of God (law, testimonies, statutes, and so on). If we are to live a life of joy, we cannot neglect the Scripture. As we see in this psalm, God's Word not only brings us joy, but it is to *be* our joy. As the psalmist says, "I have inherited Thy testimonies forever, for they are the joy of my heart" (Psalm 119:111) and "I rejoice at Thy word" (verse 162).

Besides bringing joy, God's Word is able to convict, correct, confirm, and train in righteousness (2 Timothy 3:16). Through His Word, we come to know Him as well as His will for us (Psalm 40:8); the Creator of the universe reveals Himself to us through His Word. If we don't read it, we can't really know Him. If we read it a little, we will only know Him a little. If we want to renew our minds—if we want to change our perspective, our thinking, and our attitude—we must learn to think God's thoughts and apply them to our lives. The only way to do that is to read in His Word what His thoughts are, meditate on them, and let His Spirit make them a part of us. As Bible commentator Henry H. Halley says,

> We read the Bible frequently and regularly, so that God's thoughts may be frequently and regularly in our minds; that His thoughts may become our thoughts; that our ideas may become conformed to God's ideas. To run God's thoughts through our mind often will make our mind grow like God's mind; and as our mind grows like God's mind, our whole life will be transformed into His image. It is one of the very best spiritual helps we can have.[1]

And that help is available to each one of us.

Our fountain of joy, the foundation of an abundant life, a handbook for living, our refreshment when we need to be revived, the hope of victory over sin, a source of wisdom, an avenue of fellowship with Christ, nourishment for our spirit—the

Bible is all this and more. So why is it that, all too often, we let this food get a little dusty until it is no longer appetizing? We know we should be reading His Word, but we don't. Or we don't read it consistently. We just nibble here and there, never fully tasting its flavor or truly getting nourished as He intends. This is probably one of the biggest guilt trips that we Christians take: "I know I should, but I'm not reading the Bible regularly. When will I ever get consistent?"

How do we stir our heart to hunger for God's Word? By feeding it! You know how it works in your physical body. You develop an appetite by exercising and eating regularly. Exercise strengthens our muscles (if we don't use a muscle it can atrophy) and makes us hungry. Eating fills us for a time, but then we get hungry again. In fact, we train our body to want food when we feed it regularly. I know because I've frequently been a breakfast skipper. I could go until early afternoon without eating when I was busy because my body was used to going that long without food. But when I began to eat breakfast regularly, I began to get hungry in the morning. I was amazed when, after a short time of making myself eat in the morning, I began to wake up hungry (a new experience for me). Just as we can train our bodies to be hungry, we can also turn off that hunger. As odd as it sounds, if we fast, we begin to lose our hunger pangs after an initial time of hunger.

And so it is in our spiritual body. When we regularly feed it the nourishing food of God's Word and exercise our spiritual muscles, we train our spiritual body to want more food. We develop in our spirit a craving for God's Word, and we learn to depend on it for sustenance. The opposite is true as well. We can lose our hunger for God's Word. If we fast too long—if we don't

If God's Word in your life is limited to a weekly 30-minute sermon, you won't have joy in the Christian life.

~Dave Anderson,
Pastor,
Faith Community Church,
The Woodlands, TX

open up that cover and spend time with the Lord—we won't feel hunger for that time with Him.

But regular nibbling doesn't make a dry meal a banquet, and maybe you're not finding Scripture a feast right now. That was the case for my friend Martha. She called me one day and began to tell me how she had little joy in her life. She said, "Don't try to tell me to just read my Bible. I do that almost every day and I still don't have joy. It's just so...dry." Being too busy to consistently read God's Word makes for spiritual dryness. We can't strengthen our spiritual bodies or develop a hunger for God's Word with a hit-and-miss approach of just a few minutes a day. Reading with no purpose further contributes to the feeling that this holy food has lost its flavor. Nibbling here and there without any direction in our reading deadens our taste buds for this spiritual nourishment.

For real spiritual growth to occur and our hunger for the Scriptures to be stoked, we must read consistently and with a plan. Any plan will do. Choose whatever suits you. Many Bible scholars recommend reading the Bible through in a year, and many churches and devotionals have suggestions for a reading schedule to accomplish this. Others suggest reading a book at a time or reading chronologically. It doesn't matter what your plan is—just have one! And trust the Holy Spirit to be your teacher, for "His anointing teaches you about all things" (1 John 2:27).

Also, try reading with a pen and notebook in hand to record your thoughts, insights, and questions for God, as well as your impressions of what He is saying to you. Add study materials (a concordance, Bible dictionary, or commentary) to this time of reading, take notes on what you read, and the material begins to become yours. It doesn't go just into your head; it has a chance to stay in your heart. When you go a step further and keep your notebooks or—for you more organized women—file your notes by Bible book or subject, you can go back and review what you learn. You can see where you were spiritually at a given time, and you may even be ready to teach others what God has taught you. In fact, when we study anything under the premise that we are sometime going to teach it (whether to a Sunday school class or our own kids), we retain much more. So try that approach in your study.

"Wait just a minute! How do you possibly expect me to do that?" some of you may be asking. "I have a young family, and

I scarcely find the time to get dressed every day!" Keep in mind that there are seasons of our lives. If you are in a "baby season," you may not be able to sit down every day for in-depth study. But even in the read-whenever-you-can times we can still read with a purpose. Try grabbing a few verses while you dry your hair (as a friend of mine did when her children were young), catch a few more verses during nap time, listen to Bible tapes in the car, or carry a pocket Bible in your purse for unexpected quiet moments. You and I can make time for what is important to us. Reading God's Word as purposefully and as regularly as possible—and applying what you find there—can change your life.

Yet there are times when Bible study feels more like just another "should" on the to-do list. Sometimes, and for some people (maybe you right now), reading God's Word is done merely out of a sense of duty, a sense of discipline rather than desire. If that's where you are right now, that's okay. At least start there. But if you find you don't move beyond duty to desire—to the point where you want to read God's Word—perhaps you're just reading it instead of studying it. The deeper you dig into the Word, the deeper you find yourself in soul-territory and the more compelled you are to return there. So, again, begin with prayer every time you read the Bible; ask the Holy Spirit to teach you as you try to get beyond the surface to the substance. If the desire is still lacking, you need to take this matter to the Lord in prayer and, perhaps, repentance. Sometimes we need to say, "Lord, my heart's not in it. Forgive me—and please develop in me a heart that hungers for You and Your Word." God wants our devotion, not just our discipline; He wants a heart that hungers for Him. Spending time in God's Word—starting, perhaps, as a mere discipline and moving to times of deep study—and going before Him with an open heart will help develop within you that hunger and devotion.

Consider the devotion of George Muller, the man of faith who founded many orphanages in England: "I believe that the one chief reason that I have been kept in happy useful service is that I have been a lover of Holy Scripture. It has been my habit to read the Bible through four times a year; in a prayerful spirit, to apply it to my heart, and practice what I find there. I have been for sixty-nine years a happy man."[2] Whether you read through the Bible four times a year (!), once a year, or once every

20 years, just read it! God's Word—read and obeyed—is the fountain of joy and the path to knowing Him.

2. *Praising God*

When we study God's Word and begin to get a glimpse of who He is and what He has done for us, we cannot help but praise Him. He has given us the ability to praise, and His Word is full of commands to do just that. (The call to praise God appears more than any other command in the Old Testament.) The more we know God, the more we will want to praise Him—and I'm not talking praise in a "religious" way, that semiautomatic, robotic uttering of "Praise the Lord" in response to a sermon or testimony. Praise is not something we do just in church when we are feeling particularly spiritual. We need not be able to play an instrument, have a great voice, or be a spiritual giant. We can praise God whoever and wherever we are simply because of who God is and His great love for us.

Furthermore, praise is one thing we can do that will shift our focus from ourselves and our problems to God. Have you ever been in a situation that is overwhelming? The daily grind, the busy but barren, the painful, or the disappointing days have you focused on your problems. You try to focus on the Lord, but your attitude and perspective don't change. Scripture gives us an antidote. It's praise. When we praise God, we turn our focus to who He is and what He has done for us ("He is your praise and He is your God, who has done these great and awesome things for you which your eyes have seen" [Deuteronomy 10:21]). The psalmist models when we are to praise God: "I will bless the LORD at all times; His praise shall continually be in my mouth. My soul shall make its boast in the LORD" (Psalm 34:1,2). When we look to God like this, our attitude can't help but improve. As Myrna Alexander says in *Behold Your God,*

> Praise keeps the character of God before our minds. The practice of praise forces us to relate God's character to the issues of life. The effect of praising God on our mental attitude is liberating, for praise focuses our attention on the person and work of God....Praise leads you to behold your God![3]

So what does praising God look like?

Myrna Alexander says we can praise God by describing His character and attributes and by declaring what He has done for us or in a particular situation. We can tell Him or others how awesome we think He is because of His many attributes (descriptive praise), and we can tell Him or others how blessed we are because of something He has done (declarative praise).[4] We can also praise God descriptively and declaratively with our songs. Singing alone for His ears (and our edification), we can praise Him for His character and His deeds, or we can bless others with our praise in song. (In my case, that wouldn't be much of a blessing so be glad I'm writing this and not trying to express myself on a CD!) Whether your praise is descriptive or declarative, to God alone or to others, follow the example of the psalmist who wrote, "I will give thanks to the LORD with all my heart; I will tell of all Thy wonders. I will be glad and exult in Thee; I will sing praise to Thy name, O Most High" (Psalm 9:1,2).

The psalms are an excellent place to go to learn how to praise God. Called in Hebrew the "Book of Praise," Psalms is filled with expressions of praise and commands to praise. Intended to be set to music and sung in worship, these poems were written as songs of devotion and trust in God. We see in some psalms that David could not be stopped from praising God whether his circumstances were causing him joy or anguish. One commentary describes David's attitude:

> David literally LIVED IN GOD. "Praise" was always on his lips. David was always asking God for something, and always thanking Him with his whole soul for the answers to his prayers.
>
> "Rejoice" is another favorite word. David's unceasing troubles could never dim his joy in God. Over and over he cried, "Sing," "Shout for Joy."[5]

The ultimate psalm of praise is the last one, Psalm 150. Here we are called to praise God for "His mighty deeds" (what He's done for us) and "excellent greatness" (His character). We can praise with trumpet, harp, lyre, tambourine, dancing, stringed instruments, pipe, and loud, resounding cymbals. In case that list leaves anyone out, the psalmist adds, "Let everything that has breath praise the LORD. Praise the LORD!" (verse 6). That pretty much covers it!

David knew the importance of music in praising God. He wrote, "Stringed instruments have made Thee glad" (Psalm 45:8) and, my favorite, "Sing for joy in the LORD, O you righteous ones; praise is becoming to the upright" (Psalm 33:1). If your joy is waning, take the advice of David and follow the many admonitions in Scripture and sing! Praise and singing lead to joy—even when we don't feel at all joyful. I know from experience.

When I was in college, I worked with a campus ministry in Hawaii for a summer. Friends and family had fun giving me grief about suffering for Jesus in that land of sunshine, beaches, and pineapples. To some, my assignment looked like Utopia, but in many ways it was a very difficult summer. To earn my keep, I opened oysters for tourists looking for pearls and cleaned houses before landing an office job as a receptionist. My employers were seldom there, so I was alone much of the time in that cold, dark, windowless office. (There's that "cave" scenario again. I think God's been trying to teach me something about my source of light for a long time!) I hated what I was doing as well as my work-week environment, so I had to seek my joy totally in the Lord. I always went to work early and sat in an outer office that had a wall of windows facing a beautiful mountain. There I would have my quiet time with God.

One morning the sunrise was particularly spectacular, and I began to sing, "[Lord,] in the morning will I direct my prayer unto thee, and will look up" (Psalm 5:3 KJV). Do you know what that did for me? Suddenly I was filled with joy! Indescribable joy! Tears came to my eyes as I watched the beauty God unfolded before me that morning and felt His joy descend on me as a gift. I sang my psalm of thanksgiving (as Psalms 81 and 95 describe) and became, just as His word promises, joyous! That time of praising God carried me through the long, lonely workday. Throughout the day, I hummed just a bit of that song in my mind, and the Lord comforted me with the remembrance of that special time with Him. Even now, the memory of that morning and the words of that song bring me great joy. When we praise God, we are transported from our circumstances, from our thought life with its limitations and burdens, to the very presence of God. Our focus shifts to His greatness. The praise corrects our perspective and the singing bypasses our minds, cutting straight to our heart and producing wonderful joy! Praise truly is a gift from the Father!

God knew, however, that mountaintop experiences like that would not be the norm for us. We are told to praise Him continually, but sometimes our spirits will not soar. We may try our best to get above our circumstances, but all we can think about is our problems. We don't feel like praising the Lord, let alone singing to Him. It is for moments like those that God gives us this instruction: "Through Him then, let us continually offer up a sacrifice of praise to God, that is, the fruit of lips that give thanks to His name" (Hebrews 13:15). When we don't feel like praising God, we are to offer it up anyway, in spite of our feelings, as our sacrifice of praise to Him.

A few years ago I was doing dishes and, for no particular reason, I was feeling down. My heart was heavy, and I didn't feel joy. I knew in my head that I should probably praise God, but I didn't feel like doing it. I wiped the bubbles off my hands and turned on a tape of praise music. *There. Praise.* But I immediately knew in my heart that the sounds filling my kitchen were someone else's expression of praise. It wasn't my own. I knew *I* had to praise. *But, Lord, I don't feel like it.* The sense I should be praising Him wouldn't go away. *Okay, Lord, but it's certainly going to fall into the "sacrifice" category.* Softly and without feeling, I began to sing with the tape. Then, still singing, I got involved with my dishes and by the time I had finished the last dirty plate, my sacrifice of praise had yielded the fruit of joy! *What a great trick I just played on my emotions. God's Word is so true!* And I went to my Bible and turned to this passage:

> O come, let us sing for joy to the LORD;
> Let us shout joyfully to the rock of our salvation.
> Let us come before His presence with thanksgiving;
> Let us shout joyfully to Him with psalms
>
> — (Psalm 95:1,2).

I highlighted these words in pink and circled the one *joy* and two *joyfully's*. What a simple act my praise had been! My singing was just an everyday occurrence in my kitchen, but our faithful God is always so sweet to meet us right where we are. He met me with my hands in dishwater and my spirits in the dumps, and He showed me that He is pleased even when praise is a sacrifice.

You and I can praise God anytime, anywhere, and in many ways. Our praise can come in a quiet moment of intimate adoration, a silent offering to God in church. It can be in a fun song with our children as we dance around the living room. We can praise God as we sing in the shower or with a tape in the car. We can occasionally even cut loose as David did (2 Samuel 6)! (Just watch out for your Michal, the person who—like David's wife—might be embarrassed by demonstrative expressions of praise!) You and I can cut loose to yell, cheer, scream, and express our enthusiasm at sporting events, parades, concerts, and the like, so why don't we do so in our personal praise to God?

My favorite time to cut loose is in the morning. Sometimes, before anyone's up, I put on my headphones and a praise tape while I exercise. For me, that's a wonderful way to praise the Lord with all my heart and all my body! I remember the first time I really "got into it" as I exercised. Before I knew it, my exercise was simply an expression of my praise for God as I abandoned my self-consciousness. (No one was even looking!) If we can go to jazzercise, why don't we dance before the Lord, as Scripture says, in our private moments? God's Word also tells us to "clap your hands, all peoples; shout to God with the voice of joy!" (Psalm 47:1). We are to "sing for joy" and "shout joyfully to the God of Jacob" (Psalm 81:1). Like the children's song goes, "If you want joy you must sing for it...clap for it..." Even the most timid Christian can find a way to privately sing, shout, or even dance(!) before the Lord in praise. Whether you praise with hair-flying, limb-moving exuberance or with a soft stanza of "This Is the Day That the Lord Hath Made," just do it! Praise God in the privacy of your home, car, shower, or wherever—and, oh yes, you and I are also to lift our voices in praise at church. Wherever you praise God and whether you do so with gusto or quietly, praise Him with all your heart! After all, when we know God, we can't help but praise Him. And since the Lord inhabits the praises of His people, we can enter His presence when we praise Him and find there "fullness of joy" (Psalm 16:11)!

3. *Praying to God*

If we want to get to know people, not only do we spend time in their presence, but we talk with and listen to them. And that is exactly what prayer is: two-way conversation with God. Prayer is the opportunity to approach God directly. The God who created the universe and us loves us enough to allow direct communication and, even more amazing, He deeply desires it. When we find ourselves feeling cavalier about prayer (and that's sometimes easy to do), we should remember that it is indeed a privilege. Do you exercise that privilege as often as the Father desires you to?

The ability to have direct access to God by simply lifting our voice or heart to Him in prayer is a gift, and it is one we can approach with childlike faith. When I was eight years old, I had plenty of that kind of faith. At Easter, which fell in April that year, I visited my grandparents in Oklahoma. Since they were already enjoying nice spring weather, Grandma took me downtown to buy me a new short-sleeved Easter dress. One night Grandma came to tuck me in and say my prayers with me.

"Grandma," I said, "I want to ask God for snow." I lived in a warm climate, but I knew that Grandma and Grandpa got snow in the winter.

"This year?" she asked.

"Yes. I want it to snow so I'm going to ask God. It never snows where we live."

"Well, honey, you can if you want to, but it's just the wrong time of year for that now. I don't want you to be disappointed."

Grandma said I could pray that prayer, and that was all I heard. She probably said a few more things about the impossibility of

> *My* own plan (for praying), when hard pressed, is to seize any time, and place, however unsuitable, in preference to the last waking moment.
>
> ~C.S. Lewis,
> *Letters to Malcolm: Chiefly on Prayer*

snow in April at her house, but all I remember is the asking—and, of course, the answer. The next morning Grandma came rushing into my room and very excitedly said, "Honey, have you looked outside yet?" Immediately remembering my prayer, I threw open the curtains to a very cold window and a white winter wonderland beyond—in April! I'll never forget the smile on Grandma's face and the excitement in her voice when she said, "From now on, when I need serious praying done I know who to call! God sure did answer your prayer!"

The physical reality of snow then and there, with or without my prayer, is not the issue. Would it have snowed even if I hadn't prayed? I don't care. I was eight years old and all I knew was that it was warm when I went to bed and there was snow when I awoke because I had prayed. At least that is what God allowed me to see. At that tender age, I experienced a God who was very real, a God who heard and answered my prayer, and that moment greatly influenced my faith.

But even when we experience God's dramatic intervention in our life, our prayers can still grow stale and seem quite ineffective. At those times, we can put off praying for a variety of reasons. Years ago when I was having one of those times, I thought a personal Bible study on prayer might help. The accompanying workbook was filled with wonderful information, but the study didn't really do much to change my prayer life—at first. I kept looking forward to being finished with the book. I wanted to get it all down so I could really get into prayer. Then it hit me. *How ridiculous! No wonder praying has become a burden. I'm spending more time learning about prayer than doing it!* I stopped focusing on the study and my approach to prayer and, instead, began to focus on the One to whom I was praying. I was soon filled with the desire to pray. My morning times of talking with God became much more important than my first cup of coffee. Those mornings became sweet moments of building a relationship with my Savior and Lord.

One frustration still remained, however. I wanted huge chunks of time when I could get out my prayer notecards and notebook and enter my prayer closet for some serious communication—no small feat for a busy mother of little ones. I eventually realized that my abiding in the Lord was going to be different during this season of my life. Oh, I still scheduled a morning appointment time with God, but when sleepless nights with babies prevented me from being there, I learned to have an attitude of prayer even though my body was in motion; I learned to fit in talk time with my Father wherever I could instead of berating myself for missing it. I found great delight in doing so, and this lifestyle approach to prayer became a real pleasure and a real necessity instead of another "ought to" in my life. I invite you to make that discovery, too.

I also invite you to heed the command we find in 1 Thessalonians:

> Rejoice always; pray without ceasing; in everything give thanks; for this is God's will for you in Christ Jesus (5:16-18).

Paul's simple language indicates a direct connection between the three commands God gives here: The reason we can rejoice always is because we are praying without ceasing and giving thanks in everything (*in* everything, not *for* everything). There was a time when that thought just overwhelmed me. *Yeah, right. I'm learning a lot about prayer, but "pray without ceasing"? Easy for Paul to say! He was in full-time ministry. How can I do that with all of my work and daily duties?* Then I learned the secret.

God isn't calling us to be on our knees in prayer all the day long. We couldn't do that even if He were, but we can learn to live in an attitude of prayer as we go about our daily activities. We can have an attitude of prayer as we work and play, drive and rest. We can have an ongoing dialogue with the Lord in our hearts while we attend to our business. "OK, kids! Get in the car and put on your seatbelts." *Lord, thank You that we've never had to test those.* "Does everyone have their homework? Love you, guys! Bye!" *Father, please bless their day and help Jacquelyn on her test.* "Oh, it's a gorgeous day." *Thank You, Lord, for Your handiwork.* You see how it works. This kind of praying (while it may look a little silly in print) is abiding in God; it's being connected with the heavenly Father in the dailyness of life. In addition to our "appointments" to pray, we can integrate prayer into our daily life with an ongoing heart-cry to God.

A Life-Changing Source of Joy

When we discover the power of prayer and see it bear fruit in our life, we can't help but be changed. Recognizing answers to our prayers can give us the assurance that God is holding everything together and remind us that we have access to a very powerful Source of help. Seeing God's power made manifest in answered prayer is exciting, faith building, and even life-changing. Seeing God answer prayer also brings great joy—even if His answers don't come in the timeframe we request—as my Aunt Glenna learned.

Glenna married a former Navy man who was tough both inside and out. She prayed that God would make her husband's heart soft toward Him and toward their marriage, but God didn't answer her prayers in her timing. "God has shown me His love, care, and direction so many times," Glenna now says. "Especially at a time when my marriage was very unstable, He showed me that He was all I needed. Not only did my communication with God see me through lonely days, but God honored my faithfulness, and I am so thankful."

Glenna prayed for her husband for 20 years, and in 1987 he committed his life to Christ. "God has given me the godly husband I always desired and healed my marriage," she says. "To see Him work through Duwayne has made all my heartaches and frustrations worthwhile." Today Duwayne is active in a prison ministry. God answered the persistent prayers of a faithful wife in His time and for His glory. And such answered prayer brings great joy, no matter what the timing.

Intercession—praying for other people—is another source of joy and another opportunity to see power and fruit. The apostle Paul knew that joy and wrote of it in Philippians: "I thank my God in all my remembrance of you, always offering prayer with joy in my every prayer for you all" (1:3,4). When we get outside of ourselves and beyond our own needs and lay other people's needs before God, we can experience great joy. It really is wonderful to be part of the miracle of answered prayer in another person's life—no matter how large or small the concern.

One day while working on this book, I called my editor. As a mom who works at home, she was having an unusually difficult day. Her seven-month-old baby wasn't feeling well and hadn't nursed in 24 hours. Those of you who have nursed a child know that's far too long a hunger strike for both baby and mother! I hung up and immediately prayed for them. Now there are times when you know in your spirit that God has heard your prayers, and this was one of those precious times. I decided to call her back in an hour to see if little Sarah had eaten. Thirty minutes later, Lisa called me. "Guess what?" she said. "Sarah nursed and is now fast asleep." Lisa and I both built a touchstone for our faith that day as we saw God immediately answer our prayer.

One of the most life-changing things about prayer—whether the answer is long-awaited or immediate—is the growth in our relationship with God that accompanies an active prayer life. And that greater degree of intimacy is a fundamental source of joy. I can share "grown-up" examples of incredible answered prayer (answers far more wonderful than the snow that April morning), and I can also tell you of desperate prayers that God did not answer according to my requests. Although God has the power and ability to answer any request we bring before Him, His answer is not the most important thing. The action of praying and the relationship that results from doing so is. As Oswald Chambers says, "Whenever the insistence is on the point that God answers prayer, we are off the track. The meaning of prayer is that we get hold of God, not of the answer."[6] We "get hold of God" when we spend time talking to Him. Our relationship with Him grows when we want to commune with Him, not just receive the object of our requests. If we only want our answer, we'll find it difficult to know God and His joy. But when we are able to accept His "yes," His "wait," and even His "no" and continue in our dialogue with Him, we can find great joy.

We can learn much about prayer, and the joy which results from prayer, in Scripture. God's Word teaches what to pray for, how to pray, when to pray, and it offers us models—great men and women of prayer—and stories of the results of their prayers (like Hannah who diligently prayed for a child and was so blessed [1 Samuel 1]). When we pray through ACTS (prayers of **A**doration, **C**onfession, **T**hanksgiving, **S**upplication, and then add intercession)—and when we do so with a pure heart (Psalm 66:18,19), in faith (Matthew 17:20), and in Christ's name (John 14:13), praying according to God's will, not our own (1 John

5:14)—we are approaching God as Scripture teaches. So learn what Scripture and study tools teach about prayer; let the Holy Spirit teach you, too.

Learn, too, from the methods which have helped other believers be more faithful in prayer. Some people, for instance, find it helpful to write out their prayers. When author Becky Tirabassi first committed to pray for one hour every day, she discovered that writing down her prayers helped her stay focused. She organized a notebook into different sections for different parts of her prayers (Praise, Admit [confess], Request, and Thanks) as well as a section for what God says to her in Scripture and sermons. She said, "After 12 years and more than 4,000 one-hour appointments with God, I understand firsthand that sometimes God says yes and sometimes He says no, but no matter the outcome, He still loves me."[7]

Some people's prayer notebooks serve as a pictorial reminder about what to pray for. They use pictures (and words) to remind them of specific prayer requests to pray for on specific days. Other people like to record their prayers and God's answers in a daily journal. When I began to do that—a simple act requiring only the purchase of a spiral notebook to get me going—my prayer time and spiritual life became much richer. I am now able to keep track of what I am praying for, and my record of God's answers are a written reminder of His work in my life. Also, remember that prayer and God's Word are virtually inseparable. As Andrew Murray said, "Power in the use of either depends on the presence of the other!"[8] So I write down all that's on my heart and then record what He seems to be saying to me through His Word and the impressions He lays on my heart during those silent moments I spend with Him. Prayer *and* Bible study make for a meaningful dialogue with the Lord.

Whatever approach to prayer you take, remember that the most important thing is this: Just do it! Don't wait to ascend to your ivory tower and don robes of righteousness to begin praying. Pray today, wherever you are, in whatever condition you find yourself. If you are hurting, tell God. If your life is full of pain, pour it out in words to God. If you are mad at God for something, tell Him. It's OK! Psalm 55:17 tells us, "Evening and morning and at noon, I will complain and murmur, and He will hear my voice." So open up the lines of communication. We get to know God better when we talk with Him often, and talking with Him often—walking through each day with Him—is one way of abiding in Him. Jesus Himself said, "If you abide in Me, and My words abide in you, ask whatever you wish, and it shall be done for you" (John 15:7). Abiding and prayer are closely related: Prayer is both a result of and a way to abide in our Lord and Savior.

Joy in Worship

One cannot talk about poring over God's Word, praising Him, and praying without mentioning worship. Whenever and wherever we read the Bible, praise God, and pray with (as Webster puts it) "an extravagant respect, honor, or devotion," we are indeed worshiping. We can read the Bible...and find it flat. We can praise...with lip service only. We can pray...like a robot. But when we add that "extravagant respect, honor, and devotion" of our heart and do these things as an expression of our love for God, we turn our "three P's" into acts of worship!

Each one of us was created to worship God, something my friend Kellie understands well. As our women's ministry worship leader, she is passionate about worshiping God. For her, worship is more than a religious activity or occasional experience; worship is the God-given purpose of her life on this earth. She first began to understand that one day while she was mopping the floor and listening to a man on the radio describe how God showed him that he was to be a preacher. Kellie leaned on her mop and said out loud, "Lord, what am I about? Who am I for You?" It was as if lightning pierced her heart. She knew instantly that God was speaking to her. She recalls:

> He said to me, "You're a worshiper!" I grabbed that mop, stood up straight, and said, "Yes, Lord! I am! That's it!" As I was mopping that floor, the Lord revealed my identity as a worshiper and a worship leader in spite of my inadequacies. That moment has impacted my life daily since then. I worship the Father every day. It's my passion and bliss! It's who I am!

Kellie likes to worship with her family, in the car, and when she runs in the morning, but her favorite way is in her clothes closet:

> Without any music and where no one can hear, I worship God alone. His Spirit touches my spirit and His presence comes down and envelops me. It changes me, renews my mind, and adjusts my focus back to Him and who He is. Worship fills my soul with such joy!

And that joy Kellie refers to is the joy of the Lord—a joy far deeper than external joys the world offers.

The joy of the Lord is joy straight from the Source, poured out on those who bother to sit at His feet and enter His presence. In the Bible, Jesus' friend Mary knew how to do just that, but her sister Martha was busy "doing" for Jesus. Do you remember which action He valued? "Martha, Martha, you are worried and bothered about so many things; but only a few things are necessary, really only one, for Mary has chosen the good part, which shall not be taken away from her" (Luke 10:41,42). Jesus wants us to be with Him, not just "do" for Him. When we make worship the top priority that God desires it to be, we take part in an activity that "shall not be taken away." The worship of God has eternal value.

So be careful not to relegate worship to only a Sunday church service. Instead, learn to experience His presence in times of Bible study, praise, prayer, giving, and daily living. That is what worship really is. When we do even the little things in our life out of our love for God, then all of our life becomes worship of Him. In fact, some of our most powerful

*W*e must take time to get to know Him in the quiet times of our life to be able to trust Him in the crisis.

~Lucy Mabery

times of worship can be when we do those "hidden things" for God, when we do what He has called us to do. With the right heart—with a heart tuned to God—we can be worshiping God whether we're leading a Bible study at church or sweeping the floor at home.

And that perspective on what we do—that attempt to make all that we do worship—is key to knowing joy day to day. Instead of knowing that joy right now, are you worried and bothered about many things? Perhaps you're feeling like Martha was because you're not sitting at Jesus' feet, in His presence, as Mary did. If your worship is weak, Bible reading boring, praise scant, or prayers lifeless, you are missing out on the rich, full, joy that is found by being in the presence of the Lord. Begin to discover—or rediscover—that joy by being honest with God. Acknowledge that you are feeling empty and admit that you haven't spent the time with Him that you and He both want. You may need to say, "Lord, I am so dry, but I don't know how to worship You with my whole heart. Please come and fill me up and teach me through Your Holy Spirit." Having named Jesus our Savior and Lord, we have received "the Spirit who is from God, that we might know the things freely given to us by God" (1 Corinthians 2:12). The Spirit will teach us to worship when we ask Him to. He will meet us where we are!

Poring over His word, praising Him, and praying to Him can be lackluster duties, but done with a spirit of worship, they become sparkles in the rocks of life. Has God touched your heart with a desire to know soul intimacy with Him? It is there we are able to taste the joy of the Lord. I encourage you to step up to the table today. Become intimate with the Gift-Giver, the One who gives joy.

∽≈ 8 ≈∽

Joy in the Dark
And Other Tales of Hope

Were you ever afraid of the dark? Perhaps you re-member what it felt like to be about six years old, lying in your bed at night, surrounded by darkness. The room was pitch black, and that blackness seemed to creep up on you, ready to deliver danger at any minute. You couldn't get up and run to the light for safety. Doing so would have put your ankles perilously close to whatever was under your bed. You clutched your teddy bear and tried to be calm as you strained your eyes in the inky darkness, but still your heart beat faster and faster. Suddenly fear overtook you, and you dove under the covers, leaving no part of you exposed to the monsters. Then, finally, you gathered the courage to peer out from beneath the blanket. You weren't sure about anything in that room because it was so hard to see, but gradually the total blackness gave way to shadows. Then you saw that the imminent danger was nothing more than a few scattered toys on the floor. Things that in the light are familiar and comforting become unrecognizable and frightening in the dark.

But do you know how dark, dark can be? You do if you've ever visited a cave and had the tour guide turn out the lights. When you put your hand in front of your face and move your

151

fingers, you see only blackness. To literally not be able to see your hand in front of your face—that is *really* dark. The cold, damp air of the cave and that utter blackness make the dark almost tangible.

When circumstances begin to chill the air and dim the light, the darkness of life can also be almost tangible. And all we need to do to get a glimpse of this darkness is turn on the radio or television news or pick up the newspaper. A man takes the stand in a spouse abuse trial, a 15-year-old commits suicide, cancer takes a young husband and father of three, a heart attack claims another life, a sexual abuse case rocks a small town, and a couple files for bankruptcy. That's just a sampling of the darkness from this morning's paper. There's no mistaking that we live in a fallen world; we see the evidence all around us.

Have you ever known a more personal darkness? A time when difficult circumstances surrounded you, threatening danger and causing you to strain to see things clearly? Things that in bright circumstances are familiar and comfortable can become strange and even frightening in such dark times. Sometimes monstrous circumstances make you want to dive under the covers rather than face a darkness you can almost feel. Your darkness may be so black that you can't see your hand in front of your face, or your darkness may be more shadowy, making familiar things unrecognizable. Or perhaps your days have been pretty sunny, but you know that sometime you may be called on to face the darkness. Wherever you are today, know that sparkles of joy shine in even the blackest darkness.

God Is Sovereign; God Is Good

Whether we drown in the darkness or are able to see a glimmer of joy often depends on the condition of our head and our heart *before* the light fades. Our ability to find joy depends on whether we have settled several issues before the tough times come. Have we mastered those three actions which are key to developing a great attitude and practicing contentment? Specifically, do we know how to renew our thought life? Are we remembering the Source of our strength? And are we resting in that Source's sovereignty? If we are to know joy in our dark days, we must focus especially on God's sovereignty. Knowing that God is in control and that He is good, we will be able to withstand the dark when it comes. As discussued earlier, if God is sovereign (in control of everything, capable of anything, and knowledgeable of all things) and good (in character and in His plans for us), then we can rest assured that His sovereignty and goodness will sustain us and that His intentions for us are not just for our good, but for our best even when that possibility is inconceivable.

When the darkness overtakes us, we have to believe that God in His goodness will redeem the events of our lives. In Romans 8:28, the apostle Paul tells us so: "We know that God causes all things to work together for good to those who love God, to those who are called according to His purpose." When Christians go through difficult times, this is one of the most quoted (and perhaps most misunderstood) Scriptures passed along by well-meaning family, friends, and clergy. The promise rings hollow when the fires rage, when all we see around us is evidence of pain. We want to yell, "Don't tell me that when I'm hurting ! How can any good come from this?" That's when we must read the next verse—and choose to believe it. Verse 29 explains God's "purpose" for us is that we "become conformed to the image of His Son." Sometimes we're allowed to see and understand how God brings this ultimate good out of evil, but at other times, when life seems unfair and suffering unjust, we must believe by faith that "all things" are working together to make us more like Christ. Deciding that this truth applies to our life *before* the crisis hits makes believing it *in* the crisis easier.

Crisis of Faith

When we struggle with circumstances that don't make sense and when we can see no

*&N*ever let anything so fill you with pain or sorrow, so as to make you forget the joy of Christ risen.

~Mother Teresa,
Suffering into Joy

point in the pain, we are in dangerous waters. Unwanted divorce, sudden illness, early death, and countless other tragedies in the lives of people who have loved God and served Him bring many of us to a crisis point in our faith. We become frustrated or even angry with God, and we question the very foundation of our beliefs. In *When God Doesn't Make Sense*, Dr. James Dobson writes:

> This [progression from frustration to questioning our faith] is particularly true when things happen that seem illogical and inconsistent with what had been taught or understood. Then if the Lord does not rescue [them] from the circumstances in which they are embroiled, their frustration quickly deteriorates into anger and a sense of abandonment. Finally, disillusionment sets in and the spirit begins to wither.[1]

But the spirit does not have to wither!

When we settle the faith issues of God's sovereignty and goodness before the storms hit and get to know Him deeply, we can avoid a crisis of faith when circumstances don't make sense and aren't fair. We can survive the adversity and even find joy in the dark. Scripture shows us that even when we are shaken we can make the choice to rejoice if foundational truths about God have been firmly established in our heart and mind. Hear what David says in this psalm:

> I have set the Lord continually before me;
> Because He is at my right hand, I will not be shaken.
> *Therefore my heart is glad, and my glory rejoices;*
> My flesh also will dwell securely
>
> (Psalm 16:8,9, emphasis added).

Suffering and pain bring no joy in themselves, and this passage is not saying we should be glad and rejoice in painful times simply because it is the proper thing to do as a Christian. That very presumption causes many Christians to reach the crisis point. They can't reconcile what they actually feel about their circumstances with how they think they should feel because they are serving Christ. This verse suggests—and it's true—that we can rejoice even when we are in trouble. That gladness of heart and rejoicing can come because we know that the Lord is "continually before me" and "is at my right hand." The psalmist knew that, even when his flesh was threatened, God was able, God was before him, and God was beside him. We can know that same truth today.

Nineteenth-century writer Hannah Whitall Smith knew that truth. She says this: "Better and sweeter than health, or friends, or money, or fame, or ease, or prosperity, is the adorable will of our God. It gilds the darkest hours with a divine halo, and sheds brightest sunshine on the gloomiest paths."[2] When we know that the will of God is for our good, when we rest in that fact when life doesn't make sense, then even darkness can have some sparkle to it. We must, however, choose to trust in His goodness and sovereignty—no matter what comes our way. After all, God's goodness is better than health, friends, money, fame, or prosperity—some of the many things we pray for. In His sovereignty He makes that goodness happen.

Fruit in Due Season

And that goodness will come in His perfect time or, to use the image of Psalm 1, "in its season." Psalm 1:3 says that the person who delights and meditates on God's Word "will be like a tree firmly planted by streams of water, which yields its fruit in its season." Every fruit has its season. If the season isn't right, the fruit doesn't come forth. As a fruit of the Spirit, joy will be yielded when the season is right. And, as surprising as it may be, I have found three seasons which are right for harvesting joy when dark days descend; I have found joy sprinkled through the dark, revealed after the dark, and even in the dark.

Joy Sprinkled Through the Darkness

Is your life full of rocks rather than manicured grass and beautiful flowers? Are hard, dark circumstances making your path rough? When those rocky circumstances become a mountain which towers between you and the sun, the shadow can be quite dark—as you know if you've ever stood in the shadow of a real mountain. If right now you're standing in a shadow caused by a mountain of hard circumstances, seeing no way out of the dark, look around you. Some of the rocks sparkle. Even on dark days, God sprinkles little sparkles of joy in the most unexpected places among our shadows.

I entered a shadowland when my mother's cancer was diagnosed. Suddenly our family faced imposing rocks of survival statistics, doctors' visits, therapy options, and disease management. Simple Saturday morning phone chats, frequent weekend visits, and ideas about family reunions and spring break with her grandkids suddenly became things of the past instead of pleasures of today and plans for the future. When the kids and I left our home, our belongings, and our friends to join Tim and be near my mom and dad, we also left behind a life of security—and that move cast another dark shadow. Other shadows came as my family and I learned about the mindset and strategy necessary in a battle against cancer; about adjusting to life when one's normal routine and dreams for the future are sidelined; and about trauma. In my valley, these shadows loomed large.

As my mother fought her battle, my husband's mother, Mary O'Connor, fought one of her own. She was rushed to the emergency room one Friday afternoon, and that night we watched helplessly as they loaded her into a waiting helicopter to take her to another hospital. One doctor said, "It doesn't look good" as they wheeled her past us. The strong wind from the helicopter's propeller and its lights in the night sky as it whisked off a woman we loved made the event quite surreal. That moment felt more like a scene from a movie than a scene from our life.

For a week we spent long hours at the hospital. My heart was heavy with the pain of watching her suffer and the pain of my own mother's increasingly intense battle for life. I was hurting for my mother-in-law, hurting for Tim, his sister, and his brothers, and hurting simply because I loved her. Carrying this double burden made my chest ache with real, physical pain.

At the end of that week, Mom O'Connor died. Then, three short weeks later, my mother died, too. My grief for both my mother and my mother-in-law intertwined, and the emotional and physical pain created a darkness that was almost tangible. I had read that there can be great joy in suffering, but at that time I vehemently disagreed. I was being choked by a darkness that was foreign to me. I desperately wanted to call for my mother to come turn on the light, just as she had done when I was six years old and alone in the dark.

Besides trying to offer one another comfort, Tim and I tried to be there for our children who had their own pain and their own questions after losing both of their grandmothers in the same month. And, sitting together at the kitchen table, we wrote thank-you notes after the funerals—Tim to his mother's friends and me to my mother's. We were together, yet alone, sharing the same yet separate griefs.

Now I told you earlier that God gives sparkles in the dark. Having never lived for so long in a shadow that was so dark, I didn't know that there could be sparkles in the dark. But one day during that time of intense grief, I was aching; I was physically and emotionally exhausted. As Tim and I pulled into the driveway, my toddler ran toward me for a hug, but then broke loose to grab a dandelion. Her older sister said, "Look, Mama! Flowers!"

"Honey, those aren't flowers. Those are weeds," I impulsively responded. But immediately I thought, "No, she's right. Those are flowers. They're only weeds because of my perspective." I knelt on the sidewalk and scooped up my little one, her flower firmly in her hand. Then I really looked at her and what she held. *Lord, You're right. She's right. It really is a flower and it's beautiful.* As I studied the beauty of both that flower and my daughter's sweet, innocent eyes which saw beauty in something I considered a problem, God suddenly gave me a great gift. I felt His joy! Instantly, my heart lightened and I delighted in the precious face of my child and the sweet aroma of a weed-turned-flower. Then I felt greater joy simply because I had heard God speak to my heart. My heavenly Father loved me enough to help me see beauty in ugliness and discover His perspective through my child's eyes. And—*for a moment*—the pain in my chest was replaced by a warmth in my heart. God had given me a sprinkling of His joy—a sparkle right there on the sidewalk—in the midst of my darkness.

That was not the only time He let me see the sparkle. Oh, I never felt a great fullness of joy while I was making my way through the dark, but God did open my eyes to the sparkles of joy sprinkled here and there. At that time, I didn't know great joy in the dark; I didn't have a full-fledged "go to the fountain and drink fully" experience. The joy I knew at the time was, instead, an occasional bubbling up from the wellspring of the Lord's joy, an occasional sparkle of His light. It was a comforting undercurrent, usually invisible, but strong—mostly undetected, but somehow very present. The joy of the Lord came as glimmers in the rocks when I wasn't expecting it—a shimmer of His love sprinkled throughout the pain. These sparkles were just enough to get me through and remind me that joy was not gone completely or gone forever.

Joy *After* the Dark

Not all fruit matures at the same rate. For some people and in some difficult seasons of life, the fruit of joy needs a little more time on the vine before it's ready for harvest. In some cases, therefore, the reaping of God's joy comes *after* the dark. That was the case for Dianne G.

Dianne has known more than one season of darkness. Even her childhood days were lived in a shadowland since she was abused, eventually abandoned, and placed in a children's home at age 14. After marrying later and having four of her six children, Dianne descended into despair when her 15-year-old daughter was killed in a car accident. The avalanche of pain didn't end there, however. Over the years, her husband was diagnosed with brain cancer, she discovered she was diabetic, and she was given the dismal news that she had breast cancer—twice. Despite all this pain and suffering, this woman knows and feels the joy of the Lord. She has learned much through her difficulties, some faced without God and the rest bearable because of His presence in her life.

When her daughter died, Dianne was devastated. She turned her back on God and spent years in despair. To outsiders, she appeared to be coping well, but on the inside, she suffered a faith crisis that kept her away from God for 11 years. Then she was told her husband had brain cancer. Michael's surgery revealed that the "cancer" was actually only an infection, but the surgery left him weak on one side with impaired speech, seizures, and permanent neurological damage and depression. For many months, she grieved deeply for the "old Michael," the active father of their two sons, the successful businessman. Fear and anger invaded her life and took away her joy. Believing that God didn't care, Dianne was truly suffocated by her sadness. But God had plans for her beyond the pain.

Desperate for answers, Dianne accepted a friend's invitation and began to attend Community Bible Study. Her 11-year anger with God gave way to a new relationship. She says:

> When my daughter died, I didn't ask God for His strength, but now I knew I had to turn back to Him. I couldn't change what had happened; I had to change how I was dealing with it. So I cried out to God, "Please hear me. I'm here and I need You now!" He heard and He responded. Reestablishing my relationship with God brought me out of my despair and helped me cope. God helped me understand the blessings I still had—Michael was alive, he could walk, and eventually he could even talk clearly. I began to thank God for letting him live. With this gratefulness and hope, I was more joyful. I also realized I had to stay close to God. With the peace He placed in my heart, I was able to fight my battles with breast cancer and diabetes with more joy and less fear than I had during any of my other trials. I know that to have joy anywhere in or near the darkness, you have to have God. I've tried it both ways and I won't ever leave Him again!

When Dianne turned back to God, she found peace in the midst of her darkness, and joy soon followed as the light of His presence and the passage of time brought her out of some of her darkest days.

Outside of testimonies like Dianne's, how do we know that there is joy *after* the darkness? We have God's Word on it. The psalmist says, "Weeping may last for the night, but a shout of joy comes in the morning" (Psalm 30:5b). He goes on: "Thou hast turned for me my mourning into dancing; thou hast loosed my sackcloth and girded me with gladness" (verse 11). The loss of a child or a spouse, a job or a dream can feel like a life sentence, but it isn't. Oh, we may hurt every single day, but God is able to shake loose the sackcloth of pain that suffocates us and replace it with gladness. Who else but God could turn our mourning into dancing? God does this so that our "soul may sing praise to Thee, and not be silent" (verse 12). We were created with a soul that yearns for something beyond ourselves, that needs communion with God. A silent soul is therefore perhaps more suffocating than sackcloth. When our soul is silent, how can there be joy? Wanting our souls to praise Him, God turns our mourning into dancing. He allows weeping for the night, but He doesn't leave us there. So if there is no joy in your darkness, take heart. The light of morning always follows the dark, and you have His Word that a song of joy will come.

Joy *in* the Dark

To people deeply wounded by the events of life or working through profound grief, the thought of experiencing joy while they are in the dark may be inconceivable. Please don't shake your head in disbelief and label me a Pollyanna. I'm not talking about feeling happy when you hurt. I'm talking about having hope if you're struggling through painful circumstances, straining to see in the shadows, or groping along the dark days of grief. I want you to have hope—to know that even if you feel you'll never be happy again, a measure of joy in your darkness is possible. The joy that our heavenly Father gives is available regardless of our circumstances. Know, too, that even if you have matters to work through or need time to pass before you know happiness again, the Giver of joy can bless you now. Wherever you are in the dark, He can find you. You may not be able to see your hand in front of your face, but He has no trouble. He is light (John 8:12), and when you seek Him in your darkness—when you choose to shift your focus from your pain to His presence even if only for a moment—He will bless you with a bit of joy, a tiny sparkle to keep you going.

If, however, you are angry with God and caught in a crisis of your faith, if you haven't predetermined that God is good and sovereign, you may have to wait for another season to harvest the fruit of joy. The only way I know to taste that fruit in the midst of the dark is to both know in your mind and believe in your heart—no matter what happens—that God is good and still in control even if your world is out of control. Settling this truth before a crisis comes is so important. When we do, a taste of joy is still possible even in the deepest darkness.

My good friend Susan knows this well. She and her family were just beginning to recover from dire financial circumstances when she learned that an aunt she was close to was diagnosed with breast cancer. Before her aunt was out of the hospital, Susan fell and injured her back, resulting in two months of almost total disability followed by back surgery. Three weeks later came the devastating news that her mother had incurable lung cancer, and one month later she learned that her husband, Marty, had advanced malignant melanoma. Those days were dim and difficult for Susan as she recovered physically and walked her husband and mother through illnesses that God chose not to heal. Susan was not only devastated for herself, but she also hurt deeply for her children, especially as she watched them say goodbye to their earthly father. Marty and her mother died five weeks apart. Susan's grief was intense; happiness was just a memory—but joy was not.

Well-grounded in God's Word after six years of intensive Bible study, Susan had learned that, no matter what, God is sovereign and God is good. When her crisis hit, she didn't question God's power or goodness because she had already settled those issues in her heart. The facts of His goodness and sovereignty were a part of her belief system, a part that sustained her in the darkness.

In July, a month before Marty's death, Susan once again made the hour-long drive to the hospital to visit him in intensive care. Like most other days, she was playing Christian music in her car, singing with the radio

> $\mathcal{G}$ive unto them beauty for ashes, the oil of joy for mourning, the garment of praise for the spirit of heaviness.
>
> ~Isaiah 61:3

and praising God with genuine gladness. That day, however, she was suddenly aware of the unlikelihood of someone praising God and smiling while on her way to visit her terminally ill husband. She wondered, "How can I feel this joy? Am I in denial?" No. She knew that barring a miracle her husband was about to die and she had begun to plan his funeral. So why was she able to energetically sing God's praises? As she wondered where this joy came from, God spoke to her heart. She describes what He said:

> It was then that I realized that I was praising God because I knew He could be trusted. Even in this, my husband, our children, and I were safe with the Lord. I had studied God's Word enough to know this truth deep in my heart. I was overwhelmed with gratitude that God had seen fit to reveal His goodness to me and that He had made even the discovery of Him a joyful experience. I realized that it had been in the joy of discovery that the discovery of joy had come.

When we discover something new about God, when we gain new spiritual awareness as Susan did, we discover joy. And that joy sustained Susan during her dark days. She had predetermined that God is sovereign and good regardless of what the circumstances of her life suggest. Susan reflects, "There's no way I could have disciplined my mind to dwell on a truth that wasn't settled in my heart. If the truth of God's sovereignty and goodness hadn't already been settled in my mind, it would have been a very different and joyless two years." Many times throughout this season in her life, Susan was asked why she was able to show such incredible strength. Her reply came straight from Nehemiah 8:10: "The joy of the Lord is [my] strength." Susan's joy during this time was literally translated into strength.

Is it odd to pour out our heart to God in gratitude, praise, and joy during our darkest of days? Certainly, when that darkness is all we are able to focus on. But in those moments when we can truly enter into His presence, find something (even a little something) for which to be grateful, and reflect on His goodness despite the bad, and His control amid the uncontrollable, joy is possible—even in the blackest darkness.

"Count It All Joy"

On the survey I did for this book, I asked women to "describe a time when you felt joy in an unpleasant or painful situation." Liz H. answered for mothers everywhere when she said, "Childbirth!" No other situation in life more vividly illustrates the possibility of feeling joy even as you feel pain. As difficult as the process is, the birth of a child is indeed one of life's greatest joys. (For good reason, too. If joy were absent in the birth, people would become absent on earth!) The joy of holding your newborn in your arms for the first time makes the pain of childbirth worth it. Even when we are in labor, we know that the pain will yield something wonderful.

And so can other pain in our lives. In fact, the pain and problems of life can be looked at as gifts. Paul even says that we can "exult" and find joy in our tribulations because they produce in us perseverance, character, and hope—the hope in Christ which does not disappoint (Romans 5:3-5). James writes these words: "Consider it all joy, my brethren, when you encounter various trials, knowing that the testing of your faith produces endurance. And let endurance have its perfect result, that you may be perfect and complete, lacking in nothing" (James 1:2-4). Notice that James doesn't say *if* we encounter trials; he says *when* we encounter them. Peter also reminds us that tough times are inevitable and, like James, calls us to rejoice in them: "Beloved, do not be surprised at the fiery ordeal among you, which comes upon you for your testing, as though some strange thing were happening to you; but to the degree that you share the sufferings of Christ, keep on rejoicing; so that also at the revelation of His glory, you may rejoice with exultation" (1 Peter 4:12,13).

In the Scriptures we are not told to count it all joy because our life is carefree. Instead, we are told to expect trials and to respond to that adversity with joy! This command flies in the face of our natural instincts and the world's understanding, yet we can obey it and respond with joy when we are aware that God is maturing and refining us through our trials and that our rewards are not in this life, but in His kingdom to come.

I once heard a pastor say this about darkness: "A plant always grows toward the light. Therefore the side in the darkness grows twice as fast as that in the light. Even in adversity, we grow toward the Light—God Himself—twice as fast as when we are in the light. Thank God, then, for adversity!" God doesn't waste pain or darkness in our lives. We can indeed experience great spiritual growth during those difficult times.

Still, perhaps one of the great mysteries of life is that the followers of Christ suffer. Over 800 years ago, St. Francis of Assisi addressed that issue when he said, "This is perfect joy—to share in the sufferings of the world as Christ did." And "sharing in the sufferings of the world" is exactly what Mother Teresa is doing. She has dedicated her life to serving the downcast and dying in India. Speaking about the slums where this modern-day saint serves, Eileen and Kathleen Egan write in *Suffering into Joy,* "How is it possible to emerge from such human squalor with such a message of joy? That is Mother Teresa's gift. To her, the pain and agony she relieves are that of the Savior himself. Therefore, each person she serves has an inviolable dignity and sacredness.[3] Mother Teresa ministers with joy and teaches by her life that suffering can produce joy in believers' hearts. She says this about our personal suffering: "You have suffered the passion of the cross. There is a purpose in this. Because of your suffering and pain, you will now understand the suffering and pain of the world."[4]

Another benefit of our dark times Paul identifies is that because of our suffering and pain we can indeed better understand the suffering and pain of the people around us. He writes that God "comforts us in all our affliction so that we may be able to comfort those who are in any affliction with the comfort with which we ourselves are comforted by God" (2 Corinthians 1:4). God comforts us in our pain in a way that transcends human explanation, and when we have received His comfort, we are then able to share it with others.

That's something my mother's good friend Jackie did so well. Jackie had fought off breast cancer, but two years later it was back. Within weeks of that news, her husband suffered a fatal heart attack. One would think that learning cancer had returned and losing your husband shortly thereafter would be enough to snuff out all joy. Those events were indeed devastating, but Jackie found joy again and shared it with my family.

What was one source of joy in her life after these events? First, she knew that James's desire was to be with the Lord and that he was at last with Jesus. Jackie also says this: "I woke up one day and realized that, with James gone, my pipeline to heaven had been taken away because he had discipled me. I decided that I was going to have to put into action on my own everything he had taught me. Doing that gave me great joy."

Although Jackie had many tough days, she still often served my mom with joy as they battled the same disease. She wanted to drive our family to the large cancer center—so familiar to her—the first time we had to go, and she often stopped by to visit with my Aunt Linda, who cared for my mom while Dad worked. Smiling, Jackie once asked Linda, "Do you think it would be too presumptuous for me to ask God, when I get to heaven, if I can be an angel? I really, really want to help others." My aunt smiled and said, "Jackie, you already are!"

Jackie told me, "I cling to my faith and family and friends. That's where your joy comes from." She indeed comforted others with the comfort she had received.

Degrees of Darkness

The dark which each of us encounters—brought on by the pain and problems of life—has numerous hues and intensities ranging from pale gray to pitch black. The shadows cast by looming mountains can, for instance, be as dark as a cave with the lights turned out. Sometimes the mountain is a little smaller and the shadows a little lighter, and sometimes the dark isn't a shadow as much as it is just the slight gray of an overcast day. If you've lost someone or something dear to you, you've faced a dark shadow. If painful circumstances trouble you, perhaps your mountain is a little smaller. But maybe it's not searing pain or soul-wrenching loss as much as the stuff of life clouding your day and making you wish you stood under brighter skies.

Whatever the shade of darkness, how do we find joy in the dark? What do we do to see that sparkle of joy when life has lost its luster? Remember the sidewalk, the tumbled rock, and the geode from chapter one? They—like joy in our darkness—all sparkle, but in different ways and at different times.

The Sidewalk:
The Sparkles Sprinkled Throughout

The surface of the sidewalk sparkles in the sunlight, but sometimes we miss those sparkles because we're focusing on our darkness. When we're sandwiched between dark skies above and the dim hardness of our gray path, we need to remember that—even in that gray—*Son*light is always present ["He Himself has said, 'I will never leave you nor forsake you'" (Hebrews 13:5 NKJV; Deuteronomy 31:6)]. To see sparkles on a sidewalk, we find the right angle and the right light. Likewise, to see sparkles sprinkled throughout our darkness, we must look from the angle of God's perspective (an eternal viewpoint) and in the light of the Son—Jesus Christ. The skies may still be dark and our path may still be gray, but when we adjust our perspective to match that of the Son (what would Jesus think, do, say?) and look for the sparkles (the little joys He scatters along our way), we can indeed find sprinkles of joy brightening our walk even when we tread in hard places.

We can miss sidewalk sparkles when we don't take the time to look for them. Likewise, during our dark days, we must take the time to look out across the sidewalk in the Son's light and notice the sparkle. When we take the time to notice them, we can find sparkles of joy in the external things in our life. We see sparkles when we notice the beauty of a child's face and her weedy flowers (or is it flowery weeds?), when we do something for someone we love, and when we spend two minutes watching the sunset. Look for the shimmers on the water as you drive by a pond, lake, or ocean and relish that sparkle. Look at the things of life that are all around you and notice them if only for an instant. Also, recognize the gleam of joy when you become aware of God's voice in the dark. Impressions and directions from God can illuminate our path or simply glow in our darkness. You may find sparkles of joy sprinkled through the grayness of life just like sparkles that are scattered across the sidewalk. Pay attention. These sparkles of joy really can lift your heart.

The Rock Tumbler: A Shine After a Tumble

Now consider the rock in the tumbler. Hard and sometimes ugly, it is tossed upside down and scraped and thrown against other rocks—and the end result is a beautiful shine. As I said in chapter one, the rock in the tumbler can be two different things. Sometimes the rock is a hurt or difficult circumstance that litters our life. God can smooth those circumstances and polish those rocks that lie before us—or even remove the rocky road to show us the sparkle. But at other times we ourselves are the rocks which must yield to the tumbler and allow God to polish us.

Maybe you're familiar with the rock tumbler of life. We get tossed upside down, unable to figure out which way to turn. We get in all kinds of scrapes, and we bump into all kinds of people. God can use the hard things in our life as well as the daily friction to polish us so that we may shine forth His light and reflect Jesus who lives within us. In this case, the sparkle comes *after* the tumbling, but the beauty is worth the wait. We must allow God to use those things that make us tumble (that job loss, prickly relationship, deep grief, or long-held pain) to polish us. When we allow Him to polish us, we know the fruit of joy. The process itself isn't joyful, but the fruit we taste *after* the tumbling stops is. Oh, it might be easier to watch the rock before us being polished, but I'd much rather go through the refining process myself so that afterwards I can be a reflection of Christ, polished with His touch. That's definitely a sparkle worth waiting for. Having Jesus shine from within us, reflected in our life, is a sparkle that others can see. That truly is a source of joy—and it comes after the tumbling.

For I will turn their mourning into joy, and will comfort them, and give them joy for their sorrow.

~Jeremiah 31:13

The Geode: The Sparkle from Within

Finally there is the sparkle within the geode, those beautiful crystals hidden beneath a rough exterior waiting to be revealed. If that geode's sparkle is to become visible, the crust must be broken. Pressure must be applied to shatter the hard outer shell. Likewise, if life is hard and rough and unpleasant for you right now, know that the capacity for sparkles of joy lies within you. After all, if you are a believer of Christ, you have His Holy Spirit dwelling inside you. Where His Spirit is, there is joy—although we cannot always see it or feel it in the darkness.

You might be content just knowing that joy lies within you because of Who resides within. But to fully enjoy the beauty of that joy, you must allow God to use the pressures of life to bring you to the breaking point and reveal the radiance of His light shining in you. If our hard outer crust is never penetrated—if the geode is never broken—the beauty within will never shine forth. The breaking of our crust of "self" allows God to penetrate our heart and shine in our brokenness. That is when His joy can truly sparkle from within us.

I must mention, though, that sometimes the sparkle within a geode is visible in its natural formation if we know how to look. Picture the hollow sphere of a geode having a portion of its crust missing. When we look at this geode with the crust facing us, we might think we're looking at an ordinary rock. But if we were to look at the other side, we would see the beautiful crystals exposed. Looking at that one side doesn't tell the whole story. We must change our perspective to get a complete and accurate picture of the geode. And so it is with life.

Sometimes we get so focused on the hard exterior of our life that we think that's all there is. We forget that there might be something beyond the pain and hurt and grief. Those of us who can find joy in the darkness are people who remember that the Source of that sparkle lies within us. We change our perspective and, for a time, focus on the sparkle. The rock remains as hard as ever, but it's more pleasant to look at. Seeing the joy does not make the hardness of the days disappear; it just makes that hardness easier to bear. Again, we can see that sparkle of joy in the dark because of the Light that resides *within us.*

Joy in the Dark

Joy in the dark—it really is possible. But don't expect joy to come cascading into your life abundantly in the midst of your darkness (although it can). Instead, look for the glimmers sprinkled *through* the hard circumstances like the diamond dust in the sidewalk. Choose peace while you're in the tumbler and look forward to the shine that you'll see *afterwards.* And along the way take a moment to change perspectives and enjoy the sparkles that shine forth from *within* even in the dark, hard places of life.

A few more suggestions for seeing joy in the dark.

• *Cling to the Vine*—Live as a branch grafted to the vine of Jesus Christ and remember that God is the Master Gardener. Let Him illuminate your way through the darkness as you stay close to Him by poring over His word, praising Him, and praying.

• *Be alert to the sparkles*—Sometimes we just don't notice them because we're going so fast or are too focused on the dark. Keep your eyes open to the sparkles God can bring in the little things. They can do much to lift your spirits and light your way.

• *Think on reasons to be thankful*—Even in the deepest darkness, there is always something to be thankful for. *Always.* So renew your mind by dwelling on those things for which you can give thanks (see Philippians 4:8). Look for the truth even when you're surrounded by lies. Search for the honorable even when you have been dishonored. Look for at least one thing that is right, not for all that is wrong. Focus on something that is pure when life seems tainted. Find one lovely thing outside of your unlovely situation. Think on things with a good reputation and turn away from those that are bad. Focus your mind on something that is excellent even when you're dwelling in imperfection. And find something to praise even if you'd rather curse.

• *Keep an eternal perspective*—Such a perspective is sometimes the only way to know joy in the pitch-black darkness. That was the perspective that fueled the apostle Paul's fire and gave him joy in the dark: He lived for the world to come—not this one. Follow his example and don't look for justice, fairness, and equity here. Those are waiting in the kingdom beyond this life, and they are real and more wonderful than our earthly minds can imagine. Also waiting for us is freedom from tears and pain (Revelation 21:4). Remember, too, that although this earth holds some rewards, our real rewards are in heaven. So if you are groping in the dark because of pain or grief, hold on to this eternal perspective.

I needed these tips last night as I pondered the shade of gray that had descended on my day. It certainly wasn't a dark gray, just a little cloudy. My heart was heavy and my body tired. I was a bit overwhelmed. *I'll be glad when I can see my way clear again. It's hard to write about joy when things are a little overcast.* Then, right in the middle of my thoughts about that gloom, God shined His flashlight on the "true and lovely" of my situation. Right then, I saw a sparkle in the gray of my sidewalk! A flicker of light was shining on something good, so I began to dwell on that and I found myself feeling truly thankful. Then I felt a tiny leap in my heart. (A subtle hop, actually, but nonetheless there!) That made me praise God. *Lord, You are awesome to point to the good in my clouds with the mag-light of your finger.* (So what if it doesn't sound like King David's praise? We can be creative!) As I talked with God and praised Him—an act important to life on the Vine—the clouds began to part some and the dark was a little lighter. For a millisecond, I got a glimpse of my place in these clouds and remembered God's eternal perspective. The sparkle sprinkled on my rock helped me get in touch with the sparkle within. Nothing in my circumstances had changed. I was still tired and rather overwhelmed, but I had found sparkles of joy in the gray.

Looking, Listening, and Learning in the Dark

When the darkness comes, it can seriously interrupt our daily life. Calling such a time "a disruptive moment," author Gordon MacDonald writes, "Where a disruptive moment leads is anyone's guess. But it is nevertheless a time, perhaps unlike any other, when one is more apt to move into communion with God and be receptive to the most searing truths about self and the world. When this happens, it has usually occurred at what I call the soul-level."[5]

Russian writer Alexander Solzhenitsyn experienced an eight-year "disruptive moment" when he served in labor camps, after which he was exiled for so-called "political treason." When he wrote of those experiences and the good he saw in them, he was able to say, "So bless you, prison, for having been in my life." Would that be your response or mine? Can we say "bless you" to the dark prisons that bar us from an easy, affliction-free life? Gordon MacDonald has come to agree with Mr. Solzhenitsyn: "Like [him], I have gradually become thankful for my disruptive moments. They have forced me inward and downward into soul territory. My journals suggest that almost every useful encounter I have had with God has occurred in the wake of a disruptive moment. And as a result, I have not since been the same."[6]

Nor have I. I would never choose to relive my darkest days, and I wish desperately that my mother and mother-in-law were still alive. I miss them every day. Yet, even so I am grateful for what I have learned in the tumbling process. I am realistic enough to know that darkness can be darker and come more frequently with age, but even so I am able to smile at the future.

"At times God puts us through the discipline of darkness to teach us to heed Him..." writes Oswald Chambers. "Song birds are taught to sing in the dark, and we are put into the shadow of God's hand until we learn to hear Him. When you are in the dark, listen, and God will give you a very precious message for someone else when you get into the light."[7] The dark is a time to listen. It is also a time to look. Even in our pain, we must listen to what God is wanting to teach us and look for the sparkles of joy He sprinkles throughout the dark, reveals after the tumbling, and plants within us.

*G*od whispers in our pleasures, but shouts in our pain.

~C.S. Lewis

～9～

I Didn't Lose My Joy— It's Been Stolen

Catching the Joy Thieves

I t was Tim's first year as a post-collegiate working man, and one night after work he drove his shiny new Mazda RX-7 into his driveway. He locked it and went inside. Apparently, he wasn't the only one who admired that car. The next morning it was gone!

When we have something valuable, we must be alert. When we possess something beautiful, we are at risk of having it stolen. And joy, with its ability to brighten our life, is something valuable indeed. It shines like a precious gem and must be guarded as such, for thieves lurk who wish to steal it.

A ring of bandits worse than Bonnie and Clyde or the Dalton Gang and led by an insidious mastermind is desperate to steal our joy. That mastermind—known as Satan—is a thief and a murderer, the biggest killjoy around. Interested in more than simple petty theft, Satan knows the true value of joy and he is intent on taking it from us. He knows that it is more than just a beautiful blessing. Satan knows that "the joy of the LORD is your strength" (Nehemiah 8:10b).

This prowling devil absolutely delights in weak Christians because, first, when our joy is gone, so is our witness. If we are pickle-faced, joyless Christians we can't expect the world to come clamoring to find out how they can be just like us. Second, when our joy is gone, so is our delight in Christ and in His salvation, and Jesus paid a high price for that salvation—His very life. "What was the purpose of our Lord's atonement on the cross," writes Sherwood Wirt in *The Book of Joy*, "what is the whole point of salvation from sin if there is no ultimate fulfillment and delight in the Lord?"[1] Third, when our joy is gone, we lose our ability to model it before our children. Children learn what they live and what is lived out before them. Fourth and finally, when our joy is gone so is the soaring spirit that God gives to His children and our pleasure in His gift of life. Clearly, as Nehemiah knew, when we lose our joy, we lose our strength—the strength we need to witness, to delight in the Lord, to model joy to our children, and to savor the blessing of life itself. So protect that gift of joy, dear reader, from the wiles of Satan and his den of thieves by knowing who the robbers are, how they attack, and what security systems we can install.

The Thieves

While there may be more, the primary ringleaders in the great joy heist are stress, fear, anger, sin, adversity, and depression. Although they sometimes team up to ambush the unaware, their individual attacks are quite effective. We must be on our guard against these thieves.

Stress

We are a culture that knows much about stress. These days, all of us, including children, can suffer from tension, pressure, or emotional strain—in a word, stress. Webster defines "stress" as "a factor that induces bodily or mental tension and may be a factor in disease causation; a force that tends to distort a body." Have you ever been so stressed that you knew the addition of one more stressor would "distort" you for sure? I have! And it's not a pretty picture.

And neither is the "disease causation" mentioned in the dictionary definition. Even those Webster word people know what many medical studies have found: Too much stress triggers chemical reactions in our body that are harmful to our health. When we're under great stress, these chemical reactions suppress the immune system and, according to one report, "increase our odds of contracting everything from colds to strokes to heart disease and even cancer."[2] Some researchers say that illnesses and accidents directly linked to stress comprise three-fourths of all lost work time. Author and physician Peter Hanson writes the following in *The Joy of Stress*:

> Stress is also implicated in the majority of cases seen in the doctor's office, hospital beds, and ultimately the graveyard. In spite of all the media attention to health, stress-related problems take the vast majority of people by *surprise*. They might have known that stress can harm others, but never fully realized what it could do to *them*.[3]

(Are those words a wake-up call to you?)

Yet, seemingly contrary to these statistics, all stress is not bad. Some stress is good for us; its mismanagement is what does us harm. Manageable levels of stress can, for instance, cause us to accomplish more than we would without the incentive that's causing stress. The stress of a deadline, say, can cause our productivity to increase and our mental acuity to sharpen. The stress of competition causes athletes to excel. The rush of adrenaline that comes with stress enables us to accomplish more than we would otherwise. But when additional factors enter in, causing too much stress, or when we lose our ability to control the stresses in our life, we begin to suffer from its bad effects. That's when stress can harm us physically and steal our joy.

Stress robs us in several ways. Stress can cause us to neglect certain disciplines—physical and spiritual—that help us lead balanced lives and feel good (see chapter ten). Too much stress can make us forget to take proper care of our body, and then our own biology can keep us from feeling joyful. Also, consider that stress management requires a great deal of energy. In times of stress overload, energy we would use to engage in activities that bring us joy is diverted to stress management. Stress can also rob us of joy because it tends to shift our focus to surviving and coping, rather than enjoying. Coping with life is good, but enjoying it is better. Finally, stress also causes us to focus on the things we cannot control instead of on the Source of control and of joy.

In fact, having a sense of control seems to be the biggest factor in effective stress management. One researcher had two groups of workers concentrate on a given task. Both groups were subjected to irritating background noises, but only one group was given an out. Workers in that group had a panic button in front of them that they could push at will to stop the noise. Which group do you think was more productive? Of course the group with the button—but, interestingly, not one person in that group ever pressed the button. The fact that they had control (not that they exercised it) accounted for their higher productivity.[4] When we lose control or the sense of control, our stress level increases. As we focus on the stressors that we can't control, we lose sight of the big picture: that God is in control even when our circumstances are out of control. And, as I've said before, when we focus on our seemingly out-of-control circumstances rather than on the steady and omnipotent Source of our joy, a loss of joy is inevitable. The apostle Paul—a man who knew a lot about stress—used the Greek word *thlipsis*, meaning "pressure" and translated "tribulation," when he talked about difficult times of stress. And Paul calls us to face that tribulation with joy!

Fear

Fear is one of the sneakiest robbers, creeping up on us when we least expect it and attacking despite our best defensive weapons—our reason, our intellect, and our logic. Whether or not it is based in reality, fear can prompt a full-blown battle and completely wipe out our joy. In many cases, if the thief attacks hard, joy completely retreats.

Fear can turn a strong, joyful woman into a wreck, trembling and terrified. Donna D. knows about that. Fear used to be the driving force in her life despite her head knowledge about the joy of Christ. She just couldn't seem to get that knowledge—that joy—into her heart or emotions. Consequently her fears—and they were many—were all consuming. A confrontation with a Peeping Tom when she was young led to a nearly paralyzing fear that someone was going to lift her garage door and break into her house. She sometimes stood at the top of her stairs, shaking, because she was convinced that someone was downstairs. Then one night it happened. She heard the garage door go up, but no one answered when she called downstairs. Then, while she called 911, she heard someone come in the door—only to discover moments later that the intruder was her son.

She was also fearful that her only son would be in a car accident. At one point, Donna even slept in her makeup because she "knew" she was going to be called to the hospital in the middle of the night. But that wasn't her worst fear. What terrified her most was being alone. Whenever her husband Bob had to travel, they would argue before he left because Donna could not bear to stay by herself. She was so bound up with fear that she would pin her drapes closed in the daylight and then go outside to see if you could see in. But her heavenly Father wanted to free this hostage from her fear.

After their children were out of the nest and two days after Donna and Bob moved into a new house, he had to leave the country for six weeks on a work assignment. Donna was terrified of being completely alone in a new place for that much time, but God used those six weeks to deliver her from her fear. She describes what happened:

I began to again ask God to take away this awful fear, and I said, "There's no way that I'll feel safe with Bob gone, Lord. I can't be by myself!" As I kept asking Him to remove the fear and buried myself in my Bible, God began to show me that I wasn't alone. He was with me. I got to a place where I let go of much that kept me bound because I wanted so badly to be free.

Knowing God is the best antidote to fear.

~Cheri Fuller

As I clung to God's Word and talked with Him constantly, He carried me until I was ready to step into the waters of healing and face my fears. He wonderfully healed me of my fear of being alone. Before, I couldn't say that I was a woman who could smile at the future, but now I can. Fear is gone.

Is your fear gone? Or is it robbing you of joy?

Before you answer those questions, consider the different degrees and sources of fear we can encounter. A novice skydiver standing at the plane's open door ready to jump knows fear about the impending jump. The keynote speaker soon to address an unfriendly crowd feels fear before the event. These are real fears, yet some of our fears are only played out in the arena of our mind. We fear, for instance, things in the future, things that may never happen: We fear the unknown.

I faced that kind of fear of the unknown when I was told that my ovarian cysts were probably malignant. For one week (that felt like one month) I battled fear, playing out the various scenarios of the cancer diagnosis which the doctors had suggested. That battle went fairly well for even though I tearfully poured out my heart to God and openly expressed my fears to Him, I prayed that He would make me able to bear the news—even if it were bad. Of course I knew great joy when the test results were negative.

After I lost my mother, however, I didn't do as well in another battle against fear. While my first scrimmage had been prompted by actual facts, this second bout with fear was totally groundless. Little aches and pains got my imagination stirring, and I concluded that what I was spared of the first time would now become a reality ("After all, just look at my mom."). Doctor visits confirmed that I had nothing to fear, but it was God's Word that actually freed me from fear and helped me rest in their reports of a clean bill of health. I had fought quite a battle against fear in my mind, and my joy had been stolen. It was only restored when I once again turned my trust to the Lord.

As my friend Cheri Fuller, author and speaker, teaches in her public speaking and her book *Trading Your Worry for Wonder*—and as I know from experience—fear takes a high toll: It causes us to miss the present; paralyzes our faith; zaps our physical, emotional, and spiritual energy; causes burnout; harms our relationships; confuses our thinking; and greatly limits our potential. No wonder we lose our joy when we operate in fear! So what can we do to safeguard ourselves? What battle plan can we adopt?

Cheri says, "The best weapon for fear is to refocus on God's character and His name. As we meditate on who He is, by praising Him through His many names and attributes, our joy and trust and gratefulness go up."[5] How, for instance, can we fear when we are spending time with the Alpha and the Omega (the Beginning and the End), Elohim ("the God who is my Source"), and Jehova-shammah ("the Lord who is present")? Fear recedes when we focus on our all-powerful, all-loving God.

We can also fight fear by remembering what God has done for us. The Old Testament tells that the Israelites erected stone altars as monuments of God's provision, and we need the same kind of reminders. We need to look back on what God has done in our life as a steppingstone to praise (even when we don't feel like it) and greater faith (even when we're feeling hopeless).

Finally, the greatest weapon of all for fighting fear is knowing that God's Word says "perfect love casts out all fear" (1 John 4:18). We know that perfect love through Jesus Christ and His death on the cross for us. Because God is perfect love, we can abide in Him and take Him at His word: "Fear not, for I am with you" (Isaiah 41:10 RSV).

Focusing on who God is, remembering what He has done for us, and drawing close to Jesus—these are key elements of our strategy against fear, an effective thief of joy.

Anger

Fear can issue a sneak attack and steal our joy from behind the scenes, but its cohort in crime—anger—tends to be a bit more demonstrative. Anger usually makes its presence known, sometimes quite loudly and dramatically. Anger itself is not a sin (what we do with our anger can be sinful—which is why Paul wrote, "Be angry but do not sin" [Ephesians 4:26a RSVB]), but it's almost impossible to feel joyful when we are angry. Joy doesn't necessarily leave us completely when we are angry, but it certainly goes underground. When we express our anger, we can still have the joy of the Lord within us, but the *feeling* of joy is definitely incompatible with the feeling of anger.

I know, for instance, that I would lose my feelings of joy if I burned dinner and stubbed my toe and then found out that the children had jumped on the bed where the folded laundry lay and, in the process, broke my favorite vase. I would definitely feel like expressing anger—and I wouldn't feel particularly joyful in the process. Yet if I'd had a full measure of joy before expressing my anger and I expressed my anger in a healthy way rather than letting it linger, then I could soon return to a joyful state. That return to joy comes more easily when we are truly angry but we sin not, following Jesus' example when He overturned the tables of those selling in the temple (Mark 11:15-17). Our Lord fully expressed His anger. Turning over chairs and tables is quite demonstrative, yet He did not sin. At other times, Jesus expressed His anger quietly. When the Pharisees were watching Him in the temple to see if He would heal on the Sabbath so they could accuse Him, Jesus looked "at them with anger, grieved at their hardness of heart," and healed the man's withered hand (Mark 3:5).

Although anger can definitely steal our joy, I'm not suggesting that we squash it. Instead, we are to control it in a healthy way as Jesus modeled. After all, anger is a natural reaction to grief and pain; it's how we deal with our anger that makes it right or wrong. In *Splashes of Joy in the Cesspools of Life*, Barbara Johnson tells about driving to a dump late at night to grieve over her "second deposit in Heaven," the loss of a second son. She would rant and rave at God in private, this outpouring of anger an expression of her grief. Today, in her ministry to hurting parents, she tells them that "it is okay to express these emotions and it is okay to be mad at God. When we scream in agony and rage at Him through our grief, He doesn't say, 'Off to hell with you, Sister!' Instead, He patiently loves us...carries us...wraps His blanket of tenderness around us while we are balking, hissing, and rebelling in every way."[6] God made us creatures capable of emotion, so He's not offended when we share our feelings. In fact, we're not telling Him anything He doesn't already know! That's one reason why venting is okay.

Releasing the anger that naturally arises from grief and pain is not only okay, it is important to our emotional health and healing. If we stuff our pain, thinking it wrong to express our anger, we are like a pressure cooker with a missing vent. We're building up steam and the pressure increases, but there is no release. Once my mother made rice in a pressure cooker and didn't know that the vent was clogged—until it exploded. Rice went everywhere, practically coating the kitchen. Luckily she wasn't in the room then. Can you imagine calling 911? "Please come quickly. I've been hit with a blast of exploding rice." That unvented pressure cooker could have been embarrassing, if not downright dangerous. And it is, in fact, dangerous for us if we fail to vent the pain and anger in our life.

In her book *Women and Stress,* Jean Lush teaches that when we are frustrated or angry high amounts of tension and emotional energy swirl around inside us, and energy always seeks to be discharged. How we discharge that energy varies depending on how we manage the "storage pots" which we use to contain this energy. Some people's pots are small and can't hold very much tension. These people rarely close the lid: "Whenever they are tense, they immediately unload their tension, regardless of the cost." Others have a larger capacity for this emotional energy. Since they rarely open their lids to release the tension, it gets discharged inwardly and manifests itself in psychosomatic illnesses, depression, avoidance, and procrastination.[7] Even my doctor's office distributed pamphlets describing the danger of "stuffing" anger, cautioning that it can lead to a host of physical problems.

If we rarely close the lid we will act out all of our emotions—which is not always appropriate and certainly hinders a joyful life. If we rarely open the lid we build up pressure until we explode—which is not healthy and which can also hinder a joyful life. Perhaps the balance lies in the image of a properly functioning pressure cooker with a clear and open escape vent. The lid fits properly to process what's inside, but the vent is open so pressure doesn't build to the point of explosion.

When anger does explode or when we allow it to linger, become a habit, or rage out of control, it begins to steal our joy. I have experienced the kind of lingering anger that crosses the boundary of healthy expression, and it robbed me of my joy. I felt that anger shortly after my mother died. I wasn't exactly mad at God, but I did find myself struggling with a great deal of anger. When I'd see a mother and daughter together having a good time, I'd get angry about my loss. In a movie I saw, the look a mother and daughter exchanged spoke volumes about how well they understood each other and what a unique bond they shared. My loss of that kind of relationship at a young age made me angry. I should have taken Barbara Johnson's advice and regularly vented. Instead, my "pot"—as Jean Lush describes—leaked, and I found myself expressing my anger in ways and at times that were not always in the best interest of my family. I became entangled in my anger even though in my heart I longed for joy. Sometimes little things set me off and my un-released anger exploded. (I have a chip in my stove today that's a testimony to that explosion!) Walking around with an under-current of anger is a big joy robber. A friend of mine knows about that, too.

Aware I was writing this book about when Mama ain't happy, this friend said, "You may not understand, but I struggle with anger and often feel like screaming." It's because I under-stand that struggle with anger that I venture to tell you that a life of joy is possible. That thief quit stealing my joy when I learned about the importance of releasing my anger privately (instead of in front of my children) and when I took my anger (and its some-times uncontrollable and lingering presence) to the cross. I had told God many times that I was angry and that I didn't like liv-ing in its shadow, and I'd asked Him to help me deal with it, yet I still struggled. But one day He did more than just help me con-trol it. He freed me from this joy robber.

That day, I expressed to the Lord how I felt and confessed my occasional but sinful outbursts that affected my family—something I'd done before. But then I asked a close friend to pray for me. It was during that prayer time with her that God gave me a mental image of just how free I could be. While we prayed, I pictured myself bound up, a thick rope wrapped tightly around my body (which is how the anger made me feel). As my friend asked God to untangle that rope of anger, I pictured my-self standing before Jesus at the foot of the cross. As I placed one end of my tangle of rope into His pierced hand, the entire thing began to loosen until it fell from my body in a heap...at the foot of the cross. He still held in His hand the end I'd given Him, but I was free to walk away—which I did.

Do I still get angry? Of course, but not in an out-of-control, misdirected way, and my anger no longer steals my joy. The vivid picture that the Lord gave me that day was freeing. Now, every time I'm tempted to grab that rope of anger again, I remember that Jesus took it from me. I can express my anger, but I don't have to let it bind me and cut off my joy because I left that rope with Jesus at the cross.

I use other safeguards against anger, too, and you might try them as well. First, to protect our joy, we are to be slow to anger since anger doesn't "achieve the righteousness of God" (James 1:19,20) or "make us good" (TLB). Second, remember the storage pots and the pressure cooker and be sure you have proper vents when you're under pressure so you don't explode. Third, we must acknowledge our anger and try to resolve the matter before the sun goes down (Ephesians 4:26b) so that it doesn't linger or become uncontrolled wrath. Fourth and finally, the prophet Nehemiah offers this model: "When I was angry...I consulted with myself" (Nehemiah 5:6,7). What a great thing to remember to do! Many times we would be much better off if we would "consult with ourselves" (that's akin to counting to ten!) before we react. When we contemplate our anger, we might ask ourselves, "Is the blocked goal worth the anger? Is the anger appropriate (is it righteous indignation or a response to someone who has sinned against me?) or inappropriate (is it based on selfishness or perfectionism?)? Is my expression of anger going to hurt someone else? What am I doing to resolve the issue?" If we act out our anger inappropriately or allow our anger to linger and become bitterness, it will indeed steal our joy. After all, wrongly expressing anger and harboring bitterness in our heart are sins—which moves us to the next joy robber.

Sin

"Sin" is as distasteful a word as "joy" is delightful. The word "sin" is also quite rare outside of the church. You never hear newscasters report, "There was great sin in our city today." No. They simply describe the results of our sin without any comment on the root cause. And, like the newscasters, we don't usually walk around saying, "I'm really struggling with my sin today." No, "sin" just isn't a frequently used word in our culture. For the most part, no one likes to be reminded of their sin, and many of the people doing the reminding these days don't seem to like their job either. More and more churches are getting away from talking about sin, opting instead for more ear-tickling, pew-filling, positive messages.

Webster defines "sin" as "an offense against God," and the Bible calls it unrighteousness (1 John 5:17), adding that it's something we all do (Romans 3:23). Defined as a "weakened state of human nature in which the self is estranged from God," sin is a powerful member of the joy heist gang. The estrangement that results from unconfessed or habitual sin prevents us from knowing joy in the Lord. Our sin separates us from God and damages our relationship with Him—as sinners, we cannot draw close to the true Source of joy.

Oh, we may feel a joyful thrill for a time since sin can be fun, but that momentary thrill is not true joy. If we are engaged in habitual sin—if we're doing that which we know is wrong yet we willfully continue—we are further cutting ourselves off from the joy of the Lord. The prophet Isaiah describes that cold, joyless place: "Your iniquities have made a separation between you and your God, and your sins have hidden His face from you, so that He does not hear" (Isaiah 59:2). Sin is a joy robber since it causes God to hide His face from us.

King David knew about God hiding His face after he and Bathsheba had quite the little affair. He must have thought he was pretty powerful and crafty, what with arranging to have her husband killed in battle and all, but he ultimately saw that the "joy" of their moments together was nothing compared to the joy in the Lord he had known before. When he was confronted by Nathan, David fully confessed his sin, acknowledging that his actions were sinful and asking God to "blot out my transgressions" (Psalm 51:1). He also asked God to "make me to hear joy and gladness" (verse 8) and "restore in me the joy of Thy salvation" (verse 12). And as Sherwood Wirt points out in *The Book of Joy,* "It was not God's salvation that David wanted restored; it was the joy of it. The salvation may hold, but if the joy of it slips away, something very precious is lost."[8] God heard David's confession, forgave his sin, and, as the psalms David later wrote reveal, restored his joy.

And God can do that for you and me regardless of the nature of our sin. I once saw a woman publicly confess before her church just what David did. The pain in her face and the remorse with which she asked forgiveness testified to the empty "joy" and passing thrill of sin compared to the true joy of an unbroken relationship with God. We can all know God's forgiveness and restoration, but what can we do to better maintain that unbroken relationship with Him? The safeguard God gives us human beings, who are sinners by nature, is explained in the promise of 1 John 1:9. There we learn that, "If we confess our sins, [God] is faithful and righteous to forgive us our sins and to cleanse us from all unrighteousness." Honesty in our confession is essential. We must be as real with God about our sin as we are when we tell Him we're afraid or angry. God doesn't expect us to change—He knows we need Him to accomplish that. But He does expect us to be honest, for then we demonstrate that we are willing to be molded and shaped by Him. Furthermore, God loves us so much that He doesn't reward us according to our sins, but instead, "as far as the east is from the west, so far has He removed our transgressions from us" (Psalm 103:12). Amazing grace! Confession and forgiveness are key to keeping sin from robbing us of our joy.

Adversity

One last member of the thieving joy heist gang is adversity—those unpleasant circumstances, accidents, mistakes, and misfortunes that are a part of life, that range from the minor to the catastrophic, from light afflictions to life-and-death matters. Adversity is often a very dark place that leaves us longing for the light of God's joy. You read more about that in the previous chapter, but here I'll offer the most important safeguard against allowing adverse situations to rob us of joy. We simply need to remember that adversity is merely a set of circumstances, albeit bad ones, and that our joy is not contingent on our circumstances. Then, when adversity does come, we need to remember that God's grace sustains us in seemingly hopeless situations. As Christ said, "My grace is sufficient for you, for [My] power is perfected in weakness" (2 Corinthians 12:9). That promise falls into "the peace that passes all understanding" category: We cannot fathom God's grace being all that we need in times of adversity until we experience it for ourselves.

Right after my mother-in-law died, I vacillated between hope and despair—hope that my mother might rally and win her fight for life and despair because Tim's mother hadn't, and I was afraid mine wouldn't either. I didn't see how I could possibly bear the loss of both of them at the same time. Then my dear friend reminded me of a statement by Corrie ten Boom: "You don't need the ticket until you get on the train." I struggled most to find joy in my darkness when I was living out in my mind that which had not yet happened. Picturing the worst case scenario before it even happened, I found myself unable to comprehend how God's grace would be sufficient. My friend's words reminded me that I wasn't on that train yet so I didn't need the ticket, and that God would provide it when I did. And that's exactly how it happened. God's grace was indeed sufficient as I dealt with the pain of two goodbyes.

We can safeguard ourselves and keep adversity from stealing our joy by remembering that God can use tough times to refine our faith, produce in us proven character, and show Himself strong (see 1 Peter 1:6-9). Without such testing, how will we ever know if our faith is really real? If we have a car that's supposed to be really fast but we never really open it up, opting instead for a safe 30-miles-per-hour pace, how will we know if it's as fast as the owner's manual says? God's Word tells me that He is capable of great performance at fierce speeds, on rough terrain, and in the worst of conditions. I've been in those places. I know the rough terrain of heavy afflictions (losing both my mother and mother-in-law in three short weeks) as well as the wear and tear of each day's trying circumstances, and I know how great God's faithfulness is.

> *Therefore you too now have sorrow; but I will see you again, and your heart will rejoice, and no one takes your joy away from you.*
>
> ~John 16:22

Daniel and his friends also knew how faithful God is. As they stood before a raging Nebuchadnezzar who had just threatened to throw them in a fiery furnace, they showed incredible faith, saying, "Our God whom we serve is able to deliver us...but even if He does not [we won't worship your gods]" (Daniel 3:17,18). These young men knew that God was able to deliver them from their adversity and that sometimes He chooses not to. Likewise, as he underwent severe trials at the hand of Satan, Job was able to say, "The LORD gave and the LORD has taken away. Blessed be the name of the LORD" (Job 1:21). Faith that is tested shows its true value.

When our faith is tested, the experience can alleviate any doubts that it is real. In fact, many followers of Christ throughout history—from the first-century apostles to contemporary believers like Corrie ten Boom and Mother Teresa—have undergone great adversity, resulting in powerful testimonies and vibrant faith. If we want such a testimony, we shouldn't run from the test. Besides, it is more important to know who God is and the reality of His power than to live a life of continual comfort!

Although some believers have a strong faith despite having never been called to face much adversity, I think they are the exception. Trials tend to be the forge of unshakable and contagious faith. Then there are those believers who have never faced great adversity but who live fearful that the ax will fall at any moment. If you fall into this category, consider that God may be calling you to a life of faith characterized by a calm staying power over the long haul. But if testing does come your way, don't be fearful. God enables us to respond to adversity—great or small—with joy! That thief may enter our house, but it doesn't have to take our prize!

Depression

One major joy robber for many women (and men) is depression. "Depression...black as a thousand midnights in a cypress swamp. Loneliness that is indescribable. Confusion regarding God. Frustration with life and circumstances. The feeling that you have been abandoned, that you are worthless. Unlovable. The pain is excruciating"[9]—that's how Cynthia Swindoll, executive director of Insight for Living, describes this dark thief of joy in the foreword of the book *Depression*. In *Surviving the Darkness*, Dr. Grace Ketterman says that depression is a complex mixture of "varying proportions of fear, anger, sadness, helplessness, guilt, remorse, and sometimes hopelessness" and lists the causes of depression: inherited genetic factors; family influences (learned behavior, reactions, and feelings taught within families); the impact of our environment (the coldness or warmth of our climate and of the people in our life); and the stress factor.[10] Dr. James Dobson says that low self-esteem as well as fatigue and time pressure are two of the top sources of depression in women.[11]

Depression is not only a joy robber in our own life, but—as the title of this book suggests—it robs our family of joy, too, because our emotional state affects our children. Dr. Ketterman writes, "Family influences, I believe, create the core of beliefs, emotions, and self-concept that predispose individuals to depression or health."[12] It's my opinion that this influence is not license to blame our parents (or for our children to blame us) for the way we (or they) turn out, for we all make choices that affect us throughout our life. Yet the influence of the family in which we were raised (or are raising our children) cannot be overlooked as a contributor to depression.

A friend of mine has battled depression for two years. She has experienced a lack of joy during this time and told me, "I've been asking myself, 'What can I do to make myself happier?' I've decided there were some faith issues and hurts from my past and my family of origin that I have to deal with before I can experience joy." Indeed, working through such issues, often with the help of a qualified Christian counselor, is important to our healing and recovery from depression.

Geri R. suffered from depression, too. For her, it began during adolescence and reached its peak in her early forties. She shares her struggle and ultimate return to a life of joy:

> I was full of bitterness from my failed first marriage, afraid of rejection, locked in an unhappy second marriage, forced to suppress my true self at work, and overwhelmed by guilt from an abortion. I saw no hope for my future and felt no worth for my life. I wanted to die. Through the help of a Christian

counselor and over time, the Lord healed me and restored my marriage. Through the Scriptures, prayer, and close fellowship with caring Christian friends, the Lord freed me from strongholds of bitterness, rejection, and quiet. He demonstrated Psalm 30:11,12 (NIV) in my life: "You turned my wailing into dancing, you removed my sackcloth and clothed me with joy, that my heart may sing to you and not be silent." Now, I gratefully receive His daily gift of joy and His promise of hope.

If depression in any of its complex forms is stealing your joy, know that there is indeed hope. Depression is not a place where you have to stay. As Dr. Ketterman concludes in her book, "With expert help, personal honesty, great patience, and persistence, you can win the battle against depression. I wish for you the courage to work and the steadfastness to endure until you know the joy that the Creator wants you to know!"[13]

The Thief Within

Finally, the wisdom of the cartoon character Pogo applies here: "I have seen the enemy and he is us!" Sometimes we ourselves are the thief that is robbing us of our joy. Oh, I know some folks would say that "other people" should be included in my band of joy robbers, but I contend that very few people actually intend to take away another person's joy (although there are those whom we could swear that is their sole mission in life!). When people rob us of our joy, we are usually allowing them to do so. People may treat us badly, sin against us, and make life miserable for us, but we choose how we respond to them. We can let them rain on our parade and wash away our joy, or we can choose to remain joyful in spite of them, even hoping that some of it will rub off on them!

I'm sure you know people whose cup of joy in life isn't exactly half-full or even close to bubbling over. I challenge you to consider these folks your "joy project." (I've had one of my own!) Those potential robbers may, of course, look at you funny, but keep on offering them lemonade when they hand you lemons. On those occasions when you could let those folks zap some of your joy, act as your own sentry. Guard against allowing them to take that which you have—joy in the Lord despite the circumstances of your life and despite the robbers who are attempting to take it away.

This was something that, as a new bride, I didn't know how to do. I prepared one of my best recipes from home for our first dinner together in our new apartment after our honeymoon. It was ready when Tim walked in, and I was ready for his praise. Instead, he said it was "interesting" and that it would be OK if I lost that recipe. My high hopes for domestic kudos that night were crushed, and I let him steal my joy. Today, if people at my dinner table complain about a meal, I simply tell them the short-order cook has the night off so they'd better eat—and I enjoy my dinner. While I love to please my family, I consider comments like "this looks like dog food" their problem—and I tell them they may not bless the neighbor's dog with it. They can't touch my joy with something that is their problem.

For a more recent example, I went to a gathering and greeted several women as I walked by. One of them looked at me as I called her by name, said nothing, and then quickly looked away. *I've been snubbed! How rude. What did I do to her?* I wondered. Then I decided that I didn't want to let her steal my joy. In fact, she wouldn't have been stealing anything. If I mulled over all the possible reasons why I'd been snubbed and then got angry about her rudeness, I would be *allowing* my joy to be stolen. My choice would be the thief. So, instead, I decided to enjoy my evening. As Linda T. points out, "Most things [like that snubbing] that happen have very little—if anything—to do with me. If someone fails to speak to me, then I just assume they are having a bad day. I don't think it's

> *I* learned early in life that I'm a child of the King— that makes me a princess! So why should I be discontented or ever lack self-esteem?
>
> ~Norma M.

about me." People are probably thinking about us much less than we presume.

But bigger issues make that choice to not let someone steal our joy more difficult. One person I know was the victim of a business deal gone awry—she'd been "taken" by someone she cared about. Although deeply hurt by the incident, this person chose to embrace forgiveness and release bitterness—a key to guarding our joy. She chose not to allow the other person's actions to steal her joy. That choice can be tough to live out, but we can become a guard of our joy instead of a target of robbery. It's a choice we can learn to make when we practice letting other people's problems remain their problems and when, instead of trying so hard to be a people-pleaser, we seek approval from God and find self-esteem in knowing who we are in Christ. The job of the sentry may get tough, but we don't have to let people steal our joy. Instead, we can offer to share it.

As we've seen, choices we make about our attitude and our level of contentment can make us either sentries of our joy or thieves. Many daily decisions also either contribute to our level of joy or rob us of it. The presence or lack of disciplines to help us in these decisions is the subject of the next chapter. Read on.

⇜ Part Three ⇝

Practicing Joy and Contentment in Our Homes
What We Do

❦ 10 ❧

Disciplines of a Joyful Person

Practical Tips for Practicing Joy

D iscipline and joy? What does discipline have to do with joy?" you may be thinking. Quite a lot actually! The phrase "disciplines of a joyful person" really isn't an oxymoron. Although a life of discipline certainly doesn't sound like the goal of Jovial Jane, she—and we—can pursue certain disciplines which are conducive to joy. We can make choices that will help us live more joyfully.

Still, "discipline" can be such a painful word—perhaps because it evokes images of feet hitting the floor at 5 A.M., sweat pouring off a body doing its 500th push-up, or a person sitting at the computer while her friends go to the movies. The word "discipline" also brings to mind images of the "board of education" (the kind that meets the seat!). After all, "If you disobey, you will be disciplined!" is a comment many of us have both made and experienced.

So how can the words "discipline" and "joyful" appear in the same sentence? Let me explain. Although the gift and fruit of joy is certainly from God and not something we create, we can choose to engage in certain disciplines which contribute to an attitude and feeling of joy. When these disciplines are combined with the heart issues of joy stemming from our faith

195

(issues which we've already discussed), the result is a life conducive to genuine joy and not mere happiness. When we adopt these practical disciplines of lifestyle, labor, and love, we are able to practice joyful living.

1. The Disciplines of Lifestyle

The choices we make and the disciplines we adopt shape our lifestyle, which in turn either helps or hinders our joyfulness. A simplified lifestyle that includes disciplines of the mind, body, and spirit can make joyful living possible.

The Discipline of Simplicity

Have you noticed that many Americans are reevaluating their lifestyle? We've been hearing much this decade about Americans who have traded fast-paced, whirlwind, lots-of-overtime lives for more family time and a simpler, more relaxed lifestyle often characterized by less purchasing power and less purchasing. In its January 2, 1996 edition, The *Houston Chronicle* reported the Trends Research Institute finding that this movement toward a simpler life is one of the top trends of the '90s and "probably the most fundamental shift in lifestyle changes since the depression." A *Time* cover story on "the simple life" said this about Americans: "They've been thinking hard about what really matters in their lives, and they've decided to make some changes. What matters is having time for family and friends, rest and recreation, good deeds and spirituality."[1] Sometimes simplicity can bring felicity—and increased joy in life!

Like many of those searching for a better lifestyle, I have struggled with barren busyness, being over-committed, and living a life that was anything but simple. In my quest for a joyful, contented, simplified life, I have lived the words of Erma Bombeck: "Do I have it all yet? I hope so. I'm half-dead."[2] And half-dead is a terrible way to live. I have since discovered and, as most women today know, that "having it all" (or even some of it) is a bunch of hooey. But the myth is a powerful one—which is why I totally related to Erma when she said the modern woman may have it all, but she doesn't want it anymore. She wrote:

It sounded so great when I heard there wasn't anything as a woman I couldn't do. "All" sounded so all-encompassing. Now it's turned out to be the same "all" as in one-size-fits-all. All of what?...I began hearing about what a great source of untapped energy and talent I was and that I should volunteer it for the community. I did that. Then someone suggested that I should be paid for all this expertise and get a job. I did that. The slick magazines came along and said, "Why work for someone else? You should be running the company." Running for Congress. Running for your health. Running for the bus. Running...running...running. I've been doing it ever since.[3]

Been there; done that. I know what it is to try to balance husband, children, church, home, career, social life, etc. Sometimes it's the "etcetera" that gets us—that and all that running! I know. Years ago I lived life at quite a rapid pace (some might have called it a sprint), which was manageable...for a while. Tim had a busy job, and I was running my own part-time business at home, speaking, writing, occasionally broadcasting, and volunteering at church. And I was doing all that in addition to my primary priority of raising our children and trying to be a good wife and homemaker. I never did all of these things on any given day or even in any given month, but—as crowded as it sounds—all of them were in my life. (Remember, I told you I was better at doing than being. I have lots of practice "doing"!) Every activity seemed important, and I wanted to be doing all of them. But just like the frog in the kettle that doesn't realize when his tepid bath becomes a boiling broth (and that he's dinner!), I failed to see the overall effect of all these activities—the too many etceteras—on my schedule and my life.

Ringing phones, crowded schedules, frequent deadlines, less frequent sleep, dirty laundry, and dinner-from-a-box became much too common. Too much to do in too little time had become a normal way of life for me and, although I enjoyed what I was doing, I often felt overwhelmed. But I was the frog unaware that my broth was about to boil. Oh, I knew I was in the kettle surrounded by hot water, but I didn't quite know how to get out. Besides, where I was, wasn't entirely unpleasant. So it is for the frog—right up to the point when he becomes dinner.

The first time I ever gave any serious consideration to the depth of the water and the rising temperature of my swirling lifestyle was several years before my mother became ill. I didn't really know there was a particular problem with how I was living until she came for a week's visit. She graciously helped out around the house and with the children while I worked at home. One morning, though, I walked through the kitchen and stared at the refrigerator, which she had just given the cleaning of its life. I looked at it, standing there shining in my kitchen. *Hmm. I hadn't even noticed it was that dirty.* There was also something else I hadn't noticed.

"Did you know, my dear, that you are a pack rat?" my mother asked.

"Me? A pack rat? Do you mean you think I keep too much stuff?"

"Honey, you have so much stuff you don't even know what you have. Let's clear out and clean out. Do you mind?" *Did I mind? Would you mind if I gave you a million dollars?*

"Of course not!" She began to clean out cupboards, organizing as she went. I walked back into my office, musing over this new thought. *Me a pack rat? Interesting.*

What made this possibility interesting was that I had to maintain a certain level of efficiency to keep all the balls I was juggling in the air. I found running a home business and managing a busy family a real blessing in my life, and I'd had some degree of success in that. I knew what was where in my business. I had a filing system and I kept up with my organizing notebook. I even knew where the kids' shoes were (most of the time). But I was also aware that, although things were running pretty well, there were pockets of chaos in my life that ran very deep. That awareness came into clear focus during my mother's visit.

When Tim came home from work that night, he walked through the kitchen and then stopped. "What happened to the refrigerator?" he asked.

"Mother cleaned it," I replied.

"Wow!"

The funny thing was that he had not even opened it! He just

noticed from across the room that the door was shining. A new concept!

One day, my mother asked, "Does the phone always ring this much?"

"Yes," I said. "This is the usual pace around here." She just breathed a bit deeply and gave me one of those motherly glances; she didn't say anything. *Hmmm. It does ring a lot....*

As simple as that sounds, a clean refrigerator (and a husband who noticed), the realization that I was a pack rat, and a ringing (and ringing and ringing) phone marked the beginning of a turning point in my life. The following conversation clinched it.

"So, you say things are always this busy for you?" Mother asked.

"Well, not always, but it's not unusual," I answered.

"And are you happy?"

"Yes, well...I'm glad I get to be home with the children and I like what I do. Is that what you mean?"

"No. I know you're happy about that. Are you happy with your lifestyle? Are you happy with who you are as a person?" she asked.

"Ummm..." I had to think.

"You're living at such a fast pace that you can't even enjoy the fruits of your labor." Then she told me about a letter from my aunt, who agreed with her.

We sat down and talked for a long time.

Later that afternoon while running an errand (there I was running again), I did something I hadn't done in ages. I drove slowly. I drove under the speed limit and let everyone else be the first to take off after the light turned green. *So this is how it feels.* Then I stopped and bought a key chain proclaiming my new goal: *"Slow Down."*

For me, the unwinding process after years of very tightly-wound wires was not an overnight accomplishment. Here's a case in point. About this same time I found out that I needed minor surgery (minor only if you're not the one on the operating table). My doctor told me he wanted to schedule the surgery within a few days.

"I can't, Doctor, because I'm scheduled to go to Canada for a Christian television interview." (And I already told you about *that* trip!) He suggested the next week.

"Oh, I can't then because I have a speaking engagement," I continued.

"And," he replied in a fatherly fashion, "I'm sure you've got something scheduled after that. We need to do the operation next week." As I obligingly consented, he added, "There comes a point when you must slow down and take care of yourself first!"

There it was again—"slow down." The message was crystallizing for me, but it took the insight of others to help me see that my lifestyle needed to change. The physical, emotional, and work pressures were taking their toll, and the words of my mother and my doctor got me doing some soul-searching. *Is this joyful living?* I had thought so. I enjoyed being home with my children. I enjoyed my homemaking and my work. But I did not enjoy them all at once and at the speed I was doing them. There were too many etceteras, and there was too much running. My complicated lifestyle had made me settle for far less joy than I knew was possible. I'd said yes too many times and had lost sight of a simpler lifestyle and its rich joys.

Immediately I took a few steps toward simplicity. I had a big garage sale and sold or gave away more junk than I'd realized we'd collected. I reorganized my home—with Mom's help. I dropped some of the responsibilities that I could drop and put many of the things that crowded my life on hold. I began moving toward a simpler life.

I also began to change my thinking, for the discipline of a lifestyle of simplicity starts there. From my journal:

> Lord, show me how to open up blocks of time for my family to find each other again and for me to find joy.

Another entry:

> It's taking me quite some time to slow down. I'm so used to being in a hurry everywhere I go because I was packing so much into such a short time. Even when I shouldn't have been in a rush, I usually ended up that way. But worse than that—I had that attitude.

The hurried mentality.

I drove in a hurry—I always had a knot in my stomach trying to get some place.

I ate in a hurry—often fast food.

I talked in a hurry—Why not if the brain can listen eight times faster than I can speak?

I even hurried at home—"Hurry up, kids!"

Now I'm making better choices. I find myself realizing when there's not enough time to fit "this" in before "that." I'm hurrying less and relaxing more. After a few months of this, I'm beginning to notice changes. I don't always search for that maximum speed in a minimum of time. I walk slower. I lingered at a neighbor's house yesterday. But the best thing was when I realized that I was beginning to slow down in my lifestyle and in my mind. While driving, I hit the brakes slightly in order to be sure to catch the approaching yellow-then-stop light. I smiled at my progress. However, I really don't talk any slower. I guess some things never change.

Later, I was on a radio broadcast with Dr. James Dobson discussing my book *Working at Home*. As Brenda Koinis, Posy Lough, and I talked about some of the pitfalls of working at home, Dr. Dobson said something that I had lived: "The subtleties of overcommitment never cease to amaze me. Just when you think you've gotten your time schedule under control, you say yes three times when you should have said no—and the next thing you know your own successes become a trap!" Boy, did I know that!

When we say yes too many times, we get away from a life of simplicity. Know the value of a "yes," but remember there is also value in a "no." And evaluate the timing of an opportunity. As Anne Ortlund puts it in *Disciplines of a Beautiful Woman*, one of the best ways to seriously simplify one's lifestyle is to learn to "eliminate and concentrate."[4] That's how I began my simplifying process: I eliminated the unimportant so I could concentrate on present priorities. As we simplify, we can also ask ourselves, "When do we have enough?" As we saw in Chapter 4, more is not always better; sometimes "more" just complicates life. Determining what is enough—in our home, our activities, our income—can be a starting step toward simplicity.

Disciplines of the Whole Person

Once we're taking steps toward a simpler life, we will be better able to work on the next lifestyle discipline—which I call "disciplines of the whole person." We can live a life of joy when we feed, exercise, and rest our mind, body, and spirit.

• Disciplines of the Mind

As we've already discussed, the mind is directly linked to the emotions. If we want to feel joyful, we must discipline our mind by carefully controlling what we put into it. We've heard it before: garbage in, garbage out. If we input trash—things that are disturbing or fruitless, sinful or negative—we will dwell on that trash. That's why Paul tells us to dwell on whatever is true, honorable, right, pure, lovely, of good repute, excellent, and worthy of praise (Philippians 4:8). That clearly limits what we should allow ourselves to see and hear.

For instance, I abhor the murder-and-mayhem portion of the local news, in spite of the fact that I have worked in that profession. I like keeping up with current events, but I really don't need to know the gory details of all the horrors that occur in my city each day. Television images take you to the scene and, frankly, I'd rather be just about anywhere than at some of the scenes that are piped into my living room every night in vivid color.

Years ago, when I worked in television news, I happened on a terrible head-on car accident that had just occurred. I saw a colleague's van and camera lights and I stopped. When I got to the scene, there were three injuries. When I left the scene, there were three fatalities. About to do an on-camera report, I thought, "I can't stand being here. Does anybody at home really need to be here either?" I didn't think so.

Today I carefully guard what I put into my mind and the minds of my children. Like the psalmist, my prayer is, "Turn my eyes away from worthless things" (Psalm 119:37 NIV). So, when I do choose to get my news from television, I keep the remote nearby and my younger children out of the room. One family I know guards the input in their home, particularly the movies they see, by asking, "Would I want Jesus to see this with me?" When they began asking this question, their viewing habits changed, making it easier for them to dwell on the honorable and excellent. And hear what the prophet Isaiah promises when we think on those things and limit the negative: "He who stops his ears from hearing about bloodshed, and shuts his eyes from looking upon evil; he will dwell on the heights" (Isaiah 33:15b,16a).

Some women, however, get caught up in the addictive time-waster and killjoy of daytime television. What good comes from the provocative revolving-bed soap operas and talk-show trash that fill the airwaves? These programs hardly add joy to our lives. While television offers many redeeming and informative programs, much of what is on the air simply robs us of joy. Why let input on topics like "mothers who date their daughter's boyfriends" steal your joy? I know people addicted to these shows; I've heard them hashing over these worthless subjects. When we watch these things, we can't help but dwell on them. It's human nature, but to think about them for longer than one second after the program's off is a second too long. Our lives— our thought lives—can be much richer than that.

Of course, many people aren't particularly sensitive to what is portrayed in the media, but perhaps as a nation we should be. We who are parents can shape the sensitivities of our children and we should. So guard the input carefully—be it from television, radio, movies, music, or the printed page. Trash abounds. Help your children learn the discipline of the mind by carefully selecting the input.

We mustn't merely limit the negative input. We must also supply positive input. If we want a healthy, active mind, we must feed it nourishing food, exercise it, and give it rest. We exercise as well as feed our mind when we read good books which stimulate our mind or entertain us with positive messages, listen to beautiful and edifying music, engage in thoughtful conversation, and learn something new. Learning a new task or skill actually does exercise our brain. In fact, some researchers have found that the people who live long lives and remain mentally alert are those who continue to engage their minds with challenging stimuli. Just ask Audrey Stubbart. She works a 40-hour week as a proofreader and columnist with *The Examiner* in Independence, Missouri. Audrey's smiling face was recently on the cover of *Parade* magazine—Audrey is 100 years old.[5]

As important as feeding and exercising your mind is giving it rest. We need to stop worrying and stewing about things we can't help or change (Matthew 6:25-34). At the close of each day, when it's time for our body to rest, we need to turn to God with our worries and cares, trust them all to Him, and let our mind rest, too. Besides being an act of obedience, this step of trust is an act of mental rest, a move toward freedom from burdens, and, therefore, a step toward knowing joy.

• Disciplines of the Body

Sometimes we struggle with feeling joyful simply because we don't feel well physically, and that can be directly related to some of our lifestyle choices. When we discipline our bodies by getting the proper amount of rest, exercise, and good food, we feel better physically as well as emotionally. Research reveals that people who get close to eight hours of sleep a night, engage in some type of regular physical exercise, and eat a reasonably healthy diet are happier than those who do not do these things.

Now before you happy, sedentary, junk-food-junkie nightowls ask what all this has to do with Mama's happiness, I must tell you that I have science on my side—but one foot in your camp! I like to stay up late, sleep in, and eat nachos *occasionally*, and that doesn't mean I'm living less joyfully. In fact, sometimes those things add a sparkle to my day. But in terms of my lifestyle I strive to sleep as much as I need, eat my veggies and grains, and get the ol' heart pumping as often as I can. Remember, we are talking about lifestyle disciplines here—choices that we live out habitually.

> *Obedience is the seed of joy.*
>
> ~Gloria Gaither

To begin you need to ask some questions. How much sleep do you routinely get? How many hours does your usual night's sleep last? Some people can function well on about five hours of sleep a night while others need nine or ten, but the average amount needed is eight hours per night. Some sources suggest that if we consistently need an alarm clock to wake up, we are somewhat sleep deprived—which is no shock to the millions of busy women who burn the candle on both ends in order to meet all the demands of their day. As most of us know, "A bad night [of sleep] leaves you with slower reaction times, poorer concentration, and a smaller pool of energy from which to draw the next day."[6] According to some researchers, sleep allows our body tissues a chance to rest after a day's use; others say it restores brain function. Whatever is happening while we snooze, a good night's sleep is the difference between awakening ready to seize the day or ready to seize the innocent bystander who gets between you and the coffeepot. To seize the day, seize enough sleep.

And once you're up, make time for exercise—that wonderful activity that we love to hate. Although some people simply love it and others just hate it, exercise has the ability to keep us feeling well, functioning well, and looking well. If we could ingest exercise in pill form, people would probably stand in line for hours and pay big bucks to buy the benefits contained in the bottle. The bad news is that there is no pill, but the good news is that the benefits of exercise are available to anyone willing and able to do it.

As those of us who have overcome inertia know, regular and moderate exercise increases energy; improves overall health; reduces stress, the "blues," and the risk of some diseases; boosts our immune system; increases resistance to some infection; revs up our metabolism; helps us sleep better; and elevates our mood. Studies have shown that people who exercise have improved moods and higher scores on the "happiness tests" (those tests which measure psychological well-being). All that from exercise—when we "just do it."

And did you know that we can turn an energy deficit into a surplus when we exercise? Paradoxically, using energy increases energy. That's especially true for aerobic exercise because it wakes up the nervous system and boosts our metabolism, giving us a good supply of energy and reducing our fatigue. This increased metabolism helps us burn more fat and calories, and these effects continue for hours after we exercise. The more consistent and long-term our exercising is, the greater our overall physical fitness level, which further increases our stamina and improves our health.

But knowing the benefits of exercise doesn't necessarily make it easy to start exercising. Many of us start exercise programs so we'll have better health and greater energy—only to throw the running shoes under the bed and use our cycling machine as an expensive clothes hanger. In fact, just 40 percent of Americans exercise regularly and only half of them do so vigorously enough to benefit aerobically.[7] What can you and I do personally to improve these statistics? The most important thing is finding an activity we like that fits our style, schedule, and needs. Choosing an exercise that we enjoy and can do regularly determines whether we will stick with it or not. Now, let's consider how we'll fuel that exercise.

We want to feel good. We want boundless energy. We want health. And we want it from the drive-through window when we grab a quick bite as we zip down the fast lane. Our love for the "typical American diet" coupled with our busy lives keeps many of us from fueling our bodies for optimum health and energy with that simple thing called...good food. It's not so much what we're eating that's so terrible. It's what we're *not* eating. As a nation, we opt for fast foods over good foods, get caught in the diet trap (lose weight, gain it back, lose weight, gain it back), and eat sporadically until our growling tummies and low blood sugar make us choose food that's less than the best.

I'm no nutritionist, but I know someone who is and, despite my share of driving through for Jack's "two tacos for a buck," even I can be taught. In *Food for Life*, nutritionist and author Pam Smith says, "The key to healthy eating is having the right perspective. You have to defeat the lie that says [healthy] food is boring and tasteless. Eating well is not denying yourself. It's giving yourself a precious gift. Eating well is not focusing on foods to avoid; rather it is focusing on the fresh, flavorful and fun foods that give the body energy and health—and give you better moods!"[8]

Pam encourages us to eat the right foods in the right balance and at the right time so we can have energy, think clearly, and manage the stress of our life—in her phrase, "walk in well-ness." As she declares in some of her "Secrets for Staying Fit, Fueled and Free," "Eating is better than starving—eat early, of-ten, balanced, and lean. Water is the beverage of champions—drink eight to ten glasses a day. Variety is the spice of life—a healthy variety includes good food choices over time, including whole grain, low-fat meals full of a mix of brightly colored fruits and veggies."[9]

Remember it's not the single meal that counts or even that week of meals. It's the lifestyle that counts. A lifestyle of junk food makes us feel like junk, and that inevitably leads to a Mama who ain't happy!

• Disciplines of the Spirit

Just as we must feed, exercise, and rest our bodies for op-timum efficiency, we must feed, exercise, and rest our spirit. A regular and healthy diet for our spirit gives us the solid nour-ishment we need to be God's people. We need both the milk of the Word and, as we mature, solid food (Hebrews 5:12-14). Without such nutrition, we would dry up and blow away; an anorexic spirit destroyed from malnutrition.

Poring over God's Word, praising Him, and praying to Him (the three P's for becoming intimate with God discussed in chapter 7) feed our spirit and keep it healthy. When we do these things as a discipline in our life, we are ensuring long-term growth and developing a heart of devotion as well as an appetite for being with the Lord. (After all, we usually don't need to be reminded to feed our bodies when we're hun-gry!) Adopting the three P's as a discipline will help keep us from neglecting our spiritual food by whetting our appetite for time with our heavenly Father.

Regularly reading God's Word and hearing it taught feeds our spirit and is vital to our growth. Involvement in a church that teaches the Bible, participation in group Bible studies, and lis-tening to Christian radio, television, books, tapes, music, and videos can nourish our spirit and feed our soul. Once, shortly af-ter we moved to a new city and before we became active in a church, a friend knew that I was rather lonely and could use some supplemental feedings. For a time, she sent me tapes of some sermons and guest speakers at her church with the note, "Thought you might like some extra nourishment." Another friend and I frequently trade cassettes of Christian radio programs or speakers.

Now, I'm not suggesting that we immerse ourselves in Christian culture and it alone. Much in the world that isn't necessarily labeled "Christian" is worth our attention. The Academy Award-winning film *Chariots of Fire* isn't a "Christian" movie, but it has a great message and is extremely well done. Wonderful music, literature, and art exist beyond the realm of what's labeled "Christian." After all, God is the Author of *all* creativity, and He certainly doesn't need a label. However, we shouldn't be surprised if we find ourselves feeling a little distant from God when we don't go to church, listen only to secular music, limit our reading to trashy bestsellers, and are undiscriminating about our entertainment. In that case, it's no wonder our spirit becomes anemic. Enjoy life—but watch the diet!

At the same time we're feeding our spirit God's Word, we can exercise our spirit through the discipline of thankfulness. Each of us can discipline ourselves to be grateful to God and to express that gratitude with thanksgiving. Developing this discipline will do more for increasing your joyfulness than any of the other disciplines combined, and it starts with a grateful attitude. I first learned that when I was a young teenager standing in line for an amusement ride at Astroworld with my best friend Teresa and her older sister Diana. While we stood in the hot sun complaining about some adolescent catastrophe, Diana reminded us that the apostle Paul was able to rejoice because he had a thankful attitude. She encouraged us to memorize this passage:

> Rejoice in the Lord always; again I will say, rejoice! Let your forbearing spirit be known to all men. The Lord is near. Be anxious for nothing, but in everything by prayer and supplication with *thanksgiving* let your requests be made known to God (Philippians 4:4-6, emphasis added).

Note that Paul doesn't say rejoice *for* everything, but *in* everything.

I never forgot that verse or lesson. Both are permanently seared in my mind—a video snippet of two teenagers standing in the middle of an amusement park and making up a song to memorize that bit of Scripture. Two lives were influenced that day because of one young woman's willingness to teach the value of a thankful heart.

LaJewyl S. is a Bible-study leader prone to depression and the blues. She used to wake up with a sense of foreboding, but became aware of the value of gratitude in fighting that feeling. What began as an antidote for her struggle has become a discipline of thankfulness. Every morning before her feet hit the floor, LaJewyl thanks God for seven things. Initially her thankfulness centered on material things, but as she grew in this discipline, she moved on to express gratitude for spiritual blessings. "This is the way," says LaJewyl, "that I make sure I begin the day with a grateful heart and practice the presence of the Lord the first thing in the morning." Thankfulness moves us beyond ourselves and into the place of joy and contentment.

Expressing thankfulness as LaJewyl did is a spiritual exercise. So is walking in obedience to what we learn in God's Word. Although that obedience doesn't always come easily, it can bear wonderful fruit of joy. Julie M. writes, "When the Lord directed me to stay home with the children, I felt a joyfulness that I cannot describe. I walked around for many weeks smiling all the time. I know my obedience (doing what I knew the Lord wanted me to do) played a large part in the joy I felt." Some of our deepest joys are in simple, hidden places of obedience. Maybe you know that truth from your own experience. If so, keep exercising—if not, start!

Obedience is indeed a spiritual discipline, but so is rest. We let our spirit rest when we are quiet with the Lord. God calls us to such quiet and promises to meet us there: "Be still, and know that I am God" (Psalm 46:10 NIV). He also tells of the rest we can find in the shadow of His wings (Psalm 91:1). What a precious invitation to those of us (to all of us) who are too busy, too frazzled, too burdened, too joyless.

Feeding, exercising, and resting the mind, body, and spirit—these are the disciplines of lifestyle. These are disciplines which lead to joy.

2. The Disciplines of Labor

People who greatly enjoy life tend to be those who are involved in the disciplines of labor—service and meaningful work—and balance those with fun.

Meaningful Work

Have you ever known the drudgery of having to pry yourself out of bed in the morning to face another day of doing work that you hate? Perhaps once in their lifetime everyone should have (briefly) at least one job like that in order to fully appreciate a more satisfying job and to better understand the many people who hate what they do. Feeling good about the work you do every day is certainly a big joy booster (more on this in chapter 13), but even more important to our level of joy than enjoyable work is meaningful work. Studies have shown that people who engage in interesting, challenging work that has meaning for them are happier—even if that choice of occupation means making less money. Work that is at times hard and unpleasant but valuable to the individual worker can be a great source of happiness.

Now it's been said that some people play at their work and work at their play. Although "playing at work" suggests a poor work ethic and a poor way to live, the idea is not all bad. When we find a way to work that has elements of play in it for us, we get caught in that wonderful state that some psychologists call "flow"—that marvelous spot of being challenged enough to fully captivate our mind but not enough to become frustrated. It's when we get so caught up in what we're doing that we lose track of time.

People who flow in their work as well as in their play are among the happiest, according to some reports. So consider what Herb Kelleher, chairman and CEO of Southwest Airlines, says about work in a *Fortune* magazine cover story entitled "America's Best CEO?" This hard-working man, much loved by his employees, thinks critics who accuse him of being a workaholic miss the point. He doesn't consider his job work. "I used to tell them if your vocation is your avocation as well—it's what you enjoy—it's not stress. It's not work. It's fun."[10] Happy people pursue work that has meaning, engages them, and is challenging without being overwhelming. What do you see when you look in that mirror?

Service

To give away some of our self in an act of service is another source of joy and another discipline of labor. When we serve others, we lose sight of ourselves for a moment and contribute to the good of someone or something else. The wonderful by-product of serving with a proper motive and pure heart is that helping others feels good. A life of great service is indeed a life of great joy.

And there are countless ways to serve. Several people I know spent their Thanksgiving working together at a local soup kitchen, and one of them just beamed as she told of the blessing it was to serve those appreciative people. My friend Sharon opened her home for over a year to a young woman in a crisis pregnancy. While sharing her faith with others wasn't difficult for Sharon, living out that faith on a daily basis in front of a stranger presented its challenges, but she says she wouldn't trade that experience for the world. "Even though it was hard, uncomfortable, and stretching at times, there was a deep measure of joy as only God can give because there was visible fruit. I got to see a young woman's new faith in Christ grow, and there was great joy in the baby's birth. The real joy I felt through that ministry, though, was God working in me."

I could offer countless other stories of service, ministry, and altruism from all over the world, examples of people serving where they can and in whatever ways they can—from building churches in Mexico to working in their own church nursery.

Like these people, you and I can serve our fellow human beings, the body of Christ, and Christ Himself when we keep our eyes and heart open to others and allow God to use us right where we are. Both joy and contentment come when we serve where God has us, as Sue J.'s life testifies. She and her husband,

The truest joy is in obedience. To feel His smile and to know that He is pleased—ahh, this is real joy.

~Kellie M.

Max, had moved from California to Tennessee in hopes of finding better work in the car business. Unfortunately, it took Max a while to learn he wasn't cut out to sell cars. He'd tell people, "This is a lovely car, but you can't afford it." Since that sales approach didn't help pay their bills, Sue and Max moved in with family and later into a beat-up, bug-infested trailer—the only place they could afford.

The night they moved in, as Sue sat in the middle of the clutter rocking her five-month-old baby, she saw a roach scurry across her pillow on the mattress. Rocking back and forth, she repeated over and over, "Please, God, don't make me live here. Please, God, don't make me live here." The next day she got busy deinfesting and scouring the little place, trying to make it as nice as possible. As she sought the Lord, she knew that God wanted her to live there until it was okay with her if she never left. And that is exactly how long she stayed there.

What made it okay was the purposeful work she found in serving *right where she was*. When Sue began to look for why God had put her where she was and what she could do there, she saw her neighbors, some of whom were far below the poverty level:

> I started reaching out, looking for meaningful service right there. Whatever I could do, I did. I used my cake decorating skills to bake for them. I listened to their stories, taught them God's Word, and befriended and counseled them. I jumped whole-hog into service and learned that God can use me where I am and can take all of my circumstances and shape and mold me into a unique servant. He said, "Sue, stop worrying about ministering to the hurting women around the world. Go next door!" So I did. In the process I found joy and contentment.

Where does God have you? What can you do for Him, His people, His kingdom right from where you are? That kind of service brings unbelievable joy.

Fun

It's important to work hard and to serve others, but it's also important to remember to have fun. For the sanguine socialites among us, this is among their life's mission, but many melancholy types wouldn't know fun if it came up, painted their face, and gave them a balloon. Of course, a balance between the two is the goal. Is your life in balance? Do you make time for active leisure? So-called happiness studies say that people who enjoy life make time for active forms of leisure that engage their skills. Sometimes all we seem to have the energy for is zoning out in front of the TV, but much more pleasurable is leisure that's somewhat active, that engages us or our skills in some way instead of just happening to us or in front of us. So turn off the tube and take a dance class, read a classic, rollerblade, plant some flowers, or play a game. More on this in the next chapter. Right now, just remember that the disciplines of labor are fulfilling work, service for the Lord, and time for fun.

3. The Disciplines of Love

If "the disciplines of a joyful person" sounded like an oxymoron, "disciplines of love" sounds even more like one. By the phrase "disciplines of love" I simply mean the disciplines of nurturing those whom we love, and those disciplines do make for joy.

Social psychologists have found that people who are truly fulfilled and happy in life are actively involved in loving relationships. As Ann H. says, "I lack joy when I lack intimacy." An intimate relationship with those we feel close to greatly increases joy in this life. (As we know if we've ever been in love!) One article reported, "Sadly, our increasingly individualistic society suffers from impoverished social connections, which some psychologists believe is a cause of today's epidemic levels of depression....In contrast to the interdependence valued in Asian societies, Americans celebrate independence."[11] While Hillary Clinton highlights that kind of interdependence in her book *It Takes a Village,* and "family values" are now politically correct, there is still some truth to Ronald Reagan's words that we live in "the age of the individual." This individualism makes being closely connected to people we love and nurturing those relationships so important.

Among those relationships which need our nurturing and which contribute to our joy is a lasting, loving marriage. Research shows that "married people are happier and live longer than those who are single, widowed, divorced, or who never married."[12] Reports also reveal that people who have several close, supportive friends with whom to share their lives are healthier and happier than those who don't.

Practicing the disciplines of love requires that we give priority to those whom we love and take time to nurture our relationship with them. We can do that by spending time with them, looking for ways to do things for them, not taking them for granted, letting them know we appreciate them, being kind, and sharing with them our thoughts and dreams, our hurts and hopes, to name just a few possibilities. Nurturing a relationship doesn't always come naturally, and that's where the discipline comes in.

Our Spouse: Work schedules of late have meant a season of too little "together time" in my marriage, and I have felt its withering effects. But Tim and I are dedicated to the discipline of nurturing our relationship, even when it's hard. Recently, my comment of "I feel like we don't know each other very well lately" was met by his "We don't. How could we?" That lonely moment led to a wonderful weekend together. But it might not have without the discipline of commitment and time.

Make time for your husband. Schedule a regular date night or just be at home together with the children in bed and the newspaper and bills out of sight. One woman I know couldn't afford a night out with her husband, so she put a lace tablecloth on a card table in their bedroom for a romantic, candlelight dinner. They followed that with a walk in the woods, holding hands and discussing their dreams. We can and must make time to nurture our relationship with our husband even if our days are long. Once after the children were in bed, for instance, Tim set up a tape player on the patio, and we enjoyed soft music, hot coffee, and a few minutes of time alone under the stars. Moments like that are free, don't take long, and can be fit into the busiest of schedules—and they nurture a marriage.

Our Children: We nurture our relationship with our children by regularly spending time really connecting with each child. We need to talk *with* them, not just *to* them. We need to know what they're doing as well as what's going on in their heads and hearts. Robin M. says, "One of the principles I live by in practicing joy is to be sure I spend one-on-one time with each family member throughout the week." More on children to come.

Our Friends: Years ago, a close friend and I were discussing our priorities, noting how women's priorities can differ. We went down the list.

"Let's see. God, husband, children, and so on....Wait a minute. I forgot friends. I've got to fit that in," she said.

"Well, that's not on my list. Who has time for shopping and lunch out with friends when I have a baby and all my other responsibilities?" I replied.

Yet "friends" was (and is) on my list. As a mother of young children, I didn't do many of the daytime activities that some of my friends enjoyed together, or spend hours on the phone, or go places with them in the evenings, but I did make time for that one special friend, and my life has been richer for it. We all need someone who is our "kindred spirit," a soul who knows us well, loves us still, and connects with those things dear to our heart. Nurturing such a close friendship and finding fellowship with other believers adds immeasurable joy to life.

If right now you are more familiar with loneliness than the joy of close connections, reach out! Don't sit around waiting for someone else to do the reaching. Instead of wondering why no one brings us cookies when we move into a new neighborhood or invites us to do anything when we visit a new church, we can do the cookie baking and the inviting. In fact, one of the biggest reasons we stay lonely and miss this joy is that we don't reach out—even if no one is reaching out to us. Tim Hansel puts it well in his book *Through the Wilderness of Loneliness:*

> Waiting for the world to come to you is a lonely place. I admit that it takes a lot of courage sometimes to reach out to others, but it is critical that we do so. Reaching out to others is the greatest evidence of the Power that lives within us. Joy is doubled when it's

divided. It is a great maxim that if you can't find joy, then the best thing to do is to give it away to someone else who is more in need than you are. The joy will then double back to you in ways that you never expected.[13]

You don't believe Tim's words? Try it out! Take the risk and reach out to a new or old friend—and take the time to nurture your relationship with your husband and your children as well. These disciplines of love bring love to us as well as joy.

Practice Makes Perfect (At Least It Helps!)

Joy itself is never something we can practice, but we can practice living a lifestyle that includes disciplines conducive to joyfulness. And like many things, when we practice we improve. So let me introduce you to Jovial Jane and the Fruitful Five. No, that's not a new rock group. It's my practical "joy barometer." If you're lacking joy in your life, try quizzing yourself on the Jovial Jane Fruitful Five to see if you're living the FINER life. Ask yourself: "Am I getting enough **f**un, **i**ntimacy, **n**utrition, **e**xercise, and **r**est?" (That's not necessarily the order of importance, but the initials spell a good word that way!) Being out of balance in any of those areas can explain why Mama ain't happy.

The disciplines of the mind, body, and spirit could be interpreted as a call to "live perfectly and know joy." But I'm not saying, "Watch a *Pollyanna* video, train for a marathon, eat rice cakes, go to church, and live a careful, safe life—and you'll find joy." We all know better than that. We can be joyful if we eat chocolate every day. We can even be joyful if we never go to bed before 1 A.M. But if Jovial Jane watches trash-TV, gets four hours of sleep a night but never any exercise, and habitually feeds her body and spirit junk food, it's no wonder she struggles to be joyful.

And sometimes I struggle, too. I told you earlier that this isn't an "I have arrived" book; it's an "I'm on the path too" book. Even as I wrote this chapter, I was struggling with some of these disciplines. (Old habits die hard.) The coffeepot brewed gallons

Jovial Jane's Fruitful Five
The FINER Life
Five Questions to Ask If Your Joy Has Fizzled

1. **F**un

   Am I making time for things that are enjoyable in my life? Am I balancing meaningful work and service with fun?

2. **I**ntimacy

   Am I nurturing my intimate relationships? Am I making time for God, making my spouse a priority (making time for talking and for sex), communicating with my children, and enjoying fellowship with a kindred spirit?

3. **N**utrition

   Am I eating enough good food to fuel my body? Am I getting my five-plus-eight a day? (That's five fruits and vegetables plus eight glasses of water!) Am I feeding my mind a healthy diet of books, movies, television, and music? Am I feeding my spirit with time with the Lord? Am I poring over His Word, praising Him, and praying to Him?

4. **E**xercise

   Am I recharging my energy, fitness, health, and moods with regular exercise four to six times a week? Am I exercising my mind by learning one thing new each day? Am I exercising my spirit by being thankful and walking in obedience?

5. **R**est

   Am I getting enough sleep? Do I awake rested and refreshed—or could I use an extra hour or two of sleep? Am I trusting God with my cares and concerns so that my mind can rest? Am I resting my spirit by regularly sitting quietly with God?

of caffeine, the midnight oil flowed, and, as I wrote about eating good food, I was struck with the sharp desire to jump in the car for those two tacos for a buck.

Despite the struggle to maintain these lifestyle disciplines, I am more convinced than ever that practicing them contributes to a life of joy. After years of keeping a very simple schedule, I found last fall to be quite busy. It would have been easy to get right back into the harried, hurried, joy-challenged life that I described earlier, but I worked very hard at these disciplines. Among other things, I ran or walked consistently, and each day I nourished my spirit with God's Word and my body with a good diet. And guess what? Instead of overwhelming stress and a Mama who wasn't happy, I was filled with joy! Even when life gets busy, I keep simplicity the goal—and you can, too. And during those busy times, don't neglect these disciplines. They really do add joy!

> $\mathcal{I}$ find joy in being able to rest in the Lord without worry in spite of difficult circumstances.
>
> ~Nancy K.

So what's the first step you can take to begin practicing disciplines that encourage joy? Where can you start? Perhaps with the issue that most strongly touched your heart as you read this chapter. When we simplify our life; when we feed, exercise, and rest our mind, body, and spirit; when we live with a balance of meaningful work, service, and fun; and when we nurture our intimate relationships, we are taking practical steps toward a more joyful life. Join me in the journey!

❧ 11 ❧

Laugh and Lollygag
It Lightens the Load

I grabbed my keys and headed out the door to pick up my children from school. I was thankful for a break in my difficult day. *I'll enjoy the drive,* I thought. But then I discovered that my car was so dead that the starter didn't even click, let alone turn over. One of my four "meddlers" had left a light on in the car overnight. I called a friend to help me jump it, but it still wouldn't start so she loaned me her car. No problem. I knew I could zip over and get the kids and zip right back. She asked me to drop off Teresa, her cleaning lady, at the bus stop on the way back. No problem.

I picked up my three school-aged children who crowded into the hot car along with Teresa and her baby. The car trouble had made me late to get my children, and Teresa asked me in broken English if we were going to be late for her bus. It was almost 90 degrees outside, and there were four children and two adults in a tiny car with no air conditioning and 260,000 miles of wear and tear. I could sense a problem heading my way.

As I was about to peak the hill of the freeway overpass, the car's get-up-and-go got up and went. I was stranded on an incline in the middle lane. Since the car wouldn't go forward, I had only one option—backwards. I made sure everyone had fastened their seatbelts and then eyed my goal: the gas station at the bottom of the hill behind me. I explained my plan and my passengers said, "You're going to do WHAT?" I assured them it would be "no problem" as long as everyone driving forward in the lane behind me got out of the way.

With sweaty palms and a racing heart, I rolled down my window and, like a crazy woman, made wild arm circles, sign language for "Everybody get out of the way!" Miraculously, they did until one car pulled up behind me while I was still coasting towards the station, forcing me to brake short of my goal. *What is she doing?...Oh, helping me.*

She offered me a quarter, and I called my friend to tell her the great news about her car. She said, "No problem. I'll borrow Kay's car and be right there." When she got to Kay's house, she was red-faced and breathing hard. Kay said, "Lois, did you run all the way here?"

"No," Lois gasped. "I rode my bike, but both the tires were flat."

We were certainly having our problems.

When Lois got within a block of us, she started honking the horn in "here I am to save the day" fashion and, for some reason, that struck Teresa funny and she started to laugh (which was amazing considering she'd just missed her bus). Laughing knows no language barrier, and she got me tickled. One of the children said, "Why are you laughing? I don't see a thing funny about this!" Then Lois told us about the flat tires and that did it—we all roared!

Two broken cars and two flat bike tires, hot children, frustrated women, and a missed bus—we had definite reasons to lose our cool, but we didn't. While teetering between the "I'm going to be joyful" and "I'm gonna lose it!" options, we decided to jump on the joy side and see the humor in the situation. Laughter softened our tough afternoon and made a great memory for my kids. It also gave our friends in our small Bible study an opportunity—at my expense—for a good howl. Somehow they found great humor in picturing me (and, I might add, imitating me) waving like mad while I coasted backwards downhill with sweaty, squished, scared passengers. But three cheers for laughter! It certainly helps lighten our load!

What Is Laughter?

Laughter is a "diaphragmatic, epiglottal spasm,"[1] of course! Can you imagine whispering that to your children the next time they start giggling in church: "Psssst...kids! Quit those diaphragmatic, epiglottal spasms right now!" They'd either stop immediately, wondering what language you were speaking, or they'd roll under their pew in greater hysterics. You might want to try that line at home to be on the safe side.

If you're joyful, you will laugh (at some point!) because laughter is an expression of joy. And it's also a whole lot of fun! *The Women's Study Bible* says, "Laughter is one way that the Creator gives us to switch gears and punctuate the monotony with joy....Humor is an exit from the mundane road of life...a simple, reasonable prescription for some of life's problems and most of its tedium."[2] After we've washed our fifteenth load of laundry in a week, it helps to laugh when we discover we've accidentally turned all of our husband's underwear pink and the children just dressed the dog in some of the finally clean, momentarily folded clothes.

Laughter acts as a much-needed diversion amid life's trials. When life is hard, laughter helps us cope with the pain and gives us a break from it—if only for a few seconds. When we let go to laugh, we release tension and momentarily lose ourselves in the thing that tickled us. Our moments of laughter give us a mini-vacation from the problems at hand. And laughing at our own mistakes and actions keeps us from taking ourselves too seriously. These are just a few of the reasons laughter has great value.

The Value of Laughter

Read what Scripture says about laughter and the joyful heart it springs from:

A joyful heart is good medicine, but a broken spirit dries up the bones (Proverbs 17:22).

A joyful heart makes a cheerful face, but when the heart is sad, the spirit is broken (Proverbs 15:13).

> He who is of a merry heart has a continual feast (Proverbs 15:15b NKJV).

> She shall rejoice in time to come (Proverbs 31:25 NKJV. That literally means she laughs at the future, confident in God and free of worry.)

How wonderful! Life without laughter dries up our bones, so life with laughter must be good for our body. Life with laughter lifts our spirit (that's a plus) and makes our face cheerful (another plus). And how wonderful that a heart which can laugh sits at a never-ending and (yea!) calorie-free feast of the spirit. Furthermore, God created us with the ability to laugh. Why wouldn't He enjoy hearing us laugh? Clearly, laughter is good for the body, spirit, and face! And there's more!

If you hate to jog, try laughing. It will give you a workout without all the sweat, which may be why Norman Cousins calls it "internal jogging." Sustained hilarity has great aerobic benefits. One hundred laughs are equivalent to 10 minutes of rowing, according to one article. Neck, shoulder, and abdominal muscles quickly contract and release, heart rate and blood pressure go up, and breathing quickens. When the laughter stops, the blood pressure and pulse can fall to levels lower than before the glee began. When you laugh, you use the large muscle groups in your body—making it, by the way, very difficult to pick up anything very heavy. (Just try to rearrange your sofa the next time you are convulsed with hilarity!) Laughter also combats stress and is a physical release for tension. Some even say that laughter contributes to a longer life. It also increases our ability to withstand pain, thanks to the increase in endorphins (the body's natural feel-good chemical and painkiller) that comes when we laugh.[3]

Science is also seeing that laughter is healing. A hospital in Georgia designated a "laughing room" where patients could go to watch funny movies and read funny books. The hospital staff, trying to help people get well through laughter, reports that "the laughing room decreases people's need for pain medication and serves as an antidepressant."[4]

These benefits of laughter aren't news to Norman Cousins, author of *An Anatomy of an Illness*. When he was told that he had an incurable disease of the connective tissue in his body (he describes it as "becoming unstuck"), he got involved with his doctor in determining his treatment. He reasoned that if negative emotions could harm our health, why couldn't positive emotions help it? He decided to laugh as much as possible every day, and he read funny books and watched Laurel and Hardy movies and *Candid Camera* reruns to get started. A year later he was well. Whether he would have been cured anyway is unknown, but his doctors hadn't suggested that possibility when they told him his dismal prognosis.[5]

One more note from the scientific community. Those wacky scientists have a bit of difficulty studying joy (how can you duplicate it in a lab?), but they have been able to study its expression—laughter. And they have reported on its downside—if you can imagine a downside to laughter! *The Good Health Magazine* reported:

> One paper describes a man who arrived at an emergency room in Ohio after having accidentally inhaled a mild insecticide. The patient had no symptoms beyond slight numbness, tremors and uncontrollable laughter. Doctors could find no physical or neurological damage, but the man continued to laugh for 55 minutes, to the point where he complained his abdominal muscles were killing him. He was given a tranquilizer intravenously, his laughter ceased, and the doctors sent him home—no doubt with frowns of triumph plastered firmly on their faces.[6]

Perhaps these scientists are related to *Star Trek's* Data, the character

I am all in favor of laughing.... It unfreezes pride and unwinds secrecy; it makes men forget themselves in the presence of something greater than themselves....

~G.K. Chesterton,
The Common Man

who's always searching for the reason why people laugh at jokes. I say stop analyzing and simply enjoy!

Filling the Home with Laughter

In a *Christian Parenting Today* article, John Trent says, "It's a sign of wisdom to add laughter to your home. Joyful behavior actually strengthens you and your children—physically and spiritually."[7] He also suggests that it's a mainstay in close-knit homes, as a survey of teenagers and adults supports. The survey gave 20 answers to choose from in response to the question, "In addition to growing closer to Christ, what would make your family even closer than it is today?" Spending more time together was first, but second on the list was: "Adding more laughter to our home."[8] What's the laughter level in your home?

If you want to strengthen your family's health, spirit, and closeness, simply cultivate laughter in your home. Even if laughter is scarce right now, know that this joyous gift can be developed. Here are five suggestions.

1. Cultivate friends who make you laugh.

The easiest way to start laughing more is to be around people who laugh easily. Cultivate friendships with those merry souls, those folks with a great sense of humor and a ready laugh. Their laughter can be very encouraging and quite contagious. Two of my closest friends have the gift of laughter, which I greatly enjoy whenever I'm with them. They give truth to these lines from *The Book of Joy*, "Keep company with the more cheerful sort of the godly; there is no mirth like the mirth of believers.""[9]

2. Look for the humor in life.

It's everywhere. When we're open to and looking for the humor all around us, everyday life can be very funny. But sometimes we're just too busy or too grumpy to notice. It helps to have the attitude of Linda T. who said, "A lot of things strike me funny, so I laugh easily. A good laugh can make my day—or someone else's."

Kids are often a source of a good laugh. When asked what God does all day, for instance, one child answered, "Most days he builds boats. All kinds of boats. Nobody knows why."[10] Liz H. says, "We definitely laugh in our home—my kids provide all the material!" When one of my daughters was little, she watched me applying makeup and said, "Mom, I bet it's hard to do that and stay in the lines. Try real hard, though, and do your face like you did on the back of your book—it was santational!" I laughed—and then worked very hard at staying in the lines.

I once heard a story which my friend insists is true. He once saw a lady at a gas station who was pumping gas in front of him. When she was finished she went in to pay—with the nozzle still in her gas tank. After she paid, she walked to her car and drove off. Immediately the hose broke loose from the pump and flew around in the air spraying gasoline everywhere. The woman stopped, backed up, got out of her car, and casually remarked, "I hate when that happens." As if it happened often! Be alert. Life can be funny.

3. Learn to laugh at yourself.

In the words of Ethel Barrymore, "You grow up the day you have the first real laugh at yourself."[11] In the midst of the car catastrophe I described earlier, I laughed at the situation, but later that evening when I told Tim the story, I really laughed—that time at myself. I imagined how funny we must have looked stranded in the middle of traffic with me doing my best windmill imitation out the car window. Being able to laugh at myself enabled me to join in when my friends found my adventure quite amusing. So, again, be alert! You may give yourself many reasons for a good laugh!

4. Lighten up! Life can be heavy, but we don't have to be!

Sometimes we take ourselves so seriously, but getting stuck in traffic or catching your toddler smearing the last few drops of your new makeup all over her face and the floor really isn't a big deal. Just smile—and hand her a big sponge! Yet sometimes we blow such incidents all out of proportion. While we should be "of sober spirit" about our earthly and spiritual responsibilities (1 Peter 5:8), the Bible says a lot more about being joyful than it does about being sober. After all, Christ came that we might know fullness of joy. In light of that fact, I think God must sometimes sit in the heavens and laugh (or cry!) at our mixed-up priorities and our concern about things which are unimportant in the big picture. That project or deadline that's weighing us down seems so all-important, but is it in God's scheme of things? He may be looking down on us, saying, "Lighten up, my dear child. Remember that my burden is light" (Matthew 11:30). *Translation:* Don't sweat the small stuff.

5. **Foster an atmosphere of laughter in your home.**

Create opportunities to laugh as Mary H. does. "I try to leave decks of cards around, puzzles in process, cartoon books, and other things out to encourage laughter and play. I let myself laugh. I howl over 'I Love Lucy' reruns, and I post cartoons and David Letterman's Top Ten lists on the refrigerator." Encourage laughter by having funny books and articles, videos, tapes, and cartoons in your home. The more we read, see, and hear funny things, the easier it is to laugh.

I know what a gift laughter is because I grew up in a home where corny jokes were standard fare, and my dad is keeping that tradition alive with his grandchildren. Iva H. also fosters humor in her home. She says:

> In our family, we laugh and play a lot. One time the children were all home for Christmas and the grandchildren were all in bed. All eight of the children plus Bob and I had been playing a game. It was late and everything got funnier and funnier. We were laughing at everything and getting sorer by the minute. Pretty soon Rob, our eldest, said, "I can remember when I was little and our aunts and uncles would be here. We'd be in bed trying to sleep and you all would be laughing and carrying on so loudly that I would wonder what you could possibly be doing to be laughing and having so much fun. Now I'm part of it, and I know you really don't have to be 'doing' anything. It's just the joy of being together and letting our

spirits interact." Of course, we all had to laugh again at his "sage" thoughts.

What are you doing to foster laughter in your home?

Let me add my ideas to my dad's and Iva's. In our home, we love to share cartoons with one another. Every year I buy a "Far Side" daily calendar for Tim, who frequently calls me from work to share that day's cartoon. Our children get in on the act, too. Claire recently taped a cartoon to the fridge that depicted the difference between how men and women grocery shop. The woman compares the price per unit for the best value, factoring in store brands, generics, and triple coupons. The man tastes the free sample and says, "Mmmm. Gimme eight boxes." My daughters and I chuckled and thought about putting Tim's picture over the cartoon face. As Carl Reiner said, "The absolute truth is the thing that makes people laugh."[12]

If you're struggling with being able to laugh and feel the lightness of life, remember Job 8:21: "He will fill your mouth with laughter and your lips with joyful shouting." Write this verse on an index card and stick it to your refrigerator or bathroom mirror. God filling us with laughter—isn't that a wonderful thought? So be creative, have fun, and sow seeds for laughter in your home. The harvest will be worth the effort because laughter is indeed good for the body, the spirit, and the face!

The Gift of Play

Another way to lighten life's load is to make time to play. Lollygag! If you think of lollygagging negatively (as in "wasting time"), I invite you to change your perspective. To lollygag—to enjoy the gift of play—can do much to lighten the cares of life. (Incidentally, you might want to avoid saying, "I feel like lollygagging." If you say that, people might only hear the "gagging" part and hand you an airsickness bag!)

One thing many of us can learn from children is the value of play. They don't need to be reminded to play—it's part of their nature. Often they even approach their household chores playfully. Not that most children always work cheerfully, but often without thinking they intersperse play into their work. The broom becomes a partner as they dance to a song. The dish-soap bubbles make a great beard until they decide to fling the suds into the air for the sheer pleasure of watching them "almost float." Riding down the banister is always more fun than walking down the stairs. And throwing the laundry down the stairs so they can ride the basket down is much more fun than carrying a full basket to the laundry room.

And what do we adults so often do in response to this very healthy attitude of play? "Stop, stop!" we say. "Pick up that broom and finish sweeping....Stop throwing bubbles....Walk down the stairs—don't slide...Get out of that laundry basket." Then we add our famous last words: "Right now!" These words and the attitude they reflect can teach our children that play is of little value and work is paramount. Instead, some of us would do well to learn from our kids, for not all of us know how to play like a child, completely absorbed in the fun and free to enjoy it.

In *Play: It's Not Just for Kids*, the authors describe just such a mother and child arriving at a quiet, calm beach for a weekday visit.

> I watched the boy as he shed the tightness and duty and rigid living rules that so wrap up the life of a child today. His eyes blinked and took on the loose, mind-wandering gaze that carried him everywhere at once. I watched in delight as his whole body gave over to soaking up moments of awareness with stones, shells, and water-hardened sand ridges.[13]

Carried away in the delights of the beach, the child walked and wiggled in the sand, digging in his fingers and toes. He was lost in a world of wonder, completely content—until...

> Rasping, breaking the air like a rusty knife, came his mother's irritating voice commanding him to go into the water and not to play along the beach. That's what they came for. That's what they had sacrificed money, time, and duties for. Startled, he tried to obey, but each time the hold of imaginative minutiae halted his mind and eyes and he'd slip into the world of peace.

Again and again came the rusty knife. Finally, in disgust, the mother gathered up their belongings and hauling him by one wrist, she hurried him off to the too hot, too metallic car. Under her breath she muttered about his ungratefulness and foolish response to opportunity. He followed obediently, and they drove off.

And a strange grief welled in my throat. I had seen the death of peace—the gift of peace—rejected. And I prayed for the boy, and I wept for the boy, and I heard God murmur, "I know, I know."[14]

I, too, murmur, "I know, I know" until God reminds me that I have wielded my own rusty knife. Mine may be a different style from the mom at the beach, but it's piercing just the same. Calls of "Quit dancing and pick up that broom!" or "Stop sliding down the stairs!" have the same sharp way of cutting into the beautiful spirit of play, naturally abundant in children.

Instead of cutting their play short, let's learn from our children the beauty of getting lost in the wonderment of the world. The pleasures of splashing in a puddle and picking up leaves. Lying on our backs and watching the clouds move until we're sure we can feel the earth spinning. Clinging to a merry-go-round horse and watching the world whiz by. And throwing rocks in the water for no other reason than watching them splash. We know with our head that the world is wonderful and intriguing, but too often we wait for the big, scheduled moments—that drive to the Grand Canyon or the next ski trip—to enjoy the beauty of God's creation. Instead, let's try to rediscover the child within and recapture that child's heart, a heart that's intrigued by a rain-swollen ditch or the mound of dirt in the backyard. Let's rediscover play and once again wonder at the world we live in, once again find play a way to express our joy at being alive.

The Value of Play

Some people are good at playing when the play will accomplish a purpose. Sometimes, for instance, we sit down with a child to play Monopoly because we think it's a good thing to do (which it is) and we want to spend quality time with that child (another good thing). Sometimes I play because I know that I should as a mom. I'll even get out (gag) Candy Land because I know it's fun for my child. But how long has it been since you and I played simply because *we* thought it was fun? If your assignment right now were to go play for 30 minutes, do you know what you'd do? (If I said, "Go rest," you'd have no trouble there!) Many of us need to learn that play recharges us, is part of a balanced life, is an expression and cause of joy, promotes a childlike spirit, and strengthens families.

Play recharges us. Like laughter, play has the ability to take us away from our problems and give us a momentary vacation. When we allow ourselves to be totally engaged—mind, body, and emotions—in the moment of our play, we exchange our problems for a taste of joy. Becoming absorbed in an enjoyable activity is key to preventing burnout in our less-enjoyable activities—that sense of being overwhelmed and wanting all the people in our life to take a slow boat to China. When we are frustrated to the point of burnout, we need to reconnect with our playful spirit. Doing so will help us both shift our focus from ourselves or our situation and find new energy for the challenges we face.

> $\mathcal{W}$e play games with our kids and grandkids, have water fights, and try new things. We know we're making [good] memories!
>
> ~Loretta K.

Play is part of a balanced life. All work and no play makes each of us dull. Play, like laughter, helps us keep a healthier perspective on the work and service we're doing and makes us quit taking ourselves so seriously. It helps us step out of the rat race long enough to realize that, as Lily Tomlin says, "we're still a rat." But even rats play, don't they?

Play is both an expression and a cause of joy. When we are absorbed in our play as opposed to playing out of a sense of duty, our play can be an expression of the joy that's in our heart. When we're in touch with that joy, we just might roll around in the leaves with our children on a crisp autumn day. Play can also contribute to our joy; it can cause us to feel joyful. Playing a hearty game of tennis or chasing the kids or the dog can increase our feeling of joy. Play is a way of expressing and fueling our joy at the same time.

Play promotes a childlike spirit. A childlike spirit is dear to the Father's heart. As Jesus Himself said, "Whoever does not receive the kingdom of God like a child shall not enter it at all" (Mark 10:15). Childlikeness is the state of simple trust, innocence, and sense of wonder in which our spirit is open to God. It's not to be confused with a childish spirit—an immature state which we are to avoid ("Brethren, do not be children in your thinking; yet in evil be babes, but in your thinking be mature" [1 Corinthians 14:20]). On "Insight for Living," Chuck Swindoll shared how a friend of his carries around a toy car in his pocket to remind him that he's not that far away from the child within. Play can help you stay close to your child and be childlike, not childish.

Play strengthens the family. If the family that prays together stays together, then the family that prays and plays together must not only be close, but have a great time in the process. When families take the time to enjoy one another as they play together, they strengthen their bonds in a way that nothing else can. Parents who play with their children are telling them with their actions, "I love you. I want to spend time with you. You are important"—messages which children desperately need to hear. Families that play together also create fond memories which, over the years, weave a tapestry of time and togetherness that hangs in the hearts and minds of each family member throughout their lives. To be wrapped up in the huddle of a family hug or buried in the tangle of arms and legs of a "roughhouse pile" on the floor is to be part of something greater than the fun of the moment. It is a time of bonding, another thread woven into the tapestry of the close-knit family.

Years ago, a young mother told me, "I don't have time to play with my children." She didn't say it with regret. Sadly, she made the statement in a rather factual way, reflecting her priorities. Unfortunately, even when we want to play, the true busyness that causes us to neglect playing together as a family can easily become habitual. It's all too easy to get so completely caught up in our work and grown-up life that we forget how important a mud pie and cup of pretend tea is to a child. Besides leading our children to Christ, is there anything more important than making them feel loved and special?

Recently, I walked into my six-year-old son's room. "Hi, Collin," I said.

"I need somebody to play with," he responded. Now there were three other siblings in the house. What he really meant was, "Mom, I need you to play with me."

"Sure," I said. *The laundry and other chores can wait a bit longer, I guess.* "How about building a Lincoln Log fort?" I suggested. His eyes lit up.

"A whole fort? Not just one cabin?" he asked.

"Yes," I said. We studied the picture on the box and made a less-than-perfect copy. As we balanced an Indian on Fort Smith and placed the sign on the OK Corral, I looked at my son. He was totally engrossed. I smiled. It was a moment of joy. When we finished, I asked him if he wanted to leave it up to show his dad.

"Oh yeah! He'll think it's great!" he said.

Fort Smith took center stage on his floor for several days— a testimony to play shared by a mother and her son. When I passed it, I smiled and thought, *Why don't I do that more often?* Then I silently thanked God for the blessing of play. If you don't know it already, I hope you get to know the blessings— and the benefits—of play.

Learning to Play

Some people don't take the time to play, but others genuinely don't know how to play. Unfortunately these people work at their play, and they lose its real benefits without even realizing it. These people approach their play with the same seriousness with which they approach life. To plan a picnic with the family, for instance, they make their list, check it twice, get several weather reports, inspect the location prior to the big event, and pack all the gear two days prior to leaving. Upon arriving at the predetermined spot, they check wind direction, calculate the sun's movement, note its effect on the availability of shade, and—analysis complete—determine the *perfect* site. "From 11:00 to 11:30 we'll unpack and set the picnic table. At 11:30 we can eat. At 12:00 I will set up the badminton net, Junior's field hockey set, and Susie's sand toys. Then we'll have a water and bathroom break. If we stay on schedule, we can leave right at 2:30." Is it any wonder these folks need to rest and recover from their play?

While there's great value in preparation and organization, we must not lose sight of the purpose of play—which is to have fun. Prior planning certainly helps vacations and outings run smoothly, so by all means plan, but don't be afraid to grab some fruit and cheese and jump in the car just in time to catch a magnificent sunset over the lake. Spontaneous play renews our childlike spirit. Become absorbed in the play, not in the planning and procedures.

The book *Play: It's Not Just for Kids* describes renewing play. It's when we get lost in the activity, forget any criteria for success, freely choose what we do, allow spontaneity, and feel a deep joy.[15] So let yourself be absorbed. Ignore thoughts of *I feel foolish. I must look ridiculous. Someone my age shouldn't be doing this.* You've got nothing to lose and a lot to gain! I know because I come from a family that knows how to play.

When I was little, my family gathered at Grandma and Grandpa Britton's house along with many of my dad's six brothers and sisters and their families. One summer afternoon, when they were looking for something fun to do while everyone was together, they hit on the perfect idea—grass sledding. After gathering and flattening large appliance boxes, they found a perfect long, sloping hill by the railroad trestle and began to sail down it. Never mind that sometimes the box went sideways and they continued downward! Rolling down the hill was just as much fun as sliding down it! While the little folks (including me) were home with Grandma, the big folks sledded for about two hours until everyone was worn out from the activity and laughter. Even the more reserved members of the family, not used to such frivolity, enjoyed the fun. Just hearing about that event over the years made an impact on me. *Wow. My parents and aunts and uncles sure know how to have fun. I guess you don't have to stop playing just because you grow up.*

By all means, our play needs to remain within the limits of good taste and the law, but forget about what others think is appropriate. Author and pastor Charles Swindoll finds great pleasure in riding his Harley motorcycle. He apparently doesn't worry whether people think it is appropriate for a man of his age and pastoral stature. Ride on, Reverend Swindoll! And have fun!

And you do the same! Jump on your motorcycle, make a grass sled, or find something else that floats your boat! Rejuvenating, bonding fun is to be had when we shed our self-consciousness, give ourselves wholeheartedly to our play, and find joy in the process.

Lessons for the Recreationally Challenged

1. *Pick something you enjoy that suits your needs and personality.* If you have a high-stress job, you might want to listen to music while you sit on your deck. If your job is boring or mundane, you might find play in listening to music while you *build* a deck. My point is that one person's work is another's play. Obviously different people enjoy doing different things. My husband and I are a case in point. I once asked Tim why he doesn't like amusement parks. He replied, "What's fun about standing in line with hordes of people for a ride that makes you sick?" Fun for one isn't necessarily fun for all. Find the thing that makes you smile and then...

2. *Do it!* Don't wait for chunks of leisure time. They may never come. Even if we "don't have time to play" (to picnic, garden, paint, and so on), we can still drop the broom and dance for a minute.

3. *Develop a childlike heart.* Practice having a playful spirit as you deal with everyday life. Lose yourself in the wonder. Let a child lead you—as Julie M. did one special afternoon: "I have a hard time being silly, but one time during the early fall, I went outside with my son and we jumped on the trampoline and really played. When we tired of this, we lay down on it and closed our eyes, listening to the sounds and trying to identify them. Then we played 'I Spy' with colors. It was truly a joyful moment because I allowed myself to see things through my child's eyes."

Those eyes can indeed lead to a childlike and more playful heart.

4. *Enjoy playing.* Don't fret over what you're not doing while you're playing. Freely enjoy what you are doing *right then!* As Robin M. says, "I learned from my mom that I can sit around and read with no guilt. From my dad, I learned the knack of ignoring the small stuff." Have you learned those lessons? They can help you play more freely!

5. *Plan to do it again!* Once you play, plan another session. Play can be habit forming—so let it be. Incorporate it into a balanced work/play/rest cycle in your life. You'll be glad you did—and so will your family!

Whatever play you choose, enjoy it with a childlike heart. Ride your bike, play tennis, get out the cards, plant a garden, play a game, dance, swim, paint, sew, tickle the kids, have a pillow fight...or ride a carousel. Lose yourself in the fun and watch what that does to your joy quotient!

At this point, I'm ready to follow my own advice. I just unearthed my rollerblades from the closet! And, although finishing this book has been wonderful play as well as hard work, it has edged out much of my leisure time but certainly not my playful spirit. I still managed to see a movie. I had dinner out with my husband. I laid on the floor with my eyes closed and listened to music during a few minutes of peaceful solitude. I had Claire drop her broom and we two-stepped across the kitchen, music blaring, dish-bubbles sailing, and dishes waiting (as

One of the best things about having kids is sometimes getting away with acting like one. If I take my kids to the park and go down the slide with them, we all have a great time.

~ Pat K.

they always do). I even emptied the laundry basket at the top of the stairs so the kids could slide down, but we discovered that a plastic mat is much faster and less bumpy. (Besides, it fits me better!) No rusty knife to be found here!

～12～

Candles
and Confetti
Creating an Atmosphere of Joy

W hen I was a little girl, one of my favorite places to visit was Grandma and Grandpa Britton's house. It was a place of hugs and kisses, good smells (like Grandma's biscuits) coming from the kitchen, happy family gatherings, and always much laughter. Simply decorated, their house was always clean and neat with pictures of their large brood everywhere. It was indeed a place of joy, for it was a home that reflected the joy of its inhabitants who found their joy in Christ. Grandma and Grandpa Britton are both in heaven now, but my memories of being in their home taught me that we can create an atmosphere of joy. That's what we'll look at in this chapter as we consider the ministry of joy our homes can have.

Did you even know that your home can have a ministry? In *A Place Called Simplicity,* Claire Cloninger writes that homes can and should have a ministry, a way to be used for God's kingdom: "Simple homes are gracious places that have a ministry of their own in much the same way that people do."[1] She and her husband, Spike, have a remote log cabin in Alabama, and its ministry is one of rest and refreshment. The home of a friend of hers has a wonderful ministry of prayer, but of course I especially liked another home she described:

The home of our friend Annie Hunt has a distinct ministry of joy. The wonderful, eclectic blend of furnishings, the colorful artwork, the framed photographs of Annie's children and grandchildren on every tabletop combine with the radiant personality of the hostess to present each guest with the gift of joy.[2]

Isn't that a wonderful thought—to be able to present each guest who enters your home with the gift of joy? As Marguarite M. said, "My home is my best witness of a joyful life." And wouldn't it be wonderful to live in a home which has that ministry? Well, we can! All it takes is a heart that knows joy, the willingness to put forth a little effort, and the desire to make our home reflect our heart.

The Spirit of Warmth

Picture your living room...and now imagine several lighted candles placed on the tables and a pair burning on the mantle. Besides generating a bit of light and a soft scent, the burning candles create a lovely atmosphere of warmth with their soft glow.

Candles are more than just my metaphor for a home's warm atmosphere. They really do add a charming, cozy, homey ambiance to a room. Candles gently but effectively say, "Welcome! We were expecting you!" So don't save candles just for a formal meal or a romantic evening. They can make any time more special. My children know that, and they love to light our candles—from the Yankee candle that scents a room to the tapers on the mantle—whenever company comes to visit.

At Christmastime, we were having some friends over, and Jacquelyn was helping me get ready. I decorate our home with a lot of Christmas candles during that wonderful season, and she asked to light some of them. I let her while I finished in the kitchen. About that time, the guests started arriving, so I began greeting them. At one point our friend Kirk said, "Lindsey, you've got quite a few candles going. In fact, I've never seen so many lit in one room!" Then I noticed that my daughter had lit about 40 candles. The place was aglow! She must have thought that if a few candles were good, then 40 must be hostessing brilliance in every sense of the word.

Since things were heating up quite a bit (candles add warmth both literally and figuratively!), we blew out some candles and shared a chuckle. What I remember most about that time was the joy that Jacquelyn, Claire, and I shared as we prepared our home to welcome our guests and to celebrate the season of Christ's birth. We had cooked, put a wreath on the door, and set up the nativity scene, and Jacquelyn had hung garlands that, with their little stars and circles, looked like confetti. After our guests had left, I went to blow out the candles but stopped for a moment. I looked at that "confetti" and the candles and thought what perfect symbols they were of a joyful home. Not only did they make the rooms look nice, but they represented the warmth and spirit of celebration present year-round in homes filled with the joy of the Lord.

What can we do to have our home be inviting, to have it generate a spirit of warmth and coziness whether or not candles are burning? Let me offer some basic guidelines:

Clean Up. The best first step toward creating a joyful home that has a warm, inviting spirit is to clean it well. A decorator once told me, "It doesn't matter what's in your home, expensive or not. Unless you start with a clean home, don't bother spending any money or time decorating" or—I would add, trying to create an atmosphere of joy and hospitality. A dirty house doesn't welcome people even if it's been filled with fine furnishings or elaborately decorated. Although the spirit of the people who live there is far more important than what's inside, we must begin with clean if we want our home to be inviting. Besides, clean is something that any of us can do, regardless of our budget.

But let me add that there's clean—and then there's pristine! I have known people who have been such perfectionists in this department that their houses were more like museums than homes. Every room was perfectly arranged, nothing was allowed to be out of place, and these dear people continually straightened up while you visited. That's not warmth! It may be clean—but it's cold. Then there's the other extreme. I've been greeted with great warmth and welcome and given wonderful refreshment, but struggled to find a place to sit! It was apparent that little attention or priority had been given to cleaning the house. A really dirty home is anything but warm and inviting.

The obvious goal is a balance between these two extremes. Begin with a thorough cleaning, but allow loved ones to "live" there. Then, when company comes, concentrate more on the people than on the fact that things might not be perfect (which, if you have children, is usually the case). We can strive for regular maintenance to keep our home clean, but we shouldn't always insist on "company perfection" before having people over. The folks I know never come to my house and do the white-glove test before they sit down, but I'm sure they feel more welcome in a clean house than they would in a dirty one.

Get Rid of the Clutter. If you're like most women I surveyed (and like me!), order is very important to you—and to your sense of joy. For many women, a home that's out of order is a huge negative; it detracts from their joy. Others said the same thing more positively, stating that order adds to their joy. One woman, for instance, said, "If the laundry is done and the kitchen is tidy, everything runs more smoothly. Then it's easier for me to be joyful."

The lack of order, commonly called clutter, can indeed steal a bit of our joy. In her book *Secrets to Getting More Done in Less Time,* Donna Otto says this about organization:

> We all have a basic need to be orderly. Every woman—those who are involved primarily in their homes as wives, mothers, and full-time household managers and those who work outside the home—will be able to benefit from bringing her life under control. The woman herself will be the one who will reap the rewards of being organized. She will feel better, have more energy, reach goals, and be relieved of many of the pressures she has always had to cope with. She will discover a freedom she has never had before: the freedom to use her mental energies to be creative and to have fun.[3]

And that freedom certainly adds to our joy in life.

Donna also points out that it's the things we don't do that make us tired, not the things we do.[4] I agree. Procrastination is more tiring than work because we spend so much energy worrying about and dreading the task we're avoiding (like regaining order in our home). In fact, we often spend far more energy thinking about the project than we would if we just went ahead and did whatever we're stewing over. Great freedom comes when we finally tackle that project and do something to declutter and gain order in our home.

Take the family's socks, for example. You know the routine. Everyone takes their socks off at the end of the day, three-fourths of them make it into the hamper (if you're lucky), and a third of those disappear somewhere between the washer and the dryer—and that's even when you use those plastic doodads to keep them together in the wash! For months I fought the sock war in my house, trying unsuccessfully to match scores of strays. Then one day, in utter frustration, I said, "Kids, this is it! I'll pay you for every pair you match." We gathered all the socks in the whole house and ended up matching 47 pairs—and finding 101 extra singles! They half-filled a garbage bag! When I pitched that bag, I also pitched a major source of clutter, both in the dresser drawers and in my mind. Regaining order is truly liberating.

Regaining order also contributes to a feeling of joy in a home. Have you noticed that it's often hard to feel joyful and offer this ministry of joy to others if your home is out of control? One friend of mine has a particularly peaceful, orderly home. She says the key is avoiding clutter. She throws a lot away and uses her storage space to get things out of sight. Some cupboards are very full, and a few are sometimes very messy, but the "junk" is out of sight until it's needed. She also picks up each morning and evening and always opts for very neat over very clean. She says, "When your home is neat, your spouse and your guests will assume it's clean and not notice the dusty corners. When it's messy, though, everyone will assume it's dirty and not notice the sparkling bathtub."

Standards for neatness and cleanliness differ, however. My books, scattered all over the house, would bother some people, but I love them. They add to my sense of joy. Likewise, you may love lots of antique kitchenware decorating your counters, but someone else might call that clutter. Once again, balance is key. Peace and joy come with the right balance for you. What degree of cleanliness and order is right for you? My mom knew how to achieve balance in this area. She truly lived out the adage "cleanliness is next to godliness," yet she was also extremely hospitable. Tim keeps coaxing me toward the godliness side of cleaning, and I keep coaxing him to pick up his clutter. In the meantime, he keeps the top of the fridge dust-free, and I declutter some of his junk. This teamwork brings both of us joy.

You can get organized—and when you have an organized life…you get done what you want to do. You save energy, money, and time…On an every-day basis you live the life that goes where you want it to.

~Sunny Schlenger and Roberta Roesch, *How to Be Organized in Spite of Yourself*

Decorate from Your Heart. Have you ever noticed that when you walk into an art gallery you enter an atmosphere of calm and quiet? That's no accident; that's the goal. Like the curators of a museum, we can create the atmosphere we want in our home. We can help our home have an atmosphere of joy, for instance, by the way we decorate and the things we display. Hiring an expensive decorator isn't necessary; decorating from the heart is. Our homes can be a reflection of our joy in the Lord as well as our personality.

Color is a great mood-setter. We can use color to change moods or encourage a certain state of mind. For a home of joy, decorate with the colors that make you happy and match your personality. Used harmoniously, colors can produce a feeling of peacefulness and well-being. Believe me, living in a home without much color has often been a challenge to my moods! Color—as Martha Stewart might say—it's a *good* thing!

When we accent our home with family mementos and things that are significant to us, our home reflects who we are. Paintings, china, and crystal are beautiful, but they aren't necessarily joyful. If a decorator fills our home with sparkling new things but we fail to add items that express what is in our heart, our home will be a reflection of fine taste but not necessarily joy.

In our home, one item that expresses my heart is a beautiful stoneware crock, with handpainted ivy and the words, "In thy presence is fullness of joy." This jar reminds me of my vine life in Christ and daily speaks to my heart. You undoubtedly have certain things in your home that express something about you or have special meaning to you. Pull them out of storage and use them as accents—and be creative. My mother-in-law gave me three beaded evening bags which I wasn't able to use very often. One day I got them out of my closet and hung them on a wall. Now I enjoy them every day. I have also framed old family photographs of several generations of my family and Tim's, and I'm making a shadow box of special family heirlooms.

I can't encourage you strongly enough to liberally display in your home photographs of your family and friends or other mementos that are meaningful to you. It's one of the best ways to create an ambiance that says, "This is a joyful home!" Many people have their hallway portrait galleries, but my friend Kim goes beyond that. Using one full wall and inexpensive frames, she hangs pictures practically from floor to ceiling. Guests are always drawn to these pictures of their life—fun, candid shots of everything from college days to a chronicle of their children growing up. That wall reflects the joy of the people who live there.

People who took my "joy survey" offer other ideas. Pam P. has hung a brightly-colored flier from somewhere they vacationed to remind them of the wonderful time they had. Shirley T. shows her taste for fun by displaying a bright metal chicken, while Beth A. hangs gold-framed paintings of tea cups. The things we display reflect our personality and say something about who we are. But these displays don't necessarily require much money—just some thought. What hobbies, interests, people, or family heirlooms bring you joy? Find a way to display them in your home! Frances L. does this and explains, "My home is my canvas, and everything I did, I did with the grocery money!" Money can make a home beautiful, but creativity can make it reflect joy.

And my friend Claudia—whom I have dubbed the Americana Queen—has all kinds of creative ideas for making her home a joyful place. Her home is filled with red, white, and blue Americana, from flags to crocks to checkerboard sets. Claudia's home is beautiful, orderly, and immaculate, but what makes it *joyful* is that it is a *celebration of family.* On a table near her entryway, she displays seasonal photographs of her children, both current and from days gone by. At Christmas, she sets a family photo alongside old pictures of her children on Santa's knee. In the summer she sets out their vacation shots, and on each child's birthday, she puts their pictures in this place of honor. Her friends love to see who's being featured when they visit. To keep this special display going, Claudia simply stores various pictures in envelopes labeled with the season or person. She keeps these—along with some different sized, inexpensive frames—in the table drawer on which she displays them, so it takes her just a moment to change her tabletop gallery.

Other sentimental items in Claudia's home are a reflection of her love for her family. She keeps, for instance, a big wooden bowl on her kitchen table filled with folded papers with questions on them like "What's your favorite food?" and "Share a favorite memory." She initially used these as conversation starters to get to know her children's friends better after they first moved here. Not surprisingly, her home is a frequent gathering place for many of their friends because Claudia's a fun mom who makes everyone feel welcome. Her hospitality truly focuses on people, not on entertaining, which draws attention to the event or the hostess. We can make our home a place of welcome and a reflection of our joy within when we decorate from our heart.

Don't Forget the Touches of Beauty. Some people may think that spending money or time beautifying one's surroundings is worldly and pointless. While good stewardship of our time and our finances is important, I couldn't disagree more with that viewpoint. Beauty is important to us as women. Besides enhancing our life, touches of beauty add to our sense of peace and that of our children's as well. In *Women and Stress,* Jean Lush agrees. She writes:

> Beauty and a sense of order in your home are functional. They have a purpose and are not unnecessary luxuries. Creating beauty around us gives us a sense of accomplishment, charges us with energy, and reduces tension. Beauty is not just for the rich and famous. It is right for everyone and fundamental to emotional health. You see, beauty creates energy.[5]

She also relates that American architect Frank Lloyd Wright taught his students that beauty dissolves conflicts, quiets, refreshes, consoles, and inspires us as well as creates a sense of happiness and serenity. Beauty, his lesson continued, is neither unnecessary nor impractical.[6]

A final word of caution about beauty. At the same time that we value beauty and benefit from it, we must never place too much value on our beautiful or special things. They are just *things* even though they are things that God allows us to enjoy. Years ago I gave my mother a red plate that said, "You Are Special." She used it on special occasions and inscribed on the back each guest or event for which it was used. Before she died, she gave it back to me. Now Mother was very practical, and I knew she wanted me to use the plate—which I did. Consequently, one day one of the children dropped it. Shattered glass went everywhere. Not a single word from the back of the plate was left intact. I fought back tears, but then thought, *What would my mother say right now? She'd say, "Remember, it's just stuff, honey!"* Then I cleaned up the mess and reassured my child as I knew my mother would have. As special and important as the beautiful things in our homes may be, they're just stuff!

Make Things Special. Bed-and-breakfast hostess Joycelyn Clairmonte has a knack—no, the gift—of making things beautiful or special with little money and little time. She told me, "I didn't grow up with a lot of things, but when I was young, I visited a woman who often served everyday meals on china plates and regularly used cloth napkins. If she used paper plates, she set them out in their wicker holder. And she didn't serve chips in the bag; she put them in a napkin-lined basket. She made a huge impression on me. I decided I wanted to be like that when I grew up." And she is.

When I visited their inn, Joycelyn and her husband left for church one night. She had told me she'd left me some soup on the stove and to help myself. But when I went downstairs, I found a china bowl sitting on a china plate, a cloth napkin in a napkin ring, and a matching glass. What I thought was going to be just a quick bite of soup had become a meal that nourished my spirit as well as my body. She had shown me love by making my solitary meal very special.

It really does take so little to make things special. Use the china instead of keeping it in the cabinet. Get out the table-cloth—it won't add much to your laundry. Pull things out of your kitchen cabinets and closets and use the things that have meaning and add beauty to your life. If you drink tea, use your pretty china cups. Look for ways to carve out a moment of serenity, beauty, and calm in your busy life. It brings a sparkle of joy.

Set the Mood. With just a few simple touches, we can create a definite mood in our homes. And one of the quickest ways to create a joyful mood is to be sure to fill it often with beautiful *music*. In the Bible, David gave specific instructions to God's people to "raise sounds of joy" using their voices as well as harps, lyres, and loud-sounding cymbals (1 Chronicles 15:16). We can raise sounds of joy in our homes as well.

Norma M. says, "Beautiful music wakes joy in my soul." And Posy L. adds, "Music above all else brings me great joy. Classical music and particularly great anthems of the church, like Handel and Bach, make me feel full of joy and often move me to tears." Another woman said that her family has soft Irish folk music or classical music on much of the time. In our home, we play a lot of classical and contemporary Christian music, not to mention lots of children's tapes. And on the weekends, Tim will sometimes get out his Irish CD reminiscent of his childhood or tune in a Cajun station for some lively tunes, and we have a great time. My friend Nancy has a family that enjoys music, too. She says, "Many Saturday mornings, Ron wakes up ready to *party* with the family. He's got the whole day to get stuff done, and he wants to jam while he works. So he cranks up some fun contemporary Christian music, and he and the kids dance around all day."

As I've mentioned before, *light* can affect our moods just as music can. So, whenever possible, let the sunshine in! Open the blinds, clean the windows, add additional indoor lighting to dark rooms, and even paint the walls for a lighter environment. Colleen A. did some of those things and more. She says, "I try to let in as much light as possible. In St. Louis, we moved into a house that was very dark, and it affected my mood for the worse. So I took off the curtains and the ugly wallpaper, and I painted the walls white. Then it seemed more like a happy home than a cave. I think a woman's home environment has a big impact on her joy and contentment."

Another thing we can add to our home environment are great smells. Everyone knows that fragrances are pleasant, but did you know that certain aromas may be able to influence how we feel, settle our nerves, and enhance our concentration? That's what some researchers are discovering. The article "Probing the Power of Common Scents" in *Prevention* magazine (October 1991) reported that "fragrance affects us more than previously thought. New research indicates that smells may influence our minds, our moods and our bodies." So get out the potpourri, light a candle, bake something that smells delicious, and create a welcoming atmosphere through scent. Some gift shops even sell home fragrance sprays, a big step up in quality (and price) from the grocery store air fresheners, but worth it to some people.

I remember some advice I heard years ago. This wise woman said, "You know it really doesn't take that much effort to bake a loaf of bread and put some flowers on the table. You just have to want to do it. The results are worth the effort." We can't always make time for these things, but when we do—when we add the little touches discussed in this chapter—we add to the spirit of warmth in our home, and that nourishes our soul and blesses our family.

The Spirit of Celebration

When you hear the word "confetti," what do you think of? The pessimists among us might say, "What a mess! It's sure hard to clean up." But most people think of one thing—a celebration!

And that's something almost everyone loves. A home whose inhabitants live with a spirit of celebration is a happy home. A home that celebrates is a home where love reigns, people are important, and family is center stage. A home with celebrations builds strong families. No matter what the occasion, celebrations say, "You are important! You are special! You are loved!"

Celebrations are a part of our nation's traditions—but in too many homes there isn't enough celebrating. A 1992 family behavior study by the Barna Research Group uncovered some sad statistics: "One of the most significant transitions has been the abandonment of family traditions. Those repetitive, predictable activities between parent and child that served as a mechanism allowing kids to ease into adulthood and maximize the enjoyment of youth have been lost."[7] The report also showed that simple traditions like eating together, playing games, praying and attending church as a family, and family vacations are not as common as they have been in years gone by. Some estimates, in fact, show that the typical parent only spends somewhere between 6 and 90 minutes with their child each day. With either estimate, George Barna says, "The bottom line is that children these days get cheated out of the time they need if they are to absorb the sense of personal value and societal responsibility that is viewed as healthy and beneficial."[8] Far too many children are learning that they are not as important as other people and activities in their parents' life.

But that doesn't have to be the case in your home or mine. We can make family traditions and celebrations a high priority. Our children will benefit greatly, and our family unit will be stronger. Read what Cheri Fuller writes in *Christmas Treasures of the Heart*:

> *I* received a telegram one day. It said simply: Until Further Notice—Celebrate Everything.
>
> ~Tim Hansel,
> *Holy Sweat*

Traditions say, "This is who we are and what we hold dear as a family." They help make up the glue that holds families together...."How do we keep our balance?" asks Tevye, the Jewish dairyman in the beloved musical play *Fiddler on the Roof.* "Tradition!" he rightly concludes. "Without tradition, our lives would be as shaky as a fiddler on a roof."[9]

Traditions can be as simple as a nightly butterfly or Eskimo kiss, but these celebrations are major memory-makers. And they'll definitely add joy to your home!

Celebrate often. Look for reasons to celebrate! Make up excuses! We don't have to limit our celebrations to major holidays and family birthdays. Reasons to throw a party are all around us. Here's a list for starters:

Minor holidays (Presidents' Day, St. Patrick's Day, Flag Day, Arbor Day, etc.)

Baptism

Salvation: welcoming Jesus into your heart

Spiritual birthdays ("Amy became a Christian two years ago today!")

A new birth

An adoption

Half-birthdays

A new job

A good report card

An improved report card

The first lost tooth

Learning to ride a bike or tie shoes

Learning anything new

A new season

A new year in school

A new home (dedicate it to God!)

Grandparents' Day

Anniversaries (of marriages, moving to a new house, etc.)

A goal met

An appreciation celebration

Just because! No reason at all!

Whatever reason you choose, remember that the celebration doesn't need to be elaborate. To mark her child's half-birthday, for instance, a friend came to our house with her children, some frozen pizza, a simple dessert, and some paper cups and napkins she had on hand. That turned a plain Tuesday into a special day and made her child feel special. So be creative and have fun!

Lots of money and lots of planning are not required. A woman I know wanted to give an engagement party for her friends, but she didn't have time to cook. So she bought fried chicken and two side orders, quickly put a lace tablecloth on her table, lighted a few candles, and served the food in pretty bowls. She gave them something she had sitting around to remind them of the little impromptu party, and it became a great memory for them.

When we put a decorative paper cup and napkin into our child's lunch sack along with a piece of candy and a "Way to go!" or "To remind you I love you!" note, we are sending them to school with a celebration in a sack. Throw in a sprinkle of confetti for that party feel, and your child will feel a touch of your love at school. (This same thoughtfulness works for husbands, too!)

You can get ideas from a party one woman gave which took very little planning but was a lot of fun. Her husband was turning 50 years old and three of their friends had turned 40, so she had a big celebration. She made a simple sign for the porch that greeted each guest with, "Welcome to the Home for the Aged." Each chair had a blanket on it. She set several fans around the room for the women "with mid-life crisis hot flashes," and her husband's place of honor was a rocking chair. One man had made a point of telling everyone he was only 38, so the hostess set his place setting with a rattle and a baby cup and told her guests that there was a child in their midst! Skipping the black, over-the-hill theme, they poked fun at the birthday folks and had a great time. This woman didn't have much money to spend on the party and gave only an hour or two to the preparations (including fixing the dinner). We can celebrate without spending a lot of time or money.

Anita K. often hosts simple tea parties for her granddaughter. She says, "Some of the deepest talks we've had were over cookies and tea, served in a pretty china cup. I want her to look back and remember the fun we had together." In her beautiful book *If Teacups Could Talk*, Emilie Barnes describes how she does the same thing.[10] She also gives great ideas for other tea parties, one of which I borrowed for a close friend's birthday. I got a picnic basket and filled it with some cookies, a thermos of hot water, tea bags, a candle and matches, a pretty teapot, and two china cups, saucers, and small plates. I wrapped the china in a towel, placed a folded lace tablecloth over the top of the basket, and surprised my friend at her home. I knew her children were going to be with their grandmother that day (her husband was in on the surprise), so we enjoyed a quiet tea party and made a fun memory. It really takes such little effort to make a memory.

Many of us, myself included, need ideas to draw on whether we want to do the simple or the elaborate. Don't let those "entertaining" books make you think, "I could never pull that off!" Instead, get ideas from those resources to use in your own way rather than trying to duplicate a book or magazine layout. Remember, you aren't trying to entertain anyway. You're celebrating, and that always puts the emphasis on the person or event you're honoring! Also, keep in mind how and when creativity tends to work. It's once we decide to make something special that our creative juices start flowing. We start thinking, "What have I got? What can I use? Won't it be fun to...? I might try...!" Until we make the decision to do it, the creativity doesn't start! When we do, then it comes. Choose something to celebrate and you'll see!

Remember to stay flexible. When Jim and Joycelyn Clairmonte were remodeling their family farmhouse into a bed and breakfast, they had lots of help from friends. To thank the six couples and say, "We couldn't have done this without you!" Joycelyn planned a nice dinner party—and she put a lot of planning into that celebration! She wrapped a little gift and put it on each person's plate along with a thank-you poem tied with a ribbon. Then she added those special touches to her table—candles and confetti! (When she told me this story, I smiled. She didn't even know about this chapter!) Everything was perfect—until the church flooded. The dinner had to be postponed for an hour and a half. Then, when it could finally begin, some people came dressed up, and those who had been cleaning up at the church came in work clothes. The food was warmed, and the party went on as planned. The evening was still a great success largely because the hostess stayed flexible.

Hanging on to your sense of humor and remembering why you're celebrating can help you be flexible when the best-laid plans are foiled again!

Keep it simple. Keeping celebrations simple will encourage us to look for reasons to celebrate and to celebrate often. Although we can have great fun planning and giving elaborate parties, we won't find ourselves doing these big productions very often. Besides, what we want in our home is the spirit of celebration; what we want in ourselves is a heart that's quick to look for ways to celebrate people. Here are some hints for simplifying the "confetti" part of a "candles and confetti" spirit:

> • Have candles and confetti on hand—literally! Buy them on sale and keep them in the ready position. Lighting some candles and sprinkling confetti on the table turns an ordinary dinner into an instant celebration.

> • Stock up on paper goods during after-season sales. My friend Lois is always buying items at 75 percent off after the event they celebrate has passed. A supply of plain red cups and napkins can be used for Christmas, Valentine's Day, and—throw in something blue—Memorial Day, the Fourth of July, or any other national holiday.

> • Think ahead. Don't wait until the morning of February 14 to see if you have any valentines or pink food!

> • Don't be afraid of the hassle. A celebration usually takes much less effort than we anticipate.

> • Finally—and this is the most important ingredient— bring a *joyful attitude* to your celebration. Your enthusiasm and sense of fun can set the tone for family fun.

Again, simple works! In fact, the simpler we keep our celebrations, the more often we'll look for reasons to celebrate. I have tons of great ideas, but if it's elaborate or time intensive, it'll be ready about three seasons from now. Simplicity makes celebrations happen at our house, and it can help them happen at yours too.

Involve the children. Children love planning parties as well as attending them. So let your kids be involved however they can—even if that means the quality's not quite what you would do. My children love to help set the table and make placecards for our family and guests whenever they can. Involving the children in the preparations promotes family unity and self-esteem. Their willingness to be involved is far more important than perfect presentation. Barbara M. agrees. She says, "The boys help me decorate for all the seasons. They love helping, and I've found that they're both very creative."

Sometimes we don't know our children's talents (and neither do they) because we always do it ourselves! My older children are getting to the point that I can say, "Sure, go ahead and do the whole table," and they love it. They're even coming up with their own spur-of-the-moment celebrations. On a hot August night last summer, for instance, my girls decided to surprise us and set the patio table for dinner. They added a fan to keep us from melting and they hung sheets to hide the garden tools and the neighbors' view. And, of course, they put candles on the table. Then they dragged us outside with our eyes closed to see their surprise. My husband looked at me with big eyes and whispered, "We can't eat out here. It's 98 degrees and humid enough to shower on the patio!" But we braved the heat, read a portion of a funny book aloud, and together made a great memory. After all, kids can have great ideas and a wonderful sense of fun. They seem to have a spirit of confetti quite naturally. So tap into these resources! I bet you'll be glad you did!

> *The* celebrating spirit need not limit itself to party time. This means that celebration shows itself in little moments of grace as well as in rambunctious revelry.
>
> ~Emilie Barnes,
> *The Spirit of Loveliness*

The Spirit of Love

A home needs not only candles and confetti to make it joyful—a home also needs *connection*. Candles offer the spirit of warmth. Confetti adds the spirit of celebration. And connections tie warmth and celebration together with those we love. Connections which happen through *relationships* and *activities* give our homes a spirit of togetherness. We connect through our relationships when we do the following:

Minimize strife. A joyful home is one in which such signs of strife like fighting and arguing are minimal. Achieving that goal isn't easy when we have more than one child living under our roof. Most of us with more than one child experience that challenge of parenthood known as sibling rivalry. If only we could inoculate against that right along with the DPT shot! Then, when the squabble heated up, we could simply cool everyone off with, "You know, it's about time for your anti-strife booster!" Imagine the peace!

Instead, peace and joy come to a home when parents keep their disagreements private, teach children how to solve their differences quickly, and encourage them to coexist peacefully. Such training isn't easy, but our efforts will contribute greatly to the amount of joy in our home. A home with a lot of fighting is no joy to live in or visit, no matter how many candles we light or how much confetti we sprinkle.

Maximize time together. We connect with the people in our home when we spend time with one another. Sometimes we are so busy with living—with earning a paycheck, paying bills, cleaning, and cooking, not to mention kid activities and church commitments—that our time together as a family is limited to leftovers. A joyful home, however, is one in which relationships between family members are nurtured by spending time together.

Enjoy one another. We connect through relationships when we spend time together and—just as important—when we enjoy that time. So, when you sit down on the floor to play a game with the kids, don't review your to-do list or let your frustration about unfinished work simmer on the back burner. Get into that game. Take the time and make the effort to engage your mind and your heart. Really enjoy your kids! Sometimes all that requires is a simple attitude adjustment.

Respect one another. A home where family members feel respected and respect one another is a home where joy can blossom. Without respect, it's hard for anyone to feel very secure, content, or joyful. Disrespect is a weed that chokes out the fruit of joy.

Share a loving touch. Touch is a balm that soothes souls, reinforces love, and communicates care. It is as important as nourishment to babies, children need large doses of it, teenagers want us to think they are "too old" for such things (but don't let them fool you!), and every vibrant marriage needs it. So kiss your spouse and children every day. Give lots of hugs. Pat a hand. Touch an arm while you talk. Greet visitors with an outstretched hand or open arms. Rub a family member's shoulders just because. And follow your children's lead when they initiate family hugs and then join in the laughter when the child in the middle squeals with delight.

We also connect through our activities. Here are some ideas:

Make memories from mishaps. With a little creativity and an attitude of joy, we can often turn problems into memories. When my washing machine broke this week, flooding my utility room, I mopped up the mess and loaded 12 loads of laundry and four kids into the van. A quick stop en route to the laundromat for canned Juice Fizz—and boxed Lunchables—turned a headache into a highlight. The kids thought that eating dinner at the Wash-O-Rama was one of the best things they'd done in ages. They helped me wash, dry, and fold all 12 loads and, amazingly, when we left to go home, they all shouted, "Thank you, Mother! That was fun!" A joyful attitude (and a little Juice Fizz) can go a long way!

Occasionally do the unexpected. Routine can be the framework for a life that runs smoothly, and children need the stability and predictability which it provides. But everyone needs a break from it occasionally. A joyful home is one in which routine is occasionally sidelined for something unexpected and fun. Take the kids to a dollar movie in the middle of the week. Or one day after school, instead of doing chores or homework, surprise them with an ice cream cone or a stop at the park. Do something your family would never expect you to do and watch the joy flow!

Practice J.O.Y. Joyful homes teach and practice the tried-and-true saying: joy comes by putting **J**esus first, **o**thers second, and **y**ourself third. Our children need to know that Jesus is the whole reason we can have joy in spite of circumstances and that "self" is not the number one priority in life. (Come to think of it, we adults could use a reminder from time to time!)

Connect with nature. Sometimes making the choice to rejoice is easier if we get out of the confines of our four walls and into the beauty of God's creation. So go outside! It's too easy to limit our experience in the great outdoors to the time we walk between the house and the car, the car and our destination. Sometimes making "outside" our destination results in a huge and wonderful attitude adjustment. We won't always be able to look around at a beautiful, inspiring vista to connect with God's handiwork, but we can always look straight up even if we're surrounded by skyscrapers. Just noticing the huge sky, the moving clouds, or the twinkling stars can remind us of the vastness of God—and the relative size of our problems.

Incorporate each individual's ideas of what makes a joyful home. What do your family members think makes a home joyful? I didn't know my own family's answers to that question until I asked recently. My thoughtful child said, "A clean house, good attitudes, and no fighting." My fun-loving daughter said, "Where the parents play with the children once a day." My husband smiled and made reference to the "loving touch" category. Since external sources of joy differ for individuals, we need to know what it is that makes the hearts of those we love sing.

So how connected are you with those you share your home with? I hope these ideas help you improve your relationships and reenergize your activities and, consequently, help everyone experience more joy.

Your Personal Presence

Candles, confetti, and connection—creating a warm feeling, looking for ways to celebrate, and bringing people together by nurturing relationships and sharing activities—can go far in helping us create a joyful home, but they're not the most important factors. The most important ingredient is you!

Haven't you noticed how a person's presence can create a certain atmosphere? Our attitude, countenance, words, voice, and demeanor create an environment around us, and it affects the people who come in contact with us and live with us. If we are anxious or hurried, that is the ambiance around us. But if we are calm and lighthearted, that can be the mood we set. If we know the Lord and His joy, we can create an atmosphere of joy wherever we are—in our home and elsewhere.

And, as this book teaches, we know God's joy when we dwell in Him. When we live connected to Jesus—the vine life—He can grow in us those qualities He adores, qualities that can contribute to an atmosphere of joy around us. God calls us, for instance, to focus on our inner person, "the hidden person of the heart," and to cultivate "the imperishable quality of a gentle and quiet spirit, which is precious in the sight of God" (1 Peter 3:4). We are also told to "pursue righteousness, godliness, faith, love, perseverance and gentleness" (1 Timothy 6:11). And then we are told that "the fruit of the spirit is love, joy, peace, patience, kindness, goodness, faithfulness, gentleness, self-control" (Galatians 5:22-23). As we grow in Christ and yield to Him, we see this fruit—the very likeness of Him—take shape in us. And that fruit makes for a personal presence and therefore a home characterized by love and peace with joy sandwiched right between the two, just as it is in the Galatians 5 list.

So, while it's fun to decorate our home and celebrate every occasion and non-occasion we can think of, we need to pay attention to the atmosphere we ourselves create. If our home is to welcome guests and bless its inhabitants with the gift of joy, we need to stay close to God so that we can know His joy and its presence in our life. No matter how much we decorate our homes or how many celebrations we have, no matter how much effort we put into relationships or how creatively we plan togetherness activities, we are the main ingredient in the recipe for a joy-filled home.

> *The danger is that we begin to simply endure our seasons rather than celebrate them, and we let life slip away imperceptibly. . . .*
>
> ~Tim Hansel,
> *When I Relax
> I Feel Guilty*

A Quick Inventory

As we cultivate joy in both our person and our home, we do well to consider the five senses. Are we appealing to each of them—touch, hearing, sight, smell, and taste? After all, God provided our senses for more than our protection; He provided them for our pleasure.

We can greet guests with the gift of joy, by welcoming them with a gentle touch, be it a hug or a pat on the arm, and offer them a soft chair. We can let them hear a voice that is gentle as they enter a home filled with music and void of strife. We can let them see us looking our best—neat and smiling—as we try to reflect our Savior. And perhaps let's treat them to the beauty of a lighted candle that says, "I was expecting you." We can be something of the "fragrance of Christ" as we usher them into a room that comforts with its pleasant aroma, be it from a candle, potpourri, flowers, or freshly baked anything. And why not tickle their tastebuds with good things from the kitchen—and let those things remind them that we are all to "taste and see that the Lord is good" (Psalm 34:8). Our presence can be warm and welcoming to those who visit and those who abide, and our homes truly can bless all with the gift of joy.

❧ 13 ❧

Living and Giving Joy and Contentment
Modeling These Gifts for Our Families

One day my friend was busy loading the dishwasher when her three-year-old daughter Erica looked up at her and said, "Mommy, are you happy?" Her mom replied, "Why, yes, honey, I'm happy." To which Erica replied, "Then why are your eyebrows always down?"

Happy on the inside doesn't automatically translate into joy on the outside. As Erica reminds us, "down eyebrows" speak loudly to a three-year-old, even when we're unaware they're down. Erica also reminds us that we are influencing the people in our life, either positively or negatively, whether we're aware of it or not. That truth got me wondering about the kind of influence I've had in my home.

So I recently asked my two older daughters if they could think of anything they do because of my influence—and I explained I wasn't asking about their regular responsibilities like taking a bath and making the bed, but about things not necessarily expected of them. Jacquelyn quickly said, "Oh, yes, I read all the time and drink lots of water like you. And you know how you're always trying to be happy when things aren't going so good? I try to do that, too." *Hmm. Not bad. She didn't mention a single negative.*

261

Claire then added, "I like to write in my journal and make notes on my calendar of what I have to do and what I did, and I like to read my Bible." Then she giggled and added, "I think I got that from you." *Oh, how sweet. I never realized she thought that.*

Then they decided to speak for their younger brother and sister. Jacquelyn said, "Yeah—and remember that time when Collin picked up a newspaper and pretended to read it? Then he put his feet up on the kitchen table and crossed his ankles. He was doing exactly what Daddy does." Then Claire jumped in, "And Allison, Mom—she's all the time shaving with her plastic razor like Dad and putting makeup on her face and her dolls and holding her little pink Bible upside down pretending to read to be like you." Then they were off to play. (By the way, I read my Bible right side up!)

If only that were the complete picture....I was touched that my girls could even articulate a way that they have been influenced by Tim and me. And I was thrilled that they immediately thought of the positive, as children often do. But I know all too well that we parents can also have a negative effect on our kids. I know because I have lived the "if Mama ain't happy, ain't nobody happy!" routine. I have seen what happens when I revert to communicating vocally with great expression. (Tim calls it yelling.) And I've noticed the dramatic change in the atmosphere of my home when I'm not living the FINER life (see chapter 10). How about you? What stands out most to you and your family? The times when you model joy or the times when you don't? And which times are more prevalent? The answer to those questions are a good indication of what you're modeling and how effective (for good or bad) your modeling skills are.

The Art of Modeling

We influence the people around us and especially members of our family in so many ways, but none is more powerful than the life we live before them. That's the essence of modeling—influencing those around us by the way we live. Our flesh-and-blood example impacts the people close to us far more than any words we could ever say or write. They may hear what we say, but they will do what they see. As St. Francis of Assisi said, "In all you do, be a witness. If necessary use words." Our actions speak and teach more than words ever could, so we need to be sure we're teaching joy and contentment with our actions using words only when absolutely necessary.

Learning to be a more joyful and content person is important simply because we are individuals made in the image of God. But the importance of our joy and contentment doesn't stop with us. We want to be women who model these traits before others, especially our children. In order to give joy, we have to live it. When Brenda K. was asked on her survey if she was content, she responded, "Yes! Partly because I was raised to be." Our influence carries over into our children's adult years. So let's not stop with learning to be joyful and content for our own fulfillment. Let's also learn to model these traits for our children, who then can influence others. Granted, the level of our kids' joy and contentment isn't solely our responsibility, but our example certainly helps. Living in a home with a mama (and/or daddy) who's joyful and content—and learning from her what joy is all about—is far better than living with a mama who ain't happy and learning those lessons.

So how can you and I model joy and contentment for our family and other people in our life? Here are ten ideas.

The Top Ten Ways to Model Joy and Contentment

1. Express Joy through Your Words
2. Express Joy with Your Voice
3. Sing Often
4. Smile More Often
5. Have Fun
6. Live Out a Joyful Faith
7. Share Your Joys with Others
8. Nurture a Spirit of Giving
9. Focus on the Blessings
10. Express Joy and Contentment Any Way You Can

1. Express Joy through Your Words

As the old song says, we can use words to "eliminate the negative, accentuate the positive." When we do this with the words we say and the tone of voice we use, we allow our joy in the Lord to shine through. In fact, it's very difficult for us Mamas to model joy before our child when we're not using words or a tone of voice that reflects joy. Our children need to hear us and see us being joyful. We can learn to express the joy in our heart and demonstrate our contentment by limiting the negative words we say, accentuating the positive words, and tempering our negative responses.

First, we need to limit—if not completely eliminate—the hurtful, negative words we speak. Both a complaining spirit which focuses on the negative aspects of a situation and a critical spirit which reveals our negative view of a person certainly hinder our joy and the joy of those around us, so we must be careful to watch our words. Having "roast pastor" on the way home from church, for instance, will leave a bad taste in the mouth of a child because it models a critical spirit—hardly our goal as parents. One woman wrote me and said, "We are building a new church and there have been power struggles and discontentment within the church family. God gave me this verse, 'Set a guard, O Lord, over my mouth; keep watch over the door of my lips' (Psalm 141:3). To me, that means keeping the things that come out of our mouth joyful and unto the Lord." Doing so will keep us more joyful and make us a better example for our children.

It will also keep us from presenting a double standard to our children, a risk we very human moms run. That double standard happens when, for example, we tell our children, "Be joyful!" and yet we fly off the handle when things don't go our way. Our message about joy also becomes skewed when we fall apart after leaving the beauty salon looking like we're wearing a hair hat. In that case, we may end up modeling "Mama is joyful when things go her way." We can certainly express our frustration, but we should stop short of wailing and gnashing teeth. The better option is to look at our disastrous "do" (or whatever crisis, big or small) as an opportunity to model Philippians 4:4: "Rejoice in the Lord always; again I will say, rejoice!" Besides, why not laugh? A hair hat could be quite amusing (and certainly fixable)!

At the same time that we temper our negative responses, we can model proper responses to negative things for our children. Our friends Ron and Nancy use two simple words to remind their children to go with the flow even when things aren't going well: "We teach our kids to say, 'Oh, well.' That phrase sums up the attitude I'd like them to develop!" And that attitude—that simple phrase "Oh, well"—can head off a critical, complaining spirit.

Second, we can accentuate the positive by the words we say, both to those in our home and to others. We can use words like "You're terrific," "Good job," "I knew you could do it," "I'm so proud of you," and "You're a lot of fun" to build up a child's self-esteem. And we can say those things no matter how old our children are. Lydia G. does: "I am an 85-year-old widow, mother, and grandmother living alone, but in my letters and telephone calls, I tell all [my children and grandchildren] that I love them and how special they are in God's sight as well as mine, and I encourage them in their achievements." Way to go, Lydia! Words are powerful, and we can use them either to build up or to destroy. Tamara L. agrees: "I think we have the power to make another person happy or we can crush their spirit with what we say. I try to encourage, not discourage." Amen! Let's be builders, not wreckers, in the lives of the ones we love.

2. Express Joy with Your Voice

Our tone of voice can be loud and clear in its expression of joy as well as the lack of it. I was reminded of that fact in a rather unusual way once. I was talking with a salesperson on the telephone when a child came in, got a snack out of the refrigerator, and walked

$\mathcal{K}$ids won't buy a double standard. When you give them permission to call you on the carpet for a violation, they will feel ownership of the rules.

~Kathy Peel,
The Family Manager

off leaving the door wide open. I was on hold so I told my child (a bit sharply), "Close that door."

"But I want a snack," she responded (also a bit sharply).

"You may have one, but you forgot to say 'please,'" I replied.

Suddenly to my surprise, the voice on the other end of the phone said, "But you didn't say please to her."

"Excuse me?" I said.

"You told her to close the door, and you didn't say 'please.' She was just responding to you in the way and with the tone of voice you used with her," she replied. At first I was taken aback that she heard me (hold can be tricky, you know) and that I had been rebuked through fiber optics by a stranger. But I realized that she was exactly right. My child was only living out what was being modeled before her. Now I'd like to say there's never been a problem since that phone call ten years ago, but you know better. So I try to watch my words and tone of voice...even when I'm not on hold.

Another woman I met told me about a time she was having words with her teenager. Apparently, the words weren't good, and neither was the tone of her voice. The daughter stomped off and ran up the stairs towards her room, leaving behind her a trail of less-than-respectful words. The mother yelled up the stairs, "Don't you talk to me like that! Did you forget that I'm your mother?" The daughter replied, "No—but please don't talk to me like that either. Did you forget that I'm your daughter?"

Our children really do follow the model that they see and hear as they grow up. It takes just a little thought and effort to speak gently and sweetly to the people in our lives, but the rewards are worth it. After all, the tone of voice we use can make or break someone's day and, in the long run, someone's spirit.

One day when I wasn't feeling very good, I certainly wasn't doing much on this "Top Ten" list, but I did make the effort in one area. I didn't feel like singing or having fun or smiling, but I made a conscious effort to speak with a sweet voice even though I didn't feel at all sweet inside. Later that day, Claire said, "Mom, you sure were nice today!" All I had done was weigh my words and deliver them sweetly. I had followed the advice of a sign on my friend's refrigerator: "Oh, Lord, may my words be sweet and tender, for tomorrow I may have to eat them!" We must dish nothing from the menu of our mouth that we do not wish to have served back to us!

3. Sing Often

When I asked a friend of mine if she grew up in a happy home, she said, "Oh, yes! My mother sang all the time." Funny. One of the first things we lose when we're angry or down is our song. So perhaps the first thing we should do when we're in such a state is try to find it! Besides, Scripture is full of exhortations to sing for joy :

O come, let us sing for joy to the LORD;
Let us shout joyfully to the rock of our salvation.
Let us come before His presence with thanksgiving;
Let us shout joyfully to Him with psalms (Psalm 95:1,2).

O satisfy us in the morning with Thy lovingkindness,
That we may sing for joy and be glad all our days
(Psalm 90:14).

In fact, the Hebrew word for "rejoice" means "to sing for joy." But which comes first—the singing or the joy? Neither and both! The circle is continuous. If you are joyful, you will sing. If you need joy, you must sing for it! God commands us to sing, promises joy when we obey that command, and gives reasons for constant rejoicing and continuing song. Many times when we are exhorted to sing, we are given a reason why we can sing with joy, as in this passage:

It is good to give thanks to the LORD,
And to sing praises to Thy name, O Most High...
For Thou, O LORD, has made me glad by what Thou
hast done,
I will sing for joy at the works of Thy hands
(Psalm 92:1,4).

James wrote, "Is anyone cheerful? Let him sing praises" (James 5:13b). Indeed, that's the key to truly joyful singing—letting it become praise to God. And did you know that your joy can be offered as a sacrifice to God even as it lifts your spirits?

> And now my head shall be lifted up above my en-
> emies all around me;
> Therefore I will offer sacrifices of joy in His taber-
> nacle;
> I will sing, yes, I will sing praises to the LORD
> (Psalm 27:6 NKJV).

Praise through song lifts our spirits to a place of joy like nothing else can.

Singing is not only good for us; it's also great for our kids. Most children love to sing and will do so with exuberance. Young children are especially enthusiastic because they have yet to become self-conscious. They couldn't care less how they sound to others. They just sing because it's fun. It's a natural expression of their joy. When our kids grow up, they may not remember the words we sang or how good (or bad) we sounded, but they will remember that we did it. So sing even if you can't carry a tune in a bucket. Joy comes whether or not we're right on key!

And that joy is something we model every time our children see and hear us singing, but we model much more when our singing is praise. When our songs are praise, we teach our children about God, about being in relationship with Him, as well as Scripture verses, great hymns of the church, and truths of our faith. For reasons such as these, our children need see us prais-ing God at church and at home, and we can teach them to join in our song. Lydia G. knows about the joyful fruit from singing. She says, "I was glad to make a joyful noise to God by singing in the choir for 70 years." No wonder she says she's joyful most of the time!

4. Smile More Often

Even if we feel as if we're usually a happy Mama, we can benefit from an occasional quick glance in the mirror. Are our eyebrows up or down? Sometimes we need to remind our face to reflect the joy in our heart. And that's what a smile is.

A smile is a wonderful way to model joy! It's free, immedi-ate, painless, and practically effortless. (It takes far fewer mus-cles to smile than to frown.) And just in case you thought almost everyone in old photographs was completely joyless, here's some smile trivia. Even though early American life was hard, those folks did smile—but not for pictures. The early daguerreotypes (also known as tintypes) sometimes had exposure times of up to ten minutes. Facial muscles can ache from holding a grin for that long, so be grateful for modern photography. It allows us to leave our children with a visual record of our joyful expressions, also known as "the family photo album."

And of course smiles shouldn't be reserved for pictures or "reasons" to smile—as Liz G. learned. When her son was six years old, he was sitting at the table waiting patiently for his lunch. She noticed he looked sad and somewhat fretful. When she asked him what was wrong, his response hit her like a ton of bricks. "Nothing," he said. "I was just wondering why your face had no smile on it." Liz said, "I found him feeling sad because he presumed I was sad. All the joy that had been on his face a few minutes before had faded, and what was left was the tone I had set unintentionally. I wasn't even sad that day. I just had nothing to smile about!"

My own son reminded me of the value of a mom's smile one night after I tucked him in. I was about to walk out the door, and he said, "Mom?"

"Yes, son," I said.

"Where's your smile?" I had to think about that a second. I hadn't noticed it was missing.

"Is my smile gone?" I asked him.

"Yeah—and I think mine is, too." Then I scooped him up in the biggest bear-hug-for-locating-lost-smiles possible.

"Oh, no, it's not! I see your smile!" I teased.

"And I see yours! Mom, I like it when you smile!" he said, and melted my heart. Then we made a pact. Whenever we notice the other one walking around without a smile, we inquire of its whereabouts. "Where's your smile?" is now our special game, and so far it's the best lost-smile-finder around. Works every time!

5. Have Fun

If you want a reading on your success as a family merry-maker, simply ask your children if they think your home is a fun place. What do you think your frivolity rating would be? If we're completely in the dark about what their answer might be, chances are we need to learn to have a little more fun. In the survey I did for this book, only two people said they thought they might have too much fun. Most people agreed that fun was important, and many thought they could add a bit more fun to their life. As we saw in chapter 11, there is great value in laughter and play, but I mention it again here because the ability to have fun is a great way to model joy for our children. Our children love it when we're spontaneous and silly with them. Liz H. said, "I 'play' when I read to my kids with *much* dramatics." When you read a story to your child, get into it! Don't just read a story about a bear—become the bear!

Another important source of fun is fellowship with other believers as well as those we love. Such times are not just for our own benefit (although, as we saw in chapter 10, nurturing friendship is key to a happy Mama); our children benefit, too. When they see us inviting friends over for dinner or meeting another family at a park for a picnic, they learn that there is value and enjoyment in Christian fellowship. I learned that as a very young child. I have memories from way back of my parents having people over to visit. I still remember my dad throwing his head back in laughter, and my mom making everything just perfect, even if she served hot dogs. What impressed me most was how our family and our guests would hold hands in a circle and pray before they left. I remember the warm feeling in my heart as I looked up at them as they prayed, glad to be included in this special circle of love. I learned early that there is great value in fellowship with other believers.

The apostle Paul thought so, too. He thanked God for his brothers in Christ and prayed for them with joy (Philippians 1:3,4). Fellow believers were a great joy to Paul, and he loved them deeply. He wrote, "Therefore, my beloved brethren whom I long to see, my joy and crown, so stand firm in the Lord, my beloved" (Philippians 4:1). We model the joy that comes with Christian fellowship when we take time to include it even in a busy life.

And, of course, we mustn't forget to have a sense of humor! In fact, it should be standard equipment and firmly installed before we bring a baby home from the hospital. It comes in handy over the 18 years or so that follow! Wouldn't it be nice to walk the aisles of Super Baby World and see diapers, strollers, humidifiers, and Sense-o-Humor in a box? How great it would be to run to the store to stock up when our supply runs low! And we'd never be at a loss for what to buy for a baby gift again!

Besides, a sense of humor and the ability to laugh at ourselves make for a great model of joyfulness—and my father, Paul Britton, is a great example. Many years ago, he was attending a sales convention at a prominent downtown Houston hotel. Nature called, so he went to the restroom. While in the stall, an unexpected sneeze came upon him, apparently with the force of a strong gale, and blew his denture right out of his mouth! Unfortunately, it didn't land at his feet. Instead it flew right *under* the stall door, slid across the floor, and stopped near the center drain in the middle of the bathroom.

He peeked under the door, hoping to find an empty bathroom, but to his dismay, a man stood at the sink washing his hands—steps away from the misplaced teeth. Not knowing if the man had noticed, he quietly opened the stall door. Without looking up, lest he lock eyes with someone in his Moment of Great Embarrassment, and with his trousers still at his knees, he quickly waddled the few steps to the center drain, grabbed the denture, and backed up into the blessed privacy of the stall. To this day, he doesn't know if that man ever noticed, and he's been careful ever since to keep a good supply of denture adhesive around. He never leaves home without it!

When I asked his permission to tell this story, he said, "Sure, isn't that the point you're making—that it's important to be able to laugh at yourself?" And that's something he's done often over the years. He laughs easily at himself (and his Moment of Great Embarrassment)—and we would do well to follow his example. Having fun with our kids, enjoying fellowship and fun with other believers, and laughing at ourselves—these are three ways we can model joy to those around us.

6. Live Out a Joyful Faith

Another great way to model joy is through our faith. While it's important to teach reverence, respect, and fear of the Lord, it's also important for our children (and other people in our life) to see that we find great joy in our faith. We need to show them that the Christian life is a life of joy! What better way to do that than by displaying a faith that knows how to laugh? If all our kids ever see is a solemn, grim-faced approach to Christianity, they may not stay in its ranks when they get older.

Of course we must teach our children reverence for their Creator, devotion to Christ, and the sobering, awesome truth of what Jesus did for them on the cross. We must know exactly what we believe and why so that we can teach these fundamentals to our children. But, in addition, we must also show them by our example that those beliefs do not relegate us to a life in Boresville. There's nothing ho-hum about a vibrant faith! Because of our faith, we have hope and joy today as well as the knowledge that today's joy will be overshadowed by the joy to come in His kingdom. What a wonderful privilege to be able to show our children that faith in Jesus Christ is indeed joyful!

As a child, I noticed the absence of such joy after a certain part of the worship service, so I asked my mother one Sunday why everyone in church was always so sad after the sermon. They sang joyfully at the beginning of the service, but after the preacher preached, they sang "Just As I Am" with soft, sad voices. I kept hoping that—just once—the preacher would forget to talk so everyone could stay happy. Then my mother explained to me some deeper aspects of faith, like conviction of sin and the call to discipleship.

> *Childhood is an adventure to be joined by parents whenever possible. By grabbing pockets of time together… you create pleasant memories for both you and your child.*
>
> ~Susan Newman,
> *Little Things*
> *Long Remembered*

But because my family lived out a joyful faith, I was not left with a downhearted view of the Christian life. To the contrary!

In fact, Tim and I try to offer our kids the same kind of joyful faith I grew up with. We love to have what we call "family praise and worship time." Tim will play praise songs on his guitar, sometimes accompanied by the children with their toy instruments, and we all offer up a joyful noise to the Lord. (It's a good thing it's joyful because the Von Trapp Family Singers we aren't!) We have a great deal of fun, and the children love to dance around the room to the fast songs—and we let them. Then, at one point, the mood changes, and Tim has them sit still as we focus on other aspects of our God. We're not really regular with our family praise, but we sure have a good time when we get together.

And, of course, family fun in worship can also happen with the extended church family. In our former city we were in a fellowship group that met once a month for fellowship, food, and prayer—but we also liked to have fun. For one evening meeting, we were told to bring our favorite breakfast food and come in our pajamas—and almost everyone did. (One or two folks decided to partake of our fun with their dignity untarnished. Bah humbug!) So there we were praying and praising God in our bathrobes and fuzzy slippers! We had a beautiful time sharing our needs and answered prayers, and we also had a lot of fun. As we laughed together, I thought about how God must be smiling, since He delights in our fellowship and He wants us to know His joy! I especially loved that our children saw us going to a Christian meeting and enjoying a touch of silliness. They see plenty of reverent worship done in Sunday clothes. This kind of fun showed them that we find great joy in our faith—an important thing to model.

7. Share Your Joys with Others

The expression "a joy divided is a joy multiplied" is so true. When we share our joy with others, our joy increases. And we can share our joy two ways: by telling people about it and by involving them in it. So, instead of being quick to share our complaints, let's be quicker sharing our joys. When something good happens to us, let's tell someone. When something brings you joy, share that with another person. When you find joy in learning something new about God or in reading His Word, share it with someone who encourages your faith walk. In a world filled with depressing news, sharing joy with another person is good for both the sharer and the "sharee." While it's nice to tell someone about our joys, hearing someone else tell us about their joy can be just as uplifting. Comments like, "I'm feeling so good today," "The best thing just happened..." or "Guess what the Lord just showed me?" really can make someone's day, whether that person is the speaker or the hearer. Try it. See for yourself that joy is twice as sweet when we have someone to share it with.

And there are as many ways to share our joy as there are sources of joy. A great meal at a beautiful table can be a sparkle of joy in our day, and the joy increases when that meal is shared. For me, a visit to a good bookstore is a sparkle of joy, and I often include my children on those trips. Now going to a bookstore is a joy for them as well. During my mother's illness, I wanted to give her a little sprinkle of joy, so I made her a joy basket. I bought a heart-shaped basket and filled it with things I thought would bring her joy: some books, a card, a few trinkets, an inexpensive Walkman with headphones, and a tape with Scripture set to music—and all the songs were about joy. She filled her mind with God's words about joy, and those words were a real comfort to her. In her books, Barbara Johnson suggests making such joy baskets for yourself to make you smile when the "gloomees" attack, and that can be a great way to spark some joy that you can, in turn, share with others.

We can literally give someone a basket of joy, or we can share our joy simply by telling them about the good God is doing in our life. Either way, sharing our joy offers those we know and love a sweet respite in an often gloomy world.

8. Nurture a Spirit of Giving

To nurture a generous spirit is to cultivate the gift of joy. My friend Posy learned this as a young girl. She said, "My mother taught me that it is always better to give than to receive. We didn't have much money growing up, so if we wanted to give gifts, they had to be homemade. Through her teaching and example, I learned that giving brings me great joy." No matter what we give to another—an actual gift, time, a deed—we are usually more than repaid by the joy we feel in our heart. Posy adds, "If I do something for someone else when I'm feeling down, I almost always feel better. Because my mother taught me to focus on doing for others first, I rarely feel I need to focus on myself or enter into self-pity."

Liz G. also finds great joy in doing for others, and she models this virtue for her family. She has a real soft spot for elderly people who need help with transportation. Liz will closely watch someone walking along and, after seeing that the person seems safe (for example, she isn't carrying any large bags or wearing heavy garments that could conceal something dangerous), she often pulls over and offers them a ride. "I'll never forget the day," Liz says, "when I was taking my son to afternoon kindergarten and there was the sweetest little 'bag lady' walking across the busy intersection. I quickly observed the situation, prayed for God's safety, and offered this lady a ride. She was a sweet lady who had not eaten that day and was hungry. I looked down and saw I still had half of a hamburger. I offered it to her and she gladly ate it. My son learned how to help people that day and since then we've helped others, prompted by the compassion of my little ones. It gives them—and me—great joy to help those in need."

What are you doing to model the joy of giving and to share that joy with your children?

9. **Focus on the Blessings**

One of the best ways to teach joy and contentment in—or in spite of—present circumstances is to focus on our blessings and to teach our children to do the same. When we point out our blessings and express our gratitude for them, we teach gratefulness, and a grateful heart is usually a joyful heart! Besides, it's hard to express gratitude and be discontent at the same time. When we express our gratefulness to God and to others, our children learn to do the same. And we can show our gratitude verbally, in writing, and by our attitude.

Verbally—The more we talk about our blessings, the more we teach our children to do the same. Kathy P. tries to do this with her family: "Daily, Troy and I talk with our children about all of the blessings God has blessed us with instead of dwelling on the things that are negative and not uplifting. The more good that goes into our hearts and minds, the more good comes out."

The words we speak really can affect our level of contentment as well as that of our children. If we are constantly putting things down and griping, so will our children. When we first moved into our cavelike house, I realized I'd been too verbal about my frustration when I heard my young son say, "Man, this house is the pits!" I quickly began to point out its blessings to him. As I did, he began to mirror my thankfulness with his words, reflecting a more positive outlook. Mary H. has also learned to watch what she says: "I try not to verbalize dissatisfaction with the house or our things (even when I'm thinking the sofa is looking pretty tacky). I also attempt to constantly affirm the value of things like the fact that we love each other and are so blessed."

One family I know teaches their children to be content with a simple family phrase: Be happy for what you've got! When cries of "That's not fair" or "That one's bigger" surface, they counter with "Be happy for what you've got!" Sometimes they shorten it to "BHFWYG," a fun and immediate call to contentment.

In writing—Blessings and answered prayer are always causes of great joy. Writing them down ensures that we don't find joy in them only when they happen. A written record of God's goodness to us and His activity in our life gives us the chance to go back and review the blessings. Julie C. keeps a journal to record her thoughts of thanksgiving as well as her requests. Then, when she has a bad day or life seems too much to handle, she looks back in her journal two years ago and reads about how she was feeling then. Using the beautiful gift of hindsight, she sees that what seemed so overwhelming then turned out okay and that God takes care of things. She adds that both writing and later reading her words of thanksgiving are "calming and comforting [activities], like dipping your hands in reality. I read it and realize that my problems aren't insurmountable." Julie uses pretty cloth journals and stores them on a bookshelf. As she lines them up, they add a touch of beauty to her home, but more importantly they serve as a visual reminder of the many reasons to give thanks for God's faithfulness.

In the Old Testament, God's people did the same thing, but their visual reminders of God's faithfulness and their tangible expressions of gratitude and thanksgiving to God took the shape of stone altars (Genesis 8:20) and monuments (Joshua 4:1-7). God wanted His people to remember His work in their life and to tell future generations about His faithfulness. God wanted these monuments to "be a sign among you when your children ask in time to come, saying, 'What do these stones mean to you?' Then you shall answer them" (Joshua 4:6,7a NKJV). How often we forget what God does in our life. Sometimes it's hard to remember what God did last month, let alone what He did years ago. A thanksgiving journal can be our monument to God's faithfulness and a reminder to tell our children about His goodness.

I like keeping my own personal chronological journal, and the children recently made a family thanksgiving journal. We put Joshua 4:6,7 on the front, and they decorated a page for various categories, which include family, friends, church, activities, feelings, blessings given, and blessings received. Anyone of us is free to write in our thanksgiving journal at any time, and we date each entry. We hope this book will become a permanent record of the faithfulness of God in our family—a monument of our thankfulness.

In attitude—Once, before we started our thanksgiving journal, I noticed that my older girls were beginning to compare our home and possessions with those of their friends. A red light flashed in my head, "Danger zone! Danger zone!" I know how perilous the comparison trap is for adults and our attitude, and I certainly didn't want my children to get caught up in that. So, instead of going straight home from our friend's house, I made a quick turn, crossed the tracks—literally, and drove toward a very poor part of our area. Without driving slowly enough to invade anyone's privacy, I gave my children a quick glimpse of something they'd never seen before: shacks that served as people's homes, lean-tos on shanties with broken windows, yards littered with junk, a man asleep in a broken-down pickup truck in his yard. I don't remember seeing a single flower. "Do people actually live here?" Jacquelyn asked in astonishment. "Yes, honey, they do." We rode in silence as they tried to imagine such a life.

As we got closer to home, we broke the silence and discussed what Jesus said about the poor and ways we might be able to help some of those people. As we drove into our driveway, our old house suddenly looked like a mansion. The hanging baskets of ferns and the geraniums by the front door were a glorious welcome to a home where blessings flowed. "Mom," Jacquelyn said. "We are so blessed!" My children were deeply moved. New perspective firmly in place, they talked about their blessings all afternoon, and I watched their level of joy and contentment take a big leap.

All of us get blind to God's goodness to us. When we take time to remember His faithfulness, look around at the countless ways He cares for us, and build an altar with paper and pen, we will have a wonderful source of joy. Focusing on the blessings can't help but make us joyful in our Lord.

10. **Express Joy and Contentment Any Way You Can**

If we are joyful and content in the deepest place of our being but never outwardly express those feelings, we aren't modeling these virtues for our children. By its very nature, joy needs to be expressed. Contentment may be a quieter feeling of calm satisfaction, yet it also needs to be shown if we are to help our children learn what it is to be content. If we want to teach them to our children, our joy and contentment are not to be secrets hidden in our heart.

Fortunately there are many ways to express our joy. The Bible describes several expressions of joy: singing, the use of musical instruments, praise, shouting, and even just having a joyful heart. Nancy K. expresses her joy with quite a repertoire: "I sing, yell, stomp, and clap." Katie R. says, "I always start my day with Psalm 118:24, 'This is the day which the LORD has made; We will rejoice and be glad in it' (NKJV)."

Spunky morning talk show host Kathie Lee Gifford often does the same thing when her two-year-old daughter comes to her requesting, "Hosanna, Mommy! Hosanna!" That's when she and Cassidy and five-year-old Cody march around their deck, singing, "This is the day the Lord has made. We will rejoice and be glad in it! Hosanna! Hosanna!" She's sure the people in her neighboring state hear her, but she says this:

> I don't care what they think. I believe worship
> should be fun and exciting so children can embrace it.

After all, David leaped and danced before the Lord with all his might, and sang out with joy.

We Christians don't do that enough. Often we're all so terrified of what somebody's going to say. But if you love the Lord, you should *show* it. *The joy of the Lord is your strength.*[1]

People often ask Kathie Lee where she gets her energy, and she says that what most people perceive as her energy (and she's *very* energetic) is really her strength of spirit. "It comes from the joy of knowing God, loving Him, and being loved by Him," she explains. "It's so simple we sometimes stumble past it."[2] She goes on:

That's why I jump in wholeheartedly to join Cassidy and her five-year-old brother, Cody, when we march around the deck doing our hosannas. They are learning from their earliest days that God loves them and has a plan for their lives. The joy of the Lord is *their* strength too.[3]

Is the joy of the Lord your strength as well? It can be. He wants it to be!

Maybe you're like Cindy G., who "seems to always have a little laugh right under her breath ready to come out." Or maybe your temperament is more subdued, like my mother who preferred to laugh on the inside but was quick with a quiet smile. No matter what your temperament, no matter how you express your joy and contentment, just be sure you do. After all, you are modeling these qualities—or the lack of them—for the people you love. Besides, joy shared really is joy increased—and none of us can ever have too much joy!

> *To* show a child what once delighted you, to find the child's delight added to your own—this is happiness.
>
> ~J.B. Priestley,
> *Reader's Digest*

~❧ Epilogue ❧~
Finding Purpose and Joy in the Moment

Have you ever asked yourself why you're here? More importantly, have you come to any conclusions? Also, how long has it been since you've lived? And I don't mean just breathing and having your heart beat, but really living with all your senses fully engaged, totally aware of the moment at hand? Knowing who we are and why we're here and finding joy in the moment are key to really living joyfully and with purpose—and that's an incredible way to live. It's the difference between being a "mama who ain't happy" and a mama who's making the choice to rejoice.

Knowing Who We Are and Why We're Here

Most of us know who we are unless, of course, mothering has taken its toll and Mama's desperate enough to claim amnesia if only to get a brief vacation at The Home for Misplaced Persons. Although we probably still have a handle on our name and address, most of us need to guard against spiritual amnesia—that condition where we forget who we are in Christ and the reason we can be joyful always.

Know who you are in Christ. Because I have been adopted as a child of God through Jesus' death on the cross for my sins, I have an inheritance more precious than any of earth's joys (Ephesians 1:5). As one of the women I surveyed said, "Because I am a child of the King, that makes me a princess!" True enough! I also know this about our identity in Christ: "Having also believed [in the gospel of salvation], you were sealed in Him with the Holy Spirit of promise, who is given as a pledge of our inheritance" (Ephesians 1:13,14a). And that inheritance is eternal life (John 3:16). So I'm a daughter of the King who has the Holy Spirit to guarantee that I will live forever with Jesus. God's Word also tells me that one of the fruits of the Holy Spirit is joy (Galatians 5:22). How wonderful! So, as believers in Christ, we are princesses who have an eternal future with Him and the ability to live joyfully today because of the Holy Spirit and God's grace! We need never doubt our worth to God or our ability to know joy. You and I must choose joy, but God's grace makes it possible for us to experience it.

Know who you are as an individual and why you're here. Besides knowing who we are in Christ, we need to know within that framework and on a more personal basis who we are and why we're here. Some of us learn in an instant who we are: a sudden spiritual discovery, experience, or happening shines a light on that spot in our soul that yearns to know who we are and why we're here. For others, that discovery may seem to take a lifetime. And, sadly, I'm afraid, many people just exist. They do their job, clean their house, and go to church without any real sense of their God-given mission in this world. They are missing the great joy that comes from knowing their unique purpose in life—why God made them. When we know that, we know our mission. And that mission can involve just about anything because—and it's essential to know this—no matter who we are or where we are, God wants to use us for His glory. We just have to be willing to be used. And no matter where you are in life, it's never too late to discover your mission.

I remember the first time I began to sense my purpose. I was 17 and had enjoyed writing since I was 9 years old. I was contemplating my future in communications as I prepared for college, and I learned that I could have a mission in life unrelated to "missions" in the evangelistic sense. My pastor told me, "God can certainly use Christians in secular work, especially the media. You can be called to that just as easily as someone can be called to the mission field overseas." I had begun to discover part of my individual purpose in life, and God has continued to reveal and reaffirm my calling and purpose over the years as my life has changed.

God places gifts and desires within us that we can use to serve Him, and that's key to knowing joy in this life. Sometimes people miss out on joy because they think that if they enjoy doing a certain work, then it must not be God's will for them. But it is God who gives us our gifts and works through our minds and desires to accomplish His will: "For it is God who is at work in you, both to will and to work for His good pleasure" (Philippians 2:13,14).

Acknowledging our gifts and identifying our desires are important steps toward knowing who we are, what we're here for, and how God can use us. God can accomplish His purposes through us because He uniquely created us to be used by Him in a role that only we can fill. No one else can evangelize just like Billy Graham does, no one can minister to the poor exactly as Mother Teresa does, and no one can do your job or raise your children like you can. We are uniquely qualified to influence the children God gave us. We are uniquely able to make a difference in whatever we do when we recognize that God can use us *where we are!*

Accepting this truth gives us vision and a mission for living. In *Holy Sweat,* author Tim Hansel writes about the importance of a vision for our life:

> In fact, to have an inner vision is critical if we're going to live our lives to the fullest. The good news is that you have the answer with you all the time. Where? God's imprinted it, stamped it on your being. Elizabeth O'Connor, in her book, *Eighth Day of Creation*, explains: "We ask to know the will of God without guessing that his will is written into our very beings. We perceive that will when we discern our gifts. Our obedience and surrender to God is in large part our obedience and surrender to our gifts."[1]

Having this "inner vision," this mission in life, however lofty or simple it is, makes getting up in the morning worth it. It gives reason to the mundane. No matter how simple our mission is or how ordinary we feel our specific purpose in life is, we must remember that God can use us where we are for His purposes. That truth gives meaning to whatever we do—from cleaning house and cooking meals to running a corporation. When we know God has a purpose for us and believe He wants to use us right where we are and when we follow the exhortation of Colossians 3:17 ("Whatever you do in word or deed, do all in the name of the Lord Jesus"), we can clean and cook or run a business with joy! Those acts can become our service and even worship offered up to Him, and we really can find great joy in it!

I love a story Gordon MacDonald tells in *The Life God Blesses* of having breakfast with some bus driver friends who were complaining about their job. What, if any, significance can come from driving a bus? Pastor MacDonald explained that God can make any job interesting when we believe He wants to use us in it. This is what he told his friends: "Tomorrow morning before anyone gets on your bus, close the door, face all the empty seats, and say loudly, 'In the name of Jesus, I declare this bus a sanctuary for the next eight hours. And I declare that all the people who enter this sanctuary will experience the love of Christ through me whether they realize it or not.' "[2] A few months later, one of the drivers told Gordon that following this suggestion had changed his life. He said:

> Each day I've been turning my bus into a sanctuary, and it's made all the difference in the way I do my job. Why, the other day a guy got on my bus, and he was so mad at me because I wouldn't let him off at a stop that was illegal. He cussed me out something awful. And you know? There was a day when I think I would have gotten up and let him have it. But not in a sanctuary. I let him off at the next stop and said, "Hope you have a good day, sir. Nice having you aboard." And a lady behind me said, "Charlie, how can you be so nice to a jerk like that?" I just muttered to myself that it wasn't hard if you were driving a sanctuary and not a bus.[3]

After I read that, I started making my minivan a sanctuary for afternoon car pool!

One of the greatest joys that we can experience is knowing and doing what God made us to do. We may have many roles and they may change over time as we grow, but discovering what they are and how they work together to fulfill our ultimate mission in life is a very joyful thing. My favorite movie line of all time is from *Chariots of Fire* when Olympic runner Eric Liddell says, "When I run, I feel His pleasure." I feel God's pleasure when I use my gifts to serve Him. Once, while taping a radio broadcast, I stopped and prayed, *Thank You, Lord. I feel You smiling. This work I do as worship to You.* I also feel God's pleasure in my primary role as a wife and mother. When I'm able to express joy instead of impatience with my children or view yet another load of laundry as an act of worship to God, I know He is pleased.

Let me direct you to a place that I think is one of the most joyful places on earth. It is the convergence point of who we are and who we are in Christ. It's that point on the line when the knowledge of our mission in life intersects with the realization that we can reflect who we are in Christ as we do that work. At that point of convergence, God can use us and we can know great joy. That convergence impacts how we live, the choices we make on this journey, and the amount of joy we find along the way.

Joy in the Moment

The other day I passed a man at the post office who stood out like a sore thumb. Everyone was hurrying about, but he stood perfectly still on the edge of the sidewalk, with his eyes closed and his face turned up towards the sun. He was drinking in the moment, and he looked so content. People probably thought he looked strange, but as I passed I smiled. *He's got it!* I thought. *He's enjoying the moment!*

How easily we forget to find joy in the moment. We work hard, endure difficulty, and wait for the biggies in life to bring the feeling of joy: a new baby, a new house, a vacation. We get so busy trying to live our life that sometimes in the process we forget what it means to really live.

We miss the joy in the moment when we look for joy in the future. Do these poignant words by an anonymous writer strike a little too close to home?

> First I was dying to finish high school and start college.
> And then I was dying to finish college and start working.
> And then I was dying to marry and have children.
> And then I was dying for my children to grow old enough for school so I could return to work.
> And then I was dying to retire.
> And now I am dying...and suddenly I realize I forgot to live.

As these words remind us, if we wait until tomorrow to enjoy life, we may miss out. It's so easy to get caught up in our daily schedules that we leave little room for things that can bring us joy. We must learn how to really live today. We can do simple things that give us gladness of heart. What things make your heart sing? I love to write, visit bookstores, go "antiquing," read to my children, and go on family outings, to name a few things. Making time in my life for these things brings me great joy.

If you let yourself be absorbed completely, if you surrender completely to the moments as they pass, you live more richly those moments.

~Anne Morrow Lindbergh

For Posy L., it's working in the yard. "With a name like Posy," she says, "it comes naturally. I love learning about and growing flowers. Having a beautiful yard thrills me—it's my way of glorifying and affirming God's presence in my life." One day she noticed that her then-eight-year-old son was watching her work in the yard.

"Mom, I was watching you because you are so happy when

you work with your flowers. And I think I know why."

Wondering what was coming, she asked, "Why?"

"Because you don't have a sandbox. The yard is your sand-box, Mom!" he replied. And it is. It's the place for her that each of us needs. "A place to go," Posy says, "to just mess around, where there are no right or wrong answers, where one can re-lax and open the soul to God." A place or thing that gives us gladness of heart. What or where is it for you?

We miss the joy in the moment when we look for it in the past. I was tempted to hang on to joys from the past when my mom died, and maybe you're there right now. But if we live in the past, we won't find joy today. We must live in the moment and be alert to the joys of those moments, no matter what the past was like. And, as Nicole Niederer's lyrics point out, the call of the past can be powerful.

This Is Now

Familiar feelings creeping inside of me,
Amazing how a simple conversation,
Things I thought I'd buried way back when;
Fear and insecurity, I thought that I had victory,
But tonight I face the battlefield again.
Amazing how a simple conversation
Can cause the loss of so much ground I've gained.
A long-forgotten memory, invading my stability;
At times like this, it helps for me to say,
"I'm here, this is now; I'm exactly where God wants me.
I'm here, this is now, and the past no longer taunts me."
It's really very clear, all that matters is I'm here.
I'm here and this is now.[4]

You and I are here and this is now—and the now really can have its own sparkle. We must get beyond the past and keep a vision for the future and, as we do so, find our joy in the mo-ment that is now! The present is not just what we pass through on the way to the future. It is filled with what one writer calls "real moments." She says, "What was missing from my life were more 'real moments,' moments when I was not trying to get somewhere or be something, moments when I was fully experiencing and enjoying where I was, now.[5] To find such "real moments" and enjoy the present, we must slow down and be aware of what we're doing.

Slow Down and Pay Attention

We probably miss many moments of joy because we're too busy and inattentive. We must pay attention to what is going on at any given moment. When we can put our problems, our tasks, and our disruptive thoughts out of our mind long enough to totally focus on the moment at hand, we have a chance to experience joy. I remember doing that one night when my son was an infant. From my journal:

> Last night I was tired, it was late, and I just wanted to finish the dishes. But Collin screamed out and I went to get him. He wasn't feeling well, so I just sat and rocked him. I sat and stroked his velvety soft cheek and tiny jaw and felt his little hand touching my face, and I was overcome with unexpected joy. His head leaned against me, and he looked up into my eyes with total peace, contentment, and love. What a moment. I think I'll forever have that picture in my mind. Lord, show me more moments like these. Let me not be too busy to seize such moments.

Lately, I've really been practicing paying attention. The other night on my way to the store, I drove with the windows down, a 70-degree wind blowing my hair, and the radio playing—loudly. *At this very instant, I feel joy*, I thought. On another evening, I stepped outside and was still for a minute. I looked up at the sky, noticed the North Star, and for just a moment the sky was that gorgeous deep blue color that it gets right before nightfall. *Mmmm. Another bit of joy. Glad I paid attention.*

Of course some joyful moments just can't be missed. Like the other day when my son and I were driving along and he said, "Mom, I know what I'm going to be when I grow up."

"What, honey?" I asked, waiting to hear him announce his future career.

"A shepherd," he said with all the seriousness in the world.
"You mean, like...with sheep?" I stammered.

"Yep. A shepherd, " he said. Then he changed the subject
as if that were all the discussion necessary, and he began telling
a new story. I choked back a laugh. I didn't have the heart to tell
him there really wasn't much of a job market for that these days.
There was joy in that moment from both the humor of Collin's
career choice as well as the pleasure of a shared connection
with my very self-absorbed young son!

Even now as I write these words, I'm finding great joy in the
moment. Normally I write at my computer, but to close this book
I wanted to fully experience my life as a writer. I wanted to feel the
pen in my hand scratching out words on paper, my heart to yours,
with the sun on my face and God's beauty around me. So here I
sit on a park bench at the edge of a lake. I have slowed my body
and mind, wanting to be alert to the things around me. My five
senses are engaged in lifting my spirits. I see the beauty of a
tree-lined lake, and I feel the warmth of the sun. I hear the sounds
of life in the birds, the children playing, and the snippets of conversations from people walking by. I smell pine trees and fresh air,
and I just tasted a nice lunch and a little bit of life. It is just an ordinary day, but today I'm paying attention. I've been to this park
before and seen all these same things, but I didn't take them in as
I'm doing today.

So, to find joy in the moment, we must know our purpose
in Christ and we must seize the day (although sometimes we just
want to *cease* the day!). In *Carpe Diem* (Latin for "seize the
day"), Tony Campolo writes: "This book is meant for us regular
people who still believe that the miraculous is a hidden dimen-
sion of the mundane and would like to figure out how to touch
and taste it."[6] We can see the miraculous and taste the joy when
we're paying attention. But we must not make joy our goal. If
that is our goal, we will never find it. It's like that butterfly that
we can't force to land on our shoulder. We can enjoy its beauty
whenever it happens to alight if we're paying attention, but—
like knowing joy—we can't make it happen. Sometimes we are
seeking so intently, we are "so conscious of the goal," as Tim
Hansel writes, "[that we miss] the miracles along the way."[7] So
don't seek after joy, but do be alert for its sparkle. Sometimes
we find the sparkle of joy in the mundane when we're paying

attention and have relaxed our striving a bit. Remember—don't focus on the joy; focus on the journey and the joy will come.

Be a gardener. A good gardener doesn't just plant to reap the fruit. She can go buy fruit if that's all she's after. She prepares the soil, plants, cultivates, nourishes, prunes, and—all along the way—enjoys every aspect of the process. The fruit is a beautiful by-product. And so it is in our life of joy. Don't seek the fruit itself. Moments of pleasure and mere happiness can be had almost any day. But when we set out to live life to its fullest, aware of our purpose and yielding to God, and when we are alert to the extraordinary in the ordinary moments, we find the by-product of joy.

Happiness Is Overrated—Go for Joy Instead!

So what about Mama? Can we really make the choice to rejoice? Picture this: It's a "Mama ain't happy" day. She's doing her very best "state of distemper." She's grumping and doing her pit-bull-in-high-heels impression. Her eyebrows are most definitely down. Now, mentally, send her to her room to get a grip.

Next, think about the Mama we'd all like to be. She's made the choice to rejoice. She's tamed that monster of discontent, she's learned to become intimate with the Giver of Joy and how to be joyful even when she feels like a grump. She's installed her security system to protect against the joy robbers, and she's practicing Jovial Jane's FINER life. She's learned to laugh and lollygag more. She's even been trying her hand at candles and confetti. Sometimes she faces the dark, but she's learned to look for the sparkle even there. By learning and practicing these things and, more importantly, turning to God's Word to help her vine life, she's become a Mama capable of modeling joy and contentment for her family.

Which Mama do we want to be? Which Mama do we want our children to see? Not a hard choice, is it? Oh, we'll never fully achieve all of these traits, but this isn't a book about perfection. This book is about process and the fruit available along the way. We will never arrive once and for all at unshakable joy—that is, until our final, heavenly destination. Then we will be greeted by the Fullness of Joy Himself who will look at us and smile and say, "Well done, good and faithful servant....Enter into the joy of your master" (Matthew 25:21).

But, until that time, we must remember that although joy awaits us at the end of our trip, there's also joy in the journey. Since Jesus wants us to have that fullness of joy, let's take Him up on it. We can be women, wives, and mothers who have the joy of the Lord and know true contentment—visible fruit of the abundant life in Christ. But that's not all. As the Talmud says, "When you teach your son, you teach your son's son." We can make the choice to rejoice to influence our family as well as future generations. Even if Mama ain't happy, she can make the choice to rejoice—it's possible, it's worth it, and it's up to us.

*I*f you desire this gift from the Father, ask Him for it.

Until now you have asked for nothing in My name; ask and you will receive, that your joy may be made full.

~John 16:24

Sparkles in the Moment

What Brings You Joy?
Answers from my Joy Survey

Relishing God's beautiful handiwork.

Beautiful music.

Wisdom, as in skillful living and making choices that honor God.

Friends, cards, a hug from a child, a bright smile from someone whom I haven't seen in a while.

Seeing God's hand in my life; having fun with my family.

Delivering meals on wheels; taking the elderly to the doctor when necessary.

My husband who is also my best friend. My only prayer was for God to give me a husband who loved the Lord as much as me and to bless us with years to serve Him together. How can I not feel joyous having had that prayer answered?

The birth of my children.

The birth of my grandchildren.

Kisses from my children.

A hug from a grandchild.

Hearing grandchildren laughing.

I feel joy when I'm doing things well, so I find ways to constantly improve what I do but that are suited to my abilities and schedule. For example, I will never commit to cooking on Saturday, cleaning on Monday, ironing on Tuesday...I would fail if I set goals like that. Flexibility is important.

Smiling; dancing; playing.

Good smells; dancing uninhibited.

Looking at the countryside from my house.

Seeing our house clean; having friends in our home; and hosting family gatherings and special celebrations.

Walking on crisp new-fallen snow; the beauty of autumn.

Knowing I'm in God's perfect will for my life.

Reading; friends; nice perfumes; hot showers.

Fulfilling my mission statement: to help others; to strive to be the unique individual God made me; to live ecstatically and die gratefully.

Life itself.

∼ Notes ∼

A Bit About Being Joyful

1. Mary Farrar, *Choices* (Sisters, OR: Multnomah Press, 1994), p. 87.

Chapter 1—Sparkles in the Rocks

1. Barbara M. is one of the 50 people—mostly women—who completed a survey on joy for me while I was working on this book.
You'll meet many of the others on a first-name/last-initial basis throughout these pages.

Chapter 2—If Mama Ain't Happy, Ain't Nobody Happy

1. Dennis and Barbara Rainey, *Building Your Mate's Self-Esteem* (San Bernardino, CA: Here's Life Publishers, 1986), p. 38.
2. Dr. Brenda Hunter, *Home by Choice* (Portland, OR: Multnomah Press, 1991), p. 38.
3. Ibid., p. 27.
4. Anne Ortlund, *Disciplines of the Home* (Dallas: Word Publishing, 1990), p. 76.
5. World Book Encyclopedia, 1976, volume 19, s.v. thermostat.
6. Ibid.
7. Ibid.
8. Leslie Barker, "No Snooze, You Lose," in *The Dallas Morning News,* September 2, 1991, p. 3c.

Chapter 3—It's All in Our Heads

1. John Maxwell, *The Winning Attitude* (Nashville: Thomas Nelson Publishers, 1993), pp. 26, 29, 33, 36, 38, 41, 44.
2. Transcript of "Attitude, Not Aptitude, Determines Altitude," a speech by Richard L. Weaver II, at Bowling Green University, April 3, 1993, in *Vital Speeches of the Day*, p. 478.
3. Gillian Flynn, "Attitude More Valued Than Ability," in *Personnel Journal*, September 1994, p. 16.
4. Charles Swindoll, *Strenghening Your Grip* (Dallas: Word, 1982), p. 207.
5. Natalie Angier, "The Anatomy of Joy," in *New York Times Magazine*, April 26, 1992, p. 50.
6. David Levine, "The Secrets of People Who Never Get Sick," in *Good Housekeeping*, December 1995, p. 73.
7. Maxwell, *The Winning Attitude*, p. 145.

8. Dr. Frank Minirth and Dr. Paul Meier, *Happiness Is a Choice* (Grand Rapids: Baker Book House, 1978), pp. 12-13.

Chapter 4—Taming the Monster of Discontent

1. "Letter to a Daughter: Being Contented," in *Christian Century*, March 16, 1994, pp. 270-71.
2. Ibid.
3. Carol Mader, "Dare to Not Compare," in "The Proverbs 31 Homemaker" newsletter (P.O. Box 17155, Charlotte, NC, 28270), January 1996), p. 3.
4. Ibid.
5. Joe Dominguez and Vicki Robin, *Your Money or Your Life* (New York: Penguin Books, 1993), pp. 18-19.
6. George Barna, *If Things Are So Good, Why Do I Feel So Bad?* (Chicago: Moody Press, 1994), pp. 12-14.
7. Susan Gregory, *Out of the Rat Race* (Ann Arbor, MI: Vine Books, 1994), pp. 83-84.
8. Grace Merrill, "Lessons in Contentment" in *Focus on the Family* magazine, November 1995, p. 16.

Chapter 5—The Secret of Contentment

1. John Maxwell, *The Winning Attitude* (Nashville: Thomas Nelson Publishers, 1993), pp. 159-60.
2. Study notes in *The Open Bible (expanded edition), New American Standard Version* (Nashville: Thomas Nelson Publishers, 1985), p. 1141.
3. John Maxwell, Injoy Life Club tape study notes: "Content or Discontent— Which Tent Do You Live In?," p. 1.
4. Hannah Whitall Smith, *The Christian's Secret of a Happy Life* (Uhrichsville, OH: Barbour and Company, 1870, 1985), p. 29.
5. Oswald Chambers, *My Utmost for His Highest* (Uhrichsville, OH: Barbour and Company, 1935, 1963), pp. 26-27, 52-53.
6. Smith, *Christian's Secret,* p. 48.

Chapter 6—How Can I Be Joyful...

1. Innovisions (Chicago, IL), Card #986.
2. Dr. Henry Cloud and Dr. John Townsend, *False Assumptions: Twelve "Christian" Beliefs That Can Drive You Crazy* (Grand Rapids: Zondervan Publishing House, 1995), p. 59.
3. Brother Lawrence, *The Practice of the Presence of God*, quoted in Ray and Anne Ortlund, *In His Presence*, pp. 3-4.
4. Ray and Anne Ortlund, *In His Presence*, p. 5.
5. Ibid., p. 28.

Chapter 7—Three Powerful P's

1. Henry H. Halley, *Halley's Bible Handbook* (Grand Rapids: Zondervan Publishing House, 1927,1965), pp. 807, 809.
2. Ibid., p. 807.

3. Myrna Alexander, *Behold Your God* (Grand Rapids: Zondervan Publishing House, 1978), pp. 115, 122.
4. Ibid., pp. 119-20.
5. Halley, *Halley's Bible Handbook,* p. 250.
6. Oswald Chambers, *My Utmost for His Highest* (Uhrichsville, OH: Barbour and Co., 1935, 1963), p. 32.
7. Becky Tirabassi, "Let Prayer Change Your Life," in *Focus on the Family* magazine, February 1996, p. 12.
8. Andrew Murray, *The Inner Life*, quoted by Tirabassi, "Let Prayer Change Your Life," p. 12.

Chapter 8—Joy in the Dark

1. James Dobson, *When God Doesn't Make Sense* (Wheaton, IL: Tyndale House Publishers, 1993), p. 12.
2. Hannah Whitall Smith, The Christian's Secret of a Happy Life (Uhrichsville, OH: Barbour and Co., 1870, 1985), p. 29.
3. Eileen Egan and Kathleen Egan, *Suffering into Joy* (Ann Arbor, MI: Servant Publishers, 1994), p. 21.
4. Ibid., p. 19.
5. Gordon MacDonald, *The Life God Blesses* (Nashville: Thomas Nelson Publishers, 1994), pp. 26-27.
6. Ibid., p. 28.
7. Oswald Chambers, *My Utmost for His Highest* (Uhrichsville, OH: Barbour and Co., 1935, 1963), p. 32.

Chapter 9—I Didn't Lose My Joy—It's Been Stolen

1. Sherwood Eliot Wirt, *The Book of Joy* (New York: McCracken Press, 1994), pp. 23-24.
2. Bill Hendricks, "Studies Suggest That Stress Is Weakening Americans' Health," in *The Houston Chronicle*, June 4, 1995, p. 12A.
3. Peter Hanson, *The Joy of Stress* (New York: Andrews, McMeel & Parker, 1986), pp. 11-12.
4. Ibid.
5. Cheri Fuller, *Trading Your Worry for Wonder: A Woman's Guide to Overcoming Anxiety* (Nashville: Broadman & Holman), chapter 1.
6. Barbara Johnson, *Splashes of Joy in the Cesspools of Life* (Dallas: Word, 1992), pp. 40-41.
7. Jean Lush, *Women and Stress* (Grand Rapids: Fleming H. Revell, 1992), p. 18.
8. *Wirt, The Book of Joy,* p. 26.
9. Don Baker and Emery Nester, *Depression: Finding Hope and Meaning in Life's Darkest Shadow* (Portland, OR: Multnomah Press, 1983), p. 7.
10. Grace Ketterman, M.D., *Surviving the Darkness* (Nashville: Thomas Nelson Publishers, 1988, 1993), p. 1.
11. Dr. James Dobson, "Focus on the Family" radio broadcast, December 12, 1995, discussing "What Wives Wish Their Husbands Knew About Women."
12. Ketterman, *Surviving the Darkness,* p. xvii.
13. Ibid., p. 230.

Chapter 10—Disciplines of a Joyful Person

1. *Time* magazine, "The Simple Life," April 8, 1991, p. 58.
2. Erma Bombeck, "The Modern Woman: She's Tired of Having It All," Universal Press Syndicate, 1991.
3. Ibid.
4. Anne Ortlund, *Disciplines of a Beautiful Woman* (Dallas: Word, 1977), p. 69.
5. Caryl Stern, "Who Is Old," in *Parade*, January 21, 1996, p. 45.
6. "Ten Ways to Take Charge of Your Health," in *Good Housekeeping*, March 1995, pp. 194-95.
7. Pam Smith, *Food for Life* (Lake Mary, FL: Creation House, 1994), p. 137.
8. Ibid., p. 24.
9. Ibid., see page 36 and related chapters.
10. Quoted in Charles Boisseau, "Southwest's Pilot," in *The Houston Chronicle*, March 10, 1996, pp. 1-2D.
11. David G. Meyers, "Pursuing Happiness," in *Psychology Today*, July/August 1993, p. 66.
12. David Levine, "The Secrets of People Who Never Get Sick," in *Good Housekeeping*, December 1995, p. 72.
13. Tim Hansel, *Through the Wilderness of Loneliness* (Elgin, IL: David C. Cook Publishing, 1991), p. 134.

Chapter 11—Laugh and Lollygag

1. That's how John Trent describes laughter in his article "Strength Training" in *Christian Parenting Today*, July/August 1995, p. 64.
2. *The Woman's Study Bible* (Nashville: Thomas Nelson, 1995), p. 1051.
3. The following sources provided information for this chapter: Pam Smith, *Food for Life* (Lake Mary, FL: Creation House, 1994); Natalie Angier, "The Anatomy of Joy," in *New York Times Magazine,* April 26, 1992, p. 50; John Trent, "Strength Training" in *Christian Patenting Today,* July/August 1995, p. 64; Carole Mayhall, "A Laugh a Day," in *Today's Christian Woman*, January/February 1995, pp. 35-37.
4. Catherine and Loren Broadus, *Play: It's Not Just for Kids!* (Dallas: Word, 1987), p. 106.
5. Norman Cousins, *Anatomy of an Illness As Perceived by the Patient* (New York: W.W. Noton Company, 1979), pp. 39-40.
6. Natalie Angier, "The Anatomy of Joy," in *New York Times Magazine*, April 26, 1992, p. 50.
7. Trent, p. 64.
8. Ibid., p. 65.
9. Sherwood Eliot Wirt, *The Book of Joy* (New York: McCracken Press, 1994), p. 1.
10. Dandi Daley Mackall, "What Does God Do All Day?" *Kids Say the Greatest Things About God* (Wheaton, IL: Tyndale House, 1995).
11. Source unknown.

12. *Webster's 21st Century Book of Quotations* (Nashville: Thomas Nelson, 1992), p. 127.
13. Broadus and Broadus, *Play: It's Not Just for Kids*, p. 13.
14. Ibid., p. 14.
15. Ibid., pp. 99-100.

Chapter 12—Candles and Confetti

1. Claire Cloninger, *A Place Called Simplicity* (Eugene, OR: Harvest House Publishers, 1993), p. 93.
2. Ibid.
3. Donna Otto, *Secrets to Getting More Done in Less Time* (Eugene, OR: Harvest House Publishers, 1995), p. 23.
4. Ibid.
5. Jean Lush, *Women and Stress* (Grand Rapids: Fleming H. Revell, 1992), pp. 199-200.
6. Ibid.
7. Barna, pp. 160-61.
8. Ibid.
9. Cheri Fuller, *Christmas Treasures of the Heart* (Tulsa: Honor Books, 1995), pp. v, vi.
10. Emilie Barnes, *If Teacups Could Talk* (Eugene, OR: Harvest House Publishers, 1994), p. 46.

Chapter 13—Living and Giving Joy and Contentment

1. Kathie Lee Gifford, "Where Do You Get Your Energy?" *Guideposts*, January 1990, p. 6.
2. Ibid.
3. Ibid., p. 8.

Epilogue—Finding Purpose and Joy in the Moment

1. Tim Hansel, *Holy Sweat* (Dallas: Word, 1987), p. 80.
2. MacDonald, *The Life God Blesses* (Nashville: Thomas Nelson Publishers, 1994), p. 125.
3. Ibid., pp. 125-26.
4. "This Is Now" words and music by Nicole Niederer, copyright 1991. Used by permission.
5. Barbara De Angelis, Ph.D., *Real Moments* (New York: Delacorte Press, 1994), p. xi. Note: This book is very interesting, but it has a "mother earth" flavor rather than a Christian worldview.
6. Tony Campolo, *Carpe Diem* (Dallas: Word, 1994), p. 233.
7. Tim Hansel, *When I Relax, I Feel Guilty* (Elgin, IL: David C. Cook Publishing Co., 1979), p. 105.

More Great Resources from Harvest House

THE CONFIDENT WOMAN
Anabel Gillham

Do you struggle to be the "perfect Christian" for God, your family, your employer, your friends? You're not alone. But God doesn't call you to be "perfect." He calls you to be *confident*—because of His love, His acceptance, and the life of His Son, Jesus, inside you. Anabel Gillham shares with you God's plan for freedom, rest, and peace, showing you from Scripture what a truly confident woman looks like.

FINDING YOUR PURPOSE AS A MOM
Donna Otto

Life-management expert Donna Otto shares simple tips and practical insights to help you have the home of your dreams—one in which holiness reigns and rest, peace, and joy can be found.

THE MOTHERLOAD
Mary M. Byers

Moms need friends, laughter, solitude, and an active relationship with Jesus. How can they get these amid family responsibilities? Byers offers spiritual truths and practical advice to help moms survive and thrive. Includes discussion questions.

SHE'S GONNA BLOW!
Julie Ann Barnhill

Yes, you *do* love your kids—and other moms struggle with feelings of anger just like you do! A "been-there-done-that" mom herself, Julie Barnhill turns the hilarious scenes of everyday life with kids into a practical guide for anyone who's wrestling with the down-to-earth realities of being a mom. *She's Gonna Blow!* offers you hope, honest understanding, and good measures of laughter and wise biblical counsel.

10-MINUTE TIME OUTS FOR MOMS
Grace Fox

Insightful devotions from author and mother Grace Fox empower you to maintain a vital connection with God. Inspiring stories, Scripture-based prayers, and practical guidance will give you strength for your spiritual journey and day-to-day life.

SECRETS TO GETTING MORE DONE IN LESS TIME
Donna Otto

Deadlines. Clutter. Unending responsibilities. These things and many others can overwhelm the daily experience of joyful living for most women. Home and life management expert Donna Otto reveals proven methods and practices so you can master time and maximize it; use personalized planners effectively; involve the family so everybody benefits. Homeowners, newlyweds, stay-at-home moms, and women in the workforce will appreciate these easy steps to a better life.

GOT TEENS?
Jill Savage and Pam Farrel

These time-tested answers for mothers of teens and tweens come from two veteran moms: Jill Savage, founder of Hearts at Home ministries, and Pam Farrel, cofounder of Masterful Living Ministries. Their practical, biblical tools will help you turn around destructive behavior or bad habits; guide your teen's relationships with the opposite sex; and identify and develop their strengths.

GOD ANSWERS MOMS' PRAYERS
Allison Bottke

Few emotions run as deep as a mother's love for her children. This collection of brief real-life stories will inspire you to combine your love with faith and hope and pray with confidence.

PARENTING...DON'T TRY THIS AT HOME
Phil Callaway

Max Lucado says, *"This is a book you'll love."* Author and award-winning columnist Phil Callaway captures the amusing and bemusing experiences of the roller-coaster ride called "parenting." In this sparkling collection of stories you'll recognize those you love...as well as yourself! And the comedy and humanity Phil finds in family life will encourage you...whatever stage you're at in the game...to take notice of each day's gifts of humor and faith.

Harvest House Helps You
with Issues That Affect Your Family

HARRY POTTER, NARNIA, AND THE LORD OF THE RINGS
What You Need to Know About Fantasy Books and Movies
Richard Abanes

Is every fantasy story appropriate for everyone?

In this evenhanded exploration of the books of J.K. Rowling, C.S. Lewis, and J.R.R. Tolkien, as well as the films based on their writings, Richard Abanes—a fantasy fan himself—answers key questions:

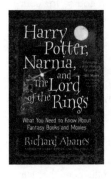

- What is inspiring and healthy in these works? What is misleading and harmful?

- Do I need to be concerned about occult influence from fantasy?

- How do movies and merchandising impact kids' minds?

Pro-literature and pro-fun, *Harry Potter, Narnia, and The Lord of the Rings* helps you evaluate fantasy's strengths and dangers from a balanced Christian perspective.

"Informative...a great resource for parents!"
—Bill Myers, bestselling youth and children's fiction author

WITCHCRAFT GOES MAINSTREAM
Uncovering Its Alarming Impact on You and Your Family
Brooks Alexander

The Halloween witch is dead. The old crone on a broomstick is gone. In her place is a young, hip, sexually magnetic woman who worships a goddess and practices socially acceptable magic.

As witchcraft goes mainstream, this new image, or some other aspect of the rapidly growing pagan religious movement, shapes the identity of more and more of your co-workers and neighbors...or maybe even your friends and family members. What do you do or say when you or your children meet someone like this?

Brooks Alexander, founder of the Spiritual Counterfeits Project, pointedly answers the tough questions:

- What do modern witches believe? Are they really following ancient pagan traditions or worshiping the devil?
- What does the widespread acceptance of witchcraft today mean for you?
- How can you respond to protect your loved ones and reach out with the love of Jesus?

Weighing our ever-changing spiritual surroundings within a biblical framework, *Witchcraft Goes Mainstream* will help you chart a course for yourself and your family and see the light of God more clearly in a darkening culture.

FEARLESS FAITH
Living Beyond the Walls of Safe Christianity
John Fischer

It's not always easy to be a Christian these days. We live in a culture that frequently challenges the very foundations of our faith. Our natural response is to flee from the criticisms and the negative influences that surround us, creating our own safe Christian environment in an unsafe world.

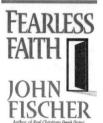

But as John Fischer reminds us, that's not what Jesus intended. In this provocative book, Fischer reminds us that we are to be *in the world*—part of the dialogue—and making a contribution to every area of our lives from a perspective of faith.

Fearless Faith will help those who desire to impact their world...

- understand the true meaning of being "in the world, but not of the world"
- find the courage to bring God's light to life's darkest corners
- learn to recognize the many ways that God is already at work in the world
- change their world by becoming constructively involved in it

SALE
$4.97
949959
Reg
$11.99
BBGN